Leigh Hunt

A Day by the Fire

Leigh Hunt

A Day by the Fire

ISBN/EAN: 9783337217754

Printed in Europe, USA, Canada, Australia, Japan

Cover: Foto ©Thomas Meinert / pixelio.de

More available books at **www.hansebooks.com**

DAY BY THE FIRE.

A

DAY BY THE FIRE;

And Other Papers,

HITHERTO UNCOLLECTED.

BY

LEIGH HUNT.

'Matchless as a fireside companion." — ELIA.

BOSTON:
ROBERTS BROTHERS.
1870.

Entered according to Act of Congress, in the year 1869, by

ROBERTS BROTHERS,

In the Clerk's Office of the District Court of the United States, for the District of Massachusetts.

CAMBRIDGE:
PRESS OF JOHN WILSON AND SON.

PREFATORY NOTE.

HE papers here first collected were originally published in "The Reflector," "The Examiner," "The Indicator,"* "The London Journal," "The Monthly Chronicle," and "The New Monthly Magazine;" and were written at widely different periods of the author's life — in his early manhood, middle life, and old age.

If there is any intelligent person who professes not to like Leigh Hunt, it is probably for precisely the same reason that Charles Lamb professed not to like the W——s, — because he did not know them. For Leigh Hunt is one of the most delightful of authors, and all who read him admire him for his scholarly tastes and literary amenities, his nimble wit, bright fancy, and subtle perception of beauty; and love him for his glad heart and sunny disposition, his large and generous sympathies, and noble, Christian faith in the innate goodness of man.

This volume of essays and sketches, — written in the author's pleasant, characteristic manner, and full of what Hawthorne happily calls "his unmeasured poetry," — will, I hope, be acceptable to the old admirers of Leigh Hunt, and introduce him to many new and appreciative readers.

J. E. B.

CHELSEA, November 18, 1869.

---

* The little weekly periodical, from which the well-known delightful work of the same name is a selection.

Something not to be replaced would be struck out of the gentler literature of our century, could the mind of Leigh Hunt cease to speak to us in a book.
EDWARD BULWER, LORD LYTTON.

Into whatever he has written he has put a living soul; and much of what he has produced is brilliant either with wit and humor, or with tenderness and beauty.
GEORGE L. CRAIK.

Leigh Hunt seems the very opposite of Hazlitt. He loves everything, he catches the sunny side of everything, and, excepting that he has a few polemical antipathies, finds everything beautiful.
HENRY CRABB ROBINSON.

He is, in truth, one of the pleasantest writers of his time, — easy, colloquial, genial, human, full of fine fancies and verbal niceties, possessing a loving if not a "learned spirit," with hardly a spice of bitterness in his composition.
E. P. WHIPPLE.

I have been reading some of Leigh Hunt's works lately, and am surprised at the freshness, and sweetness, and Christian, not lax, spirit of human benevolence and toleration which existed in the heart of one who was the contemporary, and even colleague, of Byron.
FREDERICK W. ROBERTSON.

CONTENTS.

Prefatory Note	3
A Day by the Fire	13
On Commonplace People	42
A Popular View of the Heathen Mythology	47
On the Genii of the Greeks and Romans, and the Spirit that was said to have waited on Socrates	59
On the Genii of Antiquity and the Poets	70
Fairies	81
Genii and Fairies of the East, the Arabian Nights, &c.	124
The Satyr of Mythology and the Poets	155
The Nymphs of Antiquity and of the Poets	170
The Sirens and Mermaids of the Poets	188
Tritons and Men of the Sea	206
On Giants, Ogres, and Cyclops	231
Gog and Magog, and the Wall of Dhoulkarnein	252
Aeronautics, Real and Fabulous	260
On the Talking of Nonsense	284
A Rainy Day	292
The True Enjoyment of Splendor	299

Retrospective Review — Men Wedded to Books — The
    Contest between the Nightingale and Musician . 302
The Murdered Pump 315
Christmas Eve and Christmas Day 319
New Year's Gifts 326
Sale of the late Mr. West's Pictures 331
Translation from Milton into Welsh 334
The Bull-Fight; or, The Story of Don Alphonso de
    Melos and the Jeweller's Daughter 343
Love and Will 353

A DAY BY THE FIRE.

AM one of those that delight in a fireside, and can enjoy it without even the help of a cat or a tea-kettle. To cats, indeed, I have an aversion, as animals that only affect a sociality, without caring a jot for any thing but their own luxury;* and my tea-kettle, I frankly confess, has long been displaced, or rather dismissed, by a bronze-colored and graceful urn; though, between ourselves, I am not sure that I have gained any thing by the exchange. Cowper, it is true, talks of the "bubbling and loud-hissing urn," which —

"Throws up a steamy column;"

but there was something so primitive and unaffected, so warm-hearted and unpresuming, in the tea-kettle, — its song was so much more cheerful and continued, and it kept the water so hot and comfortable as long as you wanted it, — that I sometimes feel as if I had sent off a good, plain, faithful old friend, who had but one wish to serve me, for a superficial, smooth-faced upstart of a fellow, who, after a little promising and vaporing, grows cold

---

* This was written in the early days of Leigh Hunt's literary career; but years after, when he was older and wiser, he did full and complete justice to the familiar household cat, in an admirable paper, entitled, "The Cat by the Fire," published in "The Seer." — ED.

and contemptuous, and thinks himself bound to do nothing but stand on a rug and have his person admired by the circle. To this admiration, in fact, I have been obliged to resort, in order to make myself think well of my bargain, if possible; and, accordingly, I say to myself every now and then during the tea, "A pretty look with it, — that urn;" or, "It's wonderful what a taste the Greeks had;" or, "The eye might have a great many enjoyments, if people would but look after forms and shapes." In the mean while, the urn leaves off its "bubbling and hissing," — but then there is such an air with it! My tea is made of cold water, — but then, the Greeks were such a nation!

If there is any one thing that can reconcile me to the loss of my kettle, more than another, it is that my fire has been left to itself: it has full room to breathe and to blaze, and I can poke it as I please. What recollections does that idea excite? — Poke it as I please! Think, benevolent reader, — think of the pride and pleasure of having in your hand that awful, but at the same time artless, weapon, a poker, — of putting it into the proper bar, gently levering up the coals, and seeing the instant and bustling flame above!* To what can I compare that moment? that sudden, empyreal enthusiasm? that fiery expression of vivification? that ardent acknowledgment, as it were, of the care and kindliness of the operator? Let me consider a moment: it is very odd; I was always reckoned a lively hand at a simile; but language and combination absolutely fail me here. If it is like any thing, it must be something beyond every thing in beauty and life. Oh, I have it now: think, reader, if you are one of those who

---

* Charles Lamb's friend and school-mate, Le Grice, wrote a book on the "Art of Poking the Fire." — ED.

can muster up sufficient sprightliness to engage in a game of forfeits, — on Twelfth night, for instance, — think of a blooming girl who is condemned to "open her mouth and shut her eyes, and see what heaven," in the shape of a mischievous young fellow, " will send her." Her mouth is opened accordingly, the fire of her eyes is dead, her face assumes a doleful air; up walks the aforesaid heaven or mischievous young fellow (young Ouranos, Hesiod would have called him), and, instead of a piece of paper, a thimble, or a cinder, claps into her mouth a peg of orange or a long slice of citron; then her eyes above instantly light up again, the smiles wreath about, the sparklings burst forth, and all is warmth, brilliancy, and delight. I am aware that this simile is not perfect; but if it would do for an epic poem, as I think it might, after Virgil's whipping-tops and Homer's jackasses and black-puddings, the reader, perhaps, will not quarrel with it.

But to describe my feelings in an orderly manner, I must request the reader to go with me through a day's enjoyments by the fireside. It is part of my business to look about for helps to reflection; and, for this reason, among many others, I indulge myself in keeping a good fire from morning till night. I have also a reflective turn for an easy chair, and a very thinking attachment to comfort in general. But of this as I proceed. Imprimis, then: the morning is clear and cold; time, half-past seven; scene, a breakfast-room. Some persons, by the by, prefer a thick and rainy morning, with a sobbing wind, and the clatter of pattens along the streets; but I confess, for my own part, that being a sedentary person, and too apt to sin against the duties of exercise, I have somewhat too sensitive a consciousness of bad weather, and feel a heavy sky go over me like a feather-bed, or rather like a huge brush which rubs all my nap the wrong way. I am growing better in this respect, and, by the help of a stout walk at noon, and getting, as it were, fairly into a favorite poet and a warm fire of an evening, begin to manage a cloud or an east wind tolerably well; but still, for perfection's sake on the present occasion, I must insist upon my clear morning, and will add to it, if the reader pleases, a little hoar-frost upon the windows, a bird or two coming after the crumbs, and the light smoke from the neighboring chimneys brightening up into the early sunshine. Even the dustman's bell is not unpleasant from its association; and there is something absolutely musical in the clash of the milk-pails suddenly unyoked, and the ineffable, *ad libitum* note that follows.

The waking epicure rises with an elastic anticipation; enjoys the freshening cold water which endears what is to come; and even goes placidly through the villanous scraping process which we soften down into the level and lawny appellation of shaving. He then hurries down stairs, rubbing his hands, and sawing the sharp air through his teeth; and, as he enters the breakfast-room, sees his old companion glowing through the bars, the life of the apartment, and wanting only his friendly hand to be lightened a little, and enabled to shoot up into dancing brilliancy. (I find I am getting into a quantity of epithets here, and must rein in my enthusiasm.) What need I say? The poker is applied, and would be so whether required or not, for it is impossible to resist the sudden ardor inspired by that sight? The use of the poker, on first seeing one's fire, is as natural as shaking hands with a friend. At that movement a hundred little sparkles fly up from the coal-dust that falls within, while from the masses themselves, a roaring flame mounts aloft with a deep and fitful sound as of a shaken carpet, — epithets again ; I must recur to poetry at once : —

> Then shine the bars, the cakes in smoke aspire,
> A sudden glory bursts from all the fire.
> The conscious wight, rejoicing in the heat,
> Rubs the blithe knees, and toasts th' alternate feet.*

The utility, as well as beauty, of the fire *during* breakfast, need not be pointed out to the most unphlogistic observer. A person would rather be shivering at any time of the day than at that of his first rising ; the transition would be too unnatural, — he is not prepared for it, as Barnardine says, when he objects to being hanged. If you eat plain bread and butter with your tea, it is fit that your moderation should be rewarded with a good blaze ; and if you indulge in hot rolls or toast, you will hardly keep them to their warmth without it, particularly if you read ; and then, if you take in a newspaper, what a delightful change from the wet, raw, dabbing fold of paper when you first touch it, to the dry, crackling, crisp superficies which, with a skilful spat of the finger-nails at its upper end, stands at once in your hand, and looks as if it said, "Come read me." Nor is it the look of the newspaper only which the fire must render complete : it is the interest of the ladies who may happen to form part of your family, — of your wife in particular, if you have one, — to avoid the niggling and pinching aspect of cold ; it takes away the harmony of her features, and the graces of her behavior ; while, on the other hand, there is scarcely a more interesting sight in the world than that of a neat, delicate, good-humored

---

* Parody upon part of the well-known description of night, with which Pope has swelled out the passage in Homer, and the faults of which have long been appreciated by general readers.

female presiding at your breakfast-table, with hands tapering out of her long sleeves, eyes with a touch of Sir Peter Lely in them, and a face set in a little oval frame of muslin tied under the chin, and retaining a certain tinge of the pillow without its cloudiness. This is, indeed, the finishing grace of a fireside, though it is impossible to have it at all times, and perhaps not always politic, — especially for the studious.

From breakfast to dinner, the quantity and quality of enjoyment depend very much on the nature of one's concerns; and occupation of any kind, if we pursue it properly, will hinder us from paying a critical attention to the fireside. It is sufficient, if our employments do not take us away from it, or at least from the genial warmth of a room which it adorns, — unless, indeed, we are enabled to have recourse to exercise; and in that case, I am not so unjust as to deny that walking or riding has its merits, and that the general glow they diffuse throughout the frame has something in it so extremely pleasurable and encouraging; nay, I must not scruple to confess that, without some preparation of this kind, the enjoyment of the fireside, humanly speaking, is not absolutely perfect, as I have latterly been convinced by a variety of incontestable arguments in the shape of headaches, rheumatisms, mote-haunted eyes, and other logical appeals to one's feelings which are in great use with physicians. Supposing, therefore, the morning to be passed, and the due portion of exercise to have been taken, the firesider fixes rather an early hour for dinner, particularly in the winter-time; for he has not only been early at breakfast, but there are two luxurious intervals to enjoy between dinner and the time of candles : one that supposes a party round the fire with their wine and fruit; the other, the hour of twilight, of which it has been reasonably doubted whether it is not the most luxurious point of time which a fireside can present; but opinions will naturally be divided on this as on all other subjects, and every degree of pleasure depends upon so many contingencies, and upon such a variety of associations, induced by habit and opinion, that I should be as unwilling as I am unable to decide on the matter. This, however, is certain, that no true firesider can dislike an hour so composing to his thoughts, and so cherishing to his whole faculties; and it is equally certain that he will be little inclined to protract the dinner beyond what he can help, for if ever a fireside becomes unpleasant, it is during that gross and pernicious prolongation of eating and drinking, to which this latter age has given itself up, and which threatens to make the rising generation regard a meal of repletion as the ultimatum of enjoyment.

The inconvenience to which I allude is owing to the way in which we sit at dinner, for the persons who have their backs to the fire are liable to be scorched, while, at the same time, they render the persons opposite them liable to be frozen: so that the fire becomes uncomfortable to the former, and tantalizing to the latter; and thus three evils are produced, of a most absurd and scandalous nature: in the first place, the fireside loses a degree of its character, and awakens feelings the very reverse of what it should; secondly, the position of the back towards it is a neglect and affront, which it becomes it to resent; and finally, its beauties, its proffered kindness, and its sprightly social effect are at once cut off from the company by the interposition of those invidious and idle surfaces called screens. This abuse is the more ridiculous, inasmuch as the remedy is so easy: for we have nothing to do but to use semicircular dining-tables, with the base unoccupied towards the fireplace, and the whole annoyance vanishes at once; the master or mistress might preside in the middle, as was the custom with the Romans, and thus propriety would be observed, while everybody had the sight and benefit of the fire; not to mention that, by this fashion, the table might be brought nearer to it, that the servants would have better access to the dishes, and that screens, if at all necessary, might be turned to better purpose as a general enclosure instead of a separation.

But I hasten from dinner, according to notice; and cannot but observe that, if you have a small set of visitors who enter into your feelings on this head, there is no movement so pleasant as a general one from the table to the fireside, each person taking his glass with him, and a small, slim-legged table being introduced into the circle for the purpose of holding the wine, and perhaps a poet or two, a glee-book, or a lute. If this practice should become general among those who know how to enjoy luxuries in such temperance as not to destroy conversation, it would soon gain for us another social advantage, by putting an end to the barbarous custom of sending away the ladies after dinner, — a gross violation of those chivalrous graces of life, for which modern times are so highly indebted to the persons whom they are pleased to term Gothic. And here I might digress, with no great impropriety, to show the *snug* notions that were entertained by the knights and damsels of old in all particulars relating to domestic enjoyment, especially in the article of mixed company; but I must not quit the fireside, and will only observe that, as the ladies formed its chief ornament, so they constituted its most familiar delight.

> "The minstralcie, the service at the feste,
> The grete yeftes to the most and leste,
> The riche array of Theseus' paleis,
> Ne who sate first, ne last upon the deis,
> What ladies fairest ben, or best dancing,
> Or which of hem can carole best or sing,
> Ne who most felingly speketh of love;
> What haukis sitten on the perch above,
> What houndis liggen on the flour adoun, —
> Of all this now make I no mencioun."
>
> CHAUCER.

The word *snug*, however, reminds me that amidst all the languages, ancient and modern, it belongs exclusively to our own; and that nothing but a want of ideas suggested by that soul-wrapping epithet could have induced certain frigid connoisseurs to tax our climate with want of genius, — supposing, forsooth, that because we have not the sunshine of the Southern countries, we have no other warmth for our veins, and that, because our skies are not hot enough to keep us in doors, we have no excursiveness of wit and range of imagination. It seems to me that a great deal of good argument in refutation of these calumnies has been wasted upon Monsieur du Bos and the Herr Winckelman: the one a narrow-minded, pedantic Frenchman, to whom the freedom of our genius was incomprehensible; the other, an Italianized German, who being suddenly transported into the sunshine, began frisking about with unwieldy vivacity, and concluded that nobody could be great or bewitching out of the pale of his advantages. Milton, it is true, in his "Paradise Lost," expresses an injudicious apprehension lest —

> "An age too late, or cold
> Climate, or years, damp his intended wing;"

but the very complaint which foreign critics bring against him, as well as Shakespeare, is that his wing was not damped enough, — that it was too daring and unsubdued ; and he not only avenges himself nobly of his fears by a flight beyond all Italian poetry, but shows, like the rest of his countrymen, that he could turn the coldness of his climate into a new species of inspiration, as I shall presently make manifest. Not to mention, however, that the Greeks and Romans, Homer in particular, saw a great deal worse weather than these critics would have us imagine ; the question is, would the poets themselves have thought as they did ? Would Tyrtæus, the singer of patriotism, have complained of being an Englishman ? Would Virgil, who delighted in husbandry, and whose first wish was to be a philosopher, have complained of living in our pastures, and being the countryman of Newton ? Would Homer, the observer of character, the panegyrist of freedom, the painter of storms, of landscapes, and of domestic tenderness, — aye, and the lover of snug house-room and a good dinner, — would he have complained of our humors, of our liberty, of our shifting skies, of our ever-green fields, our conjugal happiness, our firesides, and our hospitality ? I only wish the reader and I had him at this party of ours after dinner, with a lyre on his knee, and a goblet, as he says, to drink as he pleased, —

—— " Piein, hote thumos anogoi."
Odyss. lib. viii. v. 70.

I am much mistaken if our blazing fire and our freedom of speech would not give him a warmer inspiration than ever he felt in the person of Demodocus, even though placed on a lofty seat, and regaled with slices of brawn from a prince's table. The ancients, in fact, were by no means deficient in enthusiasm at sight of a good fire ; and it is to be presumed that, if they had enjoyed such firesides as ours, they would have acknowledged the advantages which our genius presents in winter, and almost been ready to conclude, with old Cleveland, that the sun himself was nothing but —

"Heaven's coalery; —
A coal-pit rampant, or a mine on flame."

The ancient hearth was generally in the middle of the room, the ceiling of which let out the smoke; it was supplied with charcoal or faggots, and consisted sometimes of a brazier or chafing-dish (the *focus* of the Romans), sometimes of a mere elevation or altar (the ἑστία or ἐσχάρα of the Greeks). We may easily imagine the smoke and annoyance which this custom must have occasioned, — not to mention the bad complexions which are caught by hanging over a fuming-pan, as the faces of the Spanish ladies bear melancholy witness. The stoves, however, in use with the countrymen of Mons. du Bos and Winckelman are, if possible, still worse, having a dull, suffocating effect, with nothing to recompense the eye. The abhorrence of them which Ariosto expresses in one of his satires, when, justifying his refusal to accompany Cardinal d'Este into Germany, he reckons up the miseries of its wintertime, may have led M. Winckelman to conclude that all the Northern resources against cold were equally intolerable to an Italian genius; but Count Alfieri, a poet, at least as warmly inclined as Ariosto, delighted in England; and the great romancer himself, in another of his satires, makes a commodious fireplace the climax of his wishes with regard to lodging. In short, what did Horace say, or rather what did he not say, of the raptures of in-door sociality, — Horace, who knew how to enjoy sunshine in all its luxury, and who nevertheless appears to have snatched a finer inspiration from absolute frost and snow?

I need not quote all those beautiful little invitations he sent to his acquaintances, telling one of them that a neat room and a sparkling fire were waiting for him; describing to another the smoke springing out of the roof in curling volumes, and even congratulating his friends in general on the opportunity of enjoyment afforded them by a stormy day; but, to take leave at once of these frigid connoisseurs, hear with what rapture he describes one of those friendly parties, in which he passed his winter evenings, and which only wanted the finish of our better morality and our patent fireplaces, to resemble the one I am now fancying.

> " Vides, ut altâ stet nive candidum
>   Soracte, nec jam sustineant onus
>   Silvæ laborantes, geluque
>   Flumina constiterint acuto:
>
> Dissolve frigus ligna super foco
> Largè reponens, atque benigniùs
>   Deprome quadrimum Sabinâ,
>   O Thaliarche, merum diotâ.
>
> Permitte Divis cætera; . .
> . . . .
> Donec virenti canities abest
> Morosa. Nunc et campus, et areæ,
>   Lenesque sub noctem susurri
>   Compositâ repetantur horâ;
>
> Nunc et latentis proditor intimo
> Gratus puellæ risus ab angulo,
>   Pignusque dereptum lacertis
>   Aut digito male pertinaci."
>   LIB. I. OD. 9.

> " Behold yon mountain's hoary height
>   Made higher with new mounts of snow;
> Again behold the winter's weight
>   Oppress the lab'ring woods below,

And streams with icy fetters bound
Benumb'd and crampt to solid ground.

With well-heap'd logs dissolve the cold,
   And feed the genial hearth with fires,
Produce the wine that makes us bold,
   And sprightly wit and mirth inspires.
For what hereafter shall betide,
Jove, if 'tis worth his care, provide.

* * * * *

Th' appointed hour of promis'd bliss,
   The pleasing whisper in the dark,
The half unwilling, willing kiss,
   The laugh that guides thee to the mark,
When the kind nymph would coyness feign,
And hides but to be found again,
These, these are joys the gods for youth ordain."

DRYDEN.

The Roman poet, however, though he occasionally boasts of his temperance, is too apt to lose sight of the intellectual part of his entertainment, or at least to make the sensual part predominate over the intellectual. Now, I reckon the nicety of social enjoyment to consist in the reverse; and, after partaking with Homer of his plentiful boiled and roast, and with Horace of his flower-crowned wine-parties, the poetical reader must come at last to us barbarians of the North for the perfection of fireside festivity, — that is to say, for the union of practical philosophy with absolute merriment, — for light meals and unintoxicating glasses ; for refection that administers to enjoyment, instead of repletions that at once constitute and contradict it. I am speaking, of course, not of our commonplace eaters and drinkers, but of our classical arbiters of pleasure, as contrasted with those of other countries ; these, it is observable, have all delighted in Horace, and copied him as far as their tastes were congenial; but, without relaxing a jot of their real comfort, how pleasingly does their native philosophy temper and adorn the freedom of their conviviality, — feeding the fire, as it were, with an equable fuel that hinders it alike from scorching and from going out, and, instead of the artificial enthusiasm of a heated body, enabling them to enjoy the healthful and unclouded predominance of a sparkling intelligence! It is curious, indeed, to see how distinct from all excess are their freest and heartiest notions of relaxation. Thus our old poet, Drayton, reminding his favorite companion of a fireside meeting, expressly unites freedom with moderation: —

> " My dearly loved friend, how oft have we
> In winter evenings, meaning to be free,
> To some well-chosen place us'd to retire,
> And there with moderate meat, and wine, and fire,
> Have pass'd the hours contentedly in chat,
> Now talk'd of this, and then discours'd of that, —
> Spoke our own verses 'twixt ourselves, — if not
> Other men's lines, which we by chance had got."
> EPISTLE TO HENRY REYNOLDS, ESQ., *of Poets and Poesy*.

And Milton, in his "Sonnet to Cyriack Skinner," one of the turns of which is plainly imitated from Horace, particularly qualifies a strong invitation to merriment by anticipating what Horace would always drive from your reflections, — the feelings of the day after : —

> " Cyriack, whose Grandsire, on the royal bench
> Of British Themis, with no mean applause
> Pronounc'd, and in his volumes taught, our laws,
> Which others at their bar so often wrench;
> *To-day deep thoughts resolve with me to drench
> In mirth. that, after, no repenting draws.*
> Let Euclid rest, and Archimedes pause,
> And what the Swede intends, and what the French
> To measure life learn thou betimes, and know
> Tow'rd solid good what leads the nearest way·

> For other things mild Heav'n a time ordains,
> And disapproves that care, though wise in show,
> That with superfluous burden loads the day,
> And when God sends a cheerful hour, refrains."

But the execution of this sonnet is not to be compared in gracefulness and a finished sociality with the one addressed to his friend Lawrence, which, as it presents us with the acme of elegant repast, may conclude the hour which I have just been describing, and conduct us complacently to our twilight, —

> " Lawrence, of virtuous father virtuous son,
> Now that the fields are dank, and ways are mire,
> Where shall we sometimes meet, and by the fire
> Help waste a sullen day, — what may be won
> From the hard season gaining? Time will run
> On smoother, till Favonius re-inspire
> The frozen earth, and clothe in fresh attire
> The lily and rose, that neither sow'd nor spun.
> What neat repast shall feast us, light and choice,
> Of Attic taste, with wine, whence we may rise
> To hear the lute well-touch'd, and artful voice
> Warble immortal notes and Tuscan air?
> He who of these delights can judge, and spare
> To interpose them oft, is not unwise."

But twilight comes: and the lover of the fireside, for the perfection of the moment, is now alone. He was reading a minute or two ago, and for some time was unconscious of the increasing dusk, till, on looking up, he perceived the objects out of doors deepening into massy outline, while the sides of his fireplace began to reflect the light of the flames, and the shadow of himself and his chair fidgeted with huge obscurity on the wall. Still wishing to read, he pushed himself nearer and nearer the window, and continued fixing on his book till he happened to take another glance out of doors, and on returning to it, could make out nothing. He therefore lays it aside, and restoring his chair to the fireplace, seats himself right before it in a reclining posture, his feet apart upon the fender, his eyes bent down towards the grate, his arms on the chair's elbows, one hand hanging down, and the palm of the other turned up and presented to the fire, — not to keep it from him, for there is no glare or scorch about it, but to intercept and have a more kindly feel of its genial warmth. It is thus that the greatest and wisest of mankind have sat and meditated; a homely truism, perhaps, but such a one as we are apt enough to forget. We talk of going to Athens or to Rome to see the precise objects which the Greeks and Romans beheld; and forget that the moon, which may be looking upon us at the moment, is the same identical planet that enchanted Homer and Virgil, and that has been contemplated and admired by all the great men and geniuses that have existed : by Socrates and Plato in Athens, by the Antonines in Rome, by the Alfreds, the l'Hospitals, the Miltons, Newtons, and Shakespeares. In like manner, we are anxious to discover how these great men and poets appeared in common, what habits they loved, in what way they talked and meditated, nay, in what postures they delighted to sit, and whether they indulged in the same tricks and little comforts that we do. Look at nature and their works, and we shall see that they did ; and that, when we act naturally and think earnestly, we are reflecting their commonest habits to the life. Thus we have seen Horace talking of his blazing hearth and snug accommodations like the jolliest of our acquaintances ; and thus we may safely imagine that Milton was in some such attitude as I have described, when he sketched that enchanting little picture which beats all the cabinet portraits that have been produced, —

> " Or if the air will not permit,
> Some still removed place will fit,
> Where glowing embers through the room
> Teach light to counterfeit a gloom,
> Far from all resort of mirth,
> Save the cricket on the hearth,
> Or the bellman's drowsy charm
> To bless the doors from nightly harm."

But to attend to our fireside. The evening is beginning to gather in. The window, which presents a large face of watery gray, intersected by strong lines, is imperceptibly becoming darker; and as that becomes darker, the fire assumes a more glowing presence. The contemplatist keeps his easy posture, absorbed in his fancies; and every thing around him is still and serene. The stillness would even ferment in his ear, and whisper, as it were, of what the air contained; but a minute coil, just sufficient to hinder that busier silence, clicks in the baking coal, while every now and then the light ashes shed themselves below, or a stronger, but still a gentle, flame flutters up with a gleam over the chimney. At length, the darker objects in the room mingle; the gleam of the fire streaks with a restless light the edges of the furniture, and reflects itself in the blackening window; while his feet take a gentle move on the fender, and then settle again, and his face comes out of the general darkness, earnest even in indolence, and pale in the very ruddiness of what it looks upon. This is the only time, perhaps, at which sheer idleness is salutary and refreshing. How observed with the smallest effort is every trick and aspect of the fire! A coal falling in, a fluttering flame, a miniature mockery of a flash of lightning, — nothing escapes the eye and the imagination. Sometimes a little flame appears at the corner of the grate like a quivering spangle; sometimes it swells out at top into a restless and brief lambency; anon it is seen only by a light beneath the grate, or it curls around one of the bars like a tongue, or darts out with a spiral thinness and a sulphurous and continued puffing as from a reed. The glowing coals meantime exhibit the shifting forms of hills and vales and gulfs, — of fiery Alps, whose heat is uninhabitable even by spirit, or of black precipices, from which swart fairies seem about to spring away on sable wings; then heat and fire are forgotten, and walled towns appear, and figures of unknown animals, and far-distant countries scarcely to be reached by human journey; then coaches and camels, and barking dogs as large as either, and forms that combine every shape and suggest every fancy, till at last, the ragged coals tumbling together, reduce the vision to chaos, and the huge profile of a gaunt and grinning face seems to make a jest of all that has passed.

During these creations of the eye, the thought roves about into a hundred abstractions, some of them suggested by the fire, some of them suggested by that suggestion, some of them arising from the general sensation of comfort and composure, contrasted with whatever the world affords of evil, or dignified by high wrought meditation on whatsoever gives hope to benevolence and inspiration to wisdom. The philosopher at such moments plans his Utopian schemes, and dreams of happy certainties which he cannot prove; the lover, happier and more certain, fancies his mistress with him, unobserved and confiding, his arm round her waist, her head upon his shoulder, and earth and heaven contained in that sweet possession; the poet, thoughtful as the one, and ardent as the other, springs off at once above the world, treads every turn of the harmonious spheres, darts up with gleaming wings through the sunshine of a thousand systems, and stops not till he has found a perfect paradise, whose fields are of young roses, and whose air is music, whose waters are the liquid diamond, whose light is as radiance through crystal, whose dwellings are laurel bowers, whose language is poetry, whose inhabitants are congenial souls, and to enter the very verge of whose atmosphere strikes beauty on the face, and felicity on the heart. Alas, that flights so lofty should ever be connected with earth by threads as slender as they are long, and that the least twitch of the most commonplace hand should be able to snatch down the viewless wanderer to existing comforts ! The entrance of a single candle dissipates at once the twilight and the sunshine, and the ambitious dreamer is summoned to his tea !

> " Now stir the fire, and close the shutters fast,
> Let fall the curtains, wheel the sofa round,
> And, while the bubbling and loud-hissing urn
> Throws up a steamy column, and the cups
> That cheer, but not inebriate, wait on each,
> So let us welcome peaceful evening in."

Never was snug hour more feelingly commenced ! Cowper was not a *great* poet ; his range was neither wide nor lofty ; but such as it was, he had it completely to himself, — he is the poet of quiet life and familiar observation. The fire, we see, is now stirred, and becomes very different from the one we have just left ; it puts on its liveliest aspect in order to welcome those to whom the tea-table is a point of meeting, and it is the business of the firesider to cherish this aspect for the remainder of the evening. How light and easy the coals look ! How ardent is the roominess within the bars ! How airily do the volumes of smoke course each other up the chimney, like so many fantastic and indefinite spirits, while the eye in vain en-

deavors to accompany any one of them! The flames are
not so fierce as in the morning, but still they are active
and powerful; and if they do not roar up the chimney,
they make a constant and playful noise, that is extremely
to the purpose. Here they come out at top with a leafy
swirl; there they dart up spirally and at once; there
they form a lambent assemblage that shifts about on its
own ground, and is continually losing and regaining its
vanishing members. I confess I take particular delight
in seeing a good blaze at top; and my impatience to produce it will sometimes lead me into great rashness in the
article of poking; that is to say, I use the poker at the
top instead of the middle of the fire, and go probing it
about in search of a flame. A lady of my acquaintance,
— "near and dear," as they say in Parliament,—will tell
me of this fault twenty times in a day, and every time so
good-humoredly that it is mere want of generosity in me
not to amend it; but somehow or other I do not. The
consequence is that, after a momentary ebullition of blaze,
the fire becomes dark and sleepy, and is in danger of going out. It is like a boy at school in the hands of a bad
master, who, thinking him dull, and being impatient to
render him brilliant, beats him about the head and ears
till he produces the very evil he would prevent. But, on
the present occasion, I forbear to use the poker; there is
no need of it: every thing is comfortable,—every thing
snug and sufficient. How equable is the warmth around
us! How cherishing this rug to one's feet! How com-
placent the cup at one's lip! What a fine broad light is
diffused from the fire over the circle, gleaming in the urn
and the polished mahogany, bringing out the white garments of the ladies, and giving a poetic warmth to their
face and hair! I need not mention all the good things

that are said at tea, — still less the gallant. Good humor never has an audience more disposed to think it wit, nor gallantry an hour of service more blameless and elegant. Ever since tea has been known, its clear and gentle powers of inspiration have been acknowledged, from Waller paying his court at the circle of Catharine of Braganza, to Dr. Johnson receiving homage at the parties of Mrs. Thrale. The former, in his lines, upon hearing it "commended by her Majesty," ranks it at once above myrtle and laurel, and her Majesty, of course, agreed with him : —

> " Venus her myrtle, Phœbus has his bays;
> Tea both excels, which she vouchsafes to praise.
> The *best of queens*, and best of herbs, we owe
> To that bold nation, which the way did show
> To the fair region where the sun does rise,
> Whose rich productions we so justly prize.
> The Muse's friend, Tea, does our fancy aid,
> Repress those vapours which the head invade,
> And keeps that palace of the soul serene,
> Fit, on her birth-day, to salute the Queen."

The eulogies pronounced on his favorite beverage by Dr. Johnson, are too well known to be repeated here ; and the commendatory inscription of the Emperor Kien Long, to an European taste at least, is somewhat too dull, unless his Majesty's teapot has been shamefully translated. For my own part, though I have the highest respect, as I have already shown, for this genial drink, which is warm to the cold, and cooling to the warm, I confess, as Montaigne would have said, that I prefer coffee, — particularly in my political capacity : —

> " Coffee, that makes the Politician wise
> To see through all things with his half-shut eyes."

There is something in it, I think, more lively, and, at the same time, more substantial. Besides, I never see it but it reminds me of the Turks and their Arabian tales, — an association infinitely preferable to any Chinese ideas; and, like the king who put his head into the tub, I am transported into distant lands the moment I dip into the coffee-cup, — at one minute ranging the valleys with Sindbad, at another encountering the fairies on the wing by moonlight, at a third exploring the haunts of the cursed Maugraby, or wrapt into the silence of that delicious solitude from which Prince Agib was carried by the fatal horse. Then, if I wish to poeticize upon it at home, there is Belinda, with her sylphs, drinking it in such state as nothing but poetry can supply: —

> "For lo! the board with cups and spoons is crown'd,
> The berries crackle, and the mill turns round:
> On shining altars of japan they raise
> The silver lamp; the fiery spirits blaze;
> From silver spouts the grateful liquors glide,
> And China's earth receives the smoking tide:
> At once they gratify the scent and taste,
> And frequent cups prolong the rich repast.
> Straight hover round the fair her airy band;
> Some, as she sipp'd, the fuming liquor fann'd;
> Some o'er her lap their careful plumes display'd,
> Trembling, and conscious of the rich brocade."

It must be acknowledged, however, that the general association of ideas is at present in favor of tea, which, on that account, has the advantage of suggesting no confinement to particular ranks or modes of life. Let there be but a fireside, and anybody, of any denomination, may be fancied enjoying the luxury of a cup of tea, from the duchess in the evening drawing-room, who makes it the instrument of displaying her white hand, to the washerwoman at her early tub, who, having had nothing to signify since five, sits down to it with her shining arms and corrugated fingers at six. If there is any one station of life in which it is enjoyed to most advantage, it is that of mediocrity: that in which all comfort is reckoned to be best appreciated, because, while there is taste to enjoy, there is necessity to earn the enjoyment; and I cannot conclude the hour before us with a better climax of snugness than is presented in the following pleasing little verses. The author, I believe, is unknown, and may not have been much of a poet in matters of fiction; but who will deny his taste for matters of reality, or say that he has not handled his subject to perfection? —

" The hearth was clean, the fire was clear,
   The kettle on for tea,
Palemon in his elbow-chair,
   As blest as man could be.

Clarinda, who his heart possess'd,
   And was his new-made bride,
With head reclin'd upon his breast
   Sat toying by his side.

Stretch'd at his feet, in happy state,
   A fav'rite dog was laid,
By whom a little sportive cat
   In wanton humour play'd.

Clarinda's hand he gently prest;
   She stole an amorous kiss,
And, blushing, modestly confess'd
   The fulness of her bliss.

Palemon, with a heart elate,
   Pray'd to Almighty Jove
That it might ever be his fate,
   Just so to live and love.

Be this eternity, he cried,
   And let no more be given:
Continue thus my lov'd fireside,
   I ask no other heaven."
           THE HAPPY FIRESIDE.

There are so many modes of spending the remainder of the evening between tea-time and bed-time (for I protest against all suppers that are not light enough to be taken on the knee), that a general description would avail me nothing, and I cannot be expected to enter into such a variety of particulars. Suffice it to say that, where the fire is duly appreciated, and the circle good humored, none of them can be unpleasant, whether the party be large or small, young or old, talkative or contemplative. If there is music, a good fire will be particularly grateful to the performers, who are often seated at the farther end of the room; for it is really shameful that a lady who is charming us all with her voice, or firing us, at the harp or piano, with the lightning of her fingers, should at the very moment be trembling with cold. As to cards, which were invented for the solace of a mad prince, and which are only tolerable, in my opinion, when we can be as mad as he was, that is to say, at a round game, I cannot by any means patronize them, as a conscientious firesider: for, not to mention all the other objections, the card-table is as awkward, in a fireside point of view, as the dinner-table, and is not to be compared with it in sociality. If it be necessary to pay so ill a compliment to the company as to have recourse to some amusement of the kind, there is chess or draughts, which may be played on a tablet by the fire; but nothing is like discourse, freely uttering the fancy as it comes, and varied, perhaps, with a little music, or with the perusal of some favorite passages which excite the comments of the circle. It is then, if tastes happen to be accordant, and the social voice is frank as well as refined, that the "sweet music of speech" is heard in its best harmony, differing only for apter sweetness, and mingling but for happier participation, while the mu-

tual sense smilingly blends in with every rising measure, —
" And female stop smoothens the charm o'er all."

This is the finished evening; this the quickener at once and the calmer of tired thought; this the spot where our better spirits await to exalt and enliven us, when the daily and vulgar ones have discharged their duty!

" Questo è il Paradiso,
Più dolce, che fra l' acque, e fra l' arene
In ciel son le Sirene."
TASSO. — *Rime Amorose.*

" Here, here is found
A sweeter Paradise of sound
Than where the Sirens take their summer stands
Among the breathing waters and glib sands."

Bright fires and joyous faces; and it is no easy thing for philosophy to say good night. But health must be enjoyed or nothing will be enjoyed, and the charm should be broken at a reasonable hour. Far be it, however, from a rational firesider not to make exceptions to the rule, when friends have been long asunder, or when some domestic celebration has called them together, or even when hours peculiarly congenial render it difficult to part. At all events, the departure must be a voluntary matter; and here I cannot help exclaiming against the gross and villanous trick which some people have, when they wish to get rid of their company, of letting their fires go down, and the snuffs of their candles run to seed: it is paltry and palpable, and argues bad policy as well as breeding; for such of their friends as have a different feeling of things, may chance to be disgusted with them altogether, while the careless or unpolite may choose to revenge themselves on the appeal, and face it out gravely till the morning. If a common visitor be inconsiderate enough, on an ordinary occasion, to sit beyond all reasonable hour, it must be reckoned as a fatality, as an ignorance of men and things, against which you cannot possibly provide: as a sort of visitation, which must be borne with patience, and which is not likely to recur often, if you know whom you invite, and those who are invited know you. But with an occasional excess of the fireside what social virtue shall quarrel? A single friend, perhaps, loiters behind the rest; you are alone in the house; you have just got upon a subject delightful to you both; the fire is of a candent brightness; the wind howls out of doors; the rain beats; the cold is piercing! Sit down. This is a time when the most melancholy temperament may defy the clouds and storms, and even extract from them a pleasure that will take no substance by daylight. The ghost of his happiness sits by him, and puts on the likeness of former hours; and if such a man can be made comfortable by the moment, what enjoyment may it not furnish to an unclouded spirit! If the excess belong not to vice, temperance does not forbid it when it only grows out of the occasion. The great poet, whom I have quoted so often for the fireside, and who will enjoy it with us to the last, was, like the rest of our great poets, an ardent recommender of temperance in all its branches; but though he practised what he preached, he could take his night out of the hands of sleep as well as the most entrenching of us. To pass over, as foreign to our subject in point of place, his noble wish that he might "*oft* outwatch the bear," with what a wrapped-up recollection of snugness, in the elegy on his friend Diodati, does he describe the fireside enjoyment of a winter's night?—

"Pectora cui credam ? Quis me lenire docebit
Mordaces curas? Quis longam fallere noctem
Dulcibus alloquiis, grato cum sibilat igni
Molle pyrum, et nucibus strepitat focus, et malus Auster
Miscet cuncta foris, et desuper intonat ulmo?"

"In whom shall I confide? Whose counsel find
A balmy med'cine for my troubled mind?
Or whose discourse, with innocent delight,
Shall fill me now, and cheat the wintry night,
When hisses on my hearth the pulpy pear,
And black'ning chestnut start and crackle there,
While storms abroad the dreary meadows whelm,
And the wind thunders through the neighb'ring elm."
COWPER'S *Translation.*

Even when left alone, there is sometimes a charm in watching out the decaying fire,—in getting closer and closer to it with tilted chair and knees against the bars, and letting the whole multitude of fancies, that work in the night silence, come whispering about the yielding faculties. The world around is silent; and for a moment the very cares of day seem to have gone with it to sleep, leaving you to catch a waking sense of disenthralment, and to commune with a thousand airy visitants that come to play with innocent thoughts. Then, for imagination's sake, not for superstition's, are recalled the stories of the Secret World and the midnight pranks of Fairyism. The fancy roams out of doors after rustics. led astray by the jack-o'-lantern, or minute laughings heard upon the wind, or the night-spirit on his horse that comes flouncing through the air on his way to a surfeited citizen, or the tiny morris-dance that springs up in the watery glimpses of the moon; or keeping at home, it finds a spirit in every room peeping at it as it opens the door, while a cry is heard from upstairs announcing the azure marks inflicted by—

"The nips of fairies upon maids' white hips,"

or hearing a snoring from below, it tiptoes down into the kitchen, and beholds where —

> ——— " Lies him down the lubber fiend,
> And stretch'd out all the chimney's length,
> Basks at the fire his hairy strength."

Presently the whole band of fairies, ancient and modern, — the demons, sylphs, gnomes, sprites, elves, peries, genii, and above all, the fairies of the fireside, the salamanders, lob-lie-by-the-fires, lars, lemures, larvæ, come flitting between the fancy's eyes, and the dying coals, some with their weapons and lights, others with grave steadfastness on book or dish, others of the softer kind with their arch looks, and their conscious pretence of attitude, while a minute music tinkles in the ear, and Oberon gives his gentle order : —

> " Through this house in glimmering light
>   By the dead and drowsy fire,
> Every elf and fairy sprite
>   Hop as light as bird from briar ;
> And this ditty, after me,
>   Sing and dance it trippingly."

Anon, the whole is vanished, and the dreamer, turning his eye down aside, almost looks for a laughing sprite gazing at him from a tiny chair, and mimicking his face and attitude. Idle fancies these, and incomprehensible to minds clogged with every-day earthliness ; but not useless, either as an exercise of the invention, or even as adding consciousness to the range and destiny of the soul. They will occupy us too, and steal us away from ourselves, when other recollections fail us or grow painful, when friends are found selfish, or better friends can but commiserate, or when the world has nothing in it to compare with what we have missed out of it. They may even lead us to higher and more solemn meditations, till we work up our way beyond the clinging and heavy atmosphere of this earthly sojourn, and look abroad upon the light that knows neither blemish nor bound, while our ears are saluted at that egress by the harmony of the skies, and our eyes behold the lost and congenial spirits that we have loved hastening to welcome us with their sparkling eyes, and their curls that are ripe with sunshine.

But earth recalls us again; the last flame is out; the fading embers tinkle with a gaping dreariness; and the chill reminds us where we should be. Another gaze on the hearth that has so cheered us, and the last, lingering action is to wind up the watch for the next day. Upon how many anxieties shall the finger of that brief chronicler strike, — and upon how many comforts too! Tomorrow our fire shall be trimmed anew; and so, gentle reader, good night: may the weariness I have caused you make sleep the pleasanter!

> "Let no lamenting cryes, nor dolefull tears,
> Be heard all night within, nor yet without;
> Ne let false whispers, breeding hidden fears,
> Break gentle sleep with misconceived doubt.
> Let no deluding dreams, nor dreadful sights,
> Make sudden, sad affrights,
> Ne let hobgoblins, names whose sense we see not,
> Fray us with things that be not;
> But let still silence true night-watches keep,
> That sacred peace may in assurance reigne,
> And timely sleep, since it is time to sleep,
> May pour his limbs forth on your pleasant plaine."
> SPENSER'S *Epithalamion*.*

---

* In the new edition of "The Round Table," published in the *Bayard Series* of books, this article is given to Hazlitt. "Our style bewrays us," says Burton; and "A Day by the Fire" is full of Leigh Hunt's peculiarities of thought and diction. The question of authorship, however, is not to be de-

ON COMMONPLACE PEOPLE.

GREEABLY to our chivalrous, as well as domestic, character, and in order to show further in what sort of spirit we shall hereafter confer blame and praise, whom we shall cut up for the benefit of humanity, and to whom apply our healing balsams, we have thought fit, in our present number, to take the part of a very numerous and ill-treated body of persons, known by the various appellations of commonplace people, — dull fellows, or people who have nothing to say.

It is perhaps wrong, indeed, to call these persons commonplace. Those who are the most vehement in objecting to them have the truest right to the title, however little they may suspect it; but of this more hereafter. It is a name by which the others are very commonly known; though they might rather be called persons of simple common sense, and, in fact, have just enough of that valuable quality to inspire them with the very quietness which brings them into so much contempt.

We need not, however, take any pains to describe a set of people so well known. They are, of course, what none of our readers are, but many are acquainted with. They are the more silent part of companies, and generally the

---

cided upon internal evidence; facts prove that the essay was written by the author of the "Story of Rimini." The prolusion was originally published in the "Reflector," with Hunt's well-known signature, — ☞. It was afterwards re-printed in the "Examiner," as one of "The Round Table" papers. When these essays were collected into a volume, Leigh Hunt's initials were printed at the end of "A Day by the Fire;" and Hazlitt, in the preface to this original edition of "The Round Table," says, "out of the fifty-two numbers, twelve are Mr. Hunt's, with the signature, L. H." — ED.

best behaved people at table. They are the best of dumb waiters near the lady of the house. They are always at leisure to help you to good things, if not to say them. They will supply your absence of mind for you while you are talking, and believe you are taking sugar for pepper. Above all, — which ought to recommend them to the very hardest of their antagonists, — they are uninquiring laughers at jokes, and most exemplary listeners.

Now, we do not say that these are the very best of companions, or that when we wished to be particularly amused or informed we should invite them to our houses, or go to see them at theirs; all we demand is that they should be kindly and respectfully treated when they are by, and not insolently left out of the pale of discourse, purely because they may not bring with them as much as they find, or say as brilliant things as we imagine we do ourselves.

This is one of the faults of over-civilization. In a stage of society like the present, there is an intellectual as well as personal coxcombry apt to prevail, which leads people to expect from each other a certain dashing turn of mind, and an appearance, at least, of having ideas, whether they can afford them or not. Their minds endeavor to put on intelligent attitudes, just as their bodies do graceful ones; and every one who, from conscious modesty, or from not thinking about the matter, does not play the same monkey tricks with his natural deficiency, is set down for a dull fellow, and treated with a sort of scornful resentment, for differing with the others. It is equally painful and amusing to see how the latter will look upon an honest fellow of this description, if they happen to find him in a company where they think he has no business. On the first entrance of one of these intolerant men of wisdom, — to see, of course, a brilliant friend of his, — he concludes that all the party are equally lustrous; but finding, by degrees, no flashes from an unfortunate gentleman on his right, he turns stiffly towards him at the first commonplace remark, measures him from head to foot with a kind of wondering indifference, and then falls to stirring his tea with a half-inquiring glance at the rest of the company, — just as much as to say, "a fellow not overburdened, eh?" or, "who the devil has Tom got here?"

Like all who are tyrannically given, and of a bullying turn of mind, — which is by no means confined to those who talk loudest, — these persons are apt to be as obsequious and dumb-stricken before men of whom they have a lofty opinion as they are otherwise in the case above mentioned. This, indeed, is not always the case; but you may sometimes find out one of the caste by seeing him waiting with open mouth and impatient eyes for the brilliant things which the great gentleman to whom he has been introduced is bound to utter. The party, perhaps, are waiting for dinner, and as silent as most Englishmen, not very well known to each other, are upon such occasions. Our hero waits with impatience to hear the celebrated person open his mouth, and is at length gratified; but not hearing very distinctly, asks his next neighbor, in a serious and earnest whisper, what it was.

"Pray, sir, what was it that Mr. W. said?"

"He says that it is particularly cold."

"Oh, — particularly cold."

The gentleman thinks this no very profound remark for so great a man, but puts on as patient a face as he can, and, refreshing himself with shifting one knee over the other, waits anxiously for the next observation. After a little silence, broken only by a hem or two, and by somebody's begging pardon of a gentleman next him for touching his shoe, Mr. W. is addressed by a friend, and the stranger is all attention.

" By the bye, W., how did you get home last night ? "

" Oh, very well, thank'ye ; I couldn't get a coach, but it was'nt very rainy, and I was soon there, and jumped into bed."

" Ah, there's nothing like bed after getting one's coat wet."

" Nothing, indeed. I had the clothes round me in a twinkling, and in two minutes was as fast as a church."

Here the conversation drops again ; and our delighter in intellect cannot hide from himself his disappointment. The description of pulling the clothes round, he thinks, might have been much more piquant; and the simile, as fast as a church, appears to him wonderfully commonplace from a man of wit. But such is his misfortune. He has no eyes but for something sparkling or violent ; and no more expects to find any thing simple in genius, than any thing tolerable in the want of it.

Persons impatient of others' deficiencies are, in fact, likely to be equally undiscerning of their merits ; and are not aware, in either case, how much they are exposing the deficiencies on their own side. Not only, however, do they get into this dilemma, but what is more, they are lowering their respectability beneath that of the dullest person in the room. They show themselves deficient, not merely in the qualities they miss in him, but in those which he really possesses, such as self-knowledge and good temper. Were they as wise as they pretend to be, they would equal him in these points, and know how to extract something good from him in spite of his deficiency in the other ; for intellectual qualities are not the only ones that excite the reflections, or conciliate the regard, of the truly intelligent, — of those who can study human nature in all its bearings, and love it, or sympathize with it, for all its affections. The best part of pleasure is the communication of it. Why must we be perpetually craving for amusement or information from others (an appetite which, after all, will be seldom acknowledged), and never think of bestowing them ourselves? Again, as the best part of pleasure is that we have just mentioned, the best proof of intellectual power is that of extracting fertility from barrenness, or so managing the least cultivated mind, which we may happen to stumble upon, as to win something from it. Setting even this talent aside, there are occasions when it is refreshing to escape from the turmoil and final nothingness of the understanding, and repose upon that contentedness of mediocrity which seems to have attained its end without the trouble of wisdom. It has often delighted me to observe a profound thinker of my acquaintance, when a good natured person of ordinary understanding has been present. He is reckoned severe, as it is called, in many of his opinions: and is thought particularly to overrate his intellectual qualities in general; and yet it is beautiful to see how he will let down his mind to the other's level, taking pleasure in his harmless enjoyment, and assenting to a thousand truisms, one after another, as familiar to him as his finger-ends. The reason is that he pierces deeper into the nature of the human being beside him, can make his very deficiencies subservient to his own speculations, and, above all, knows that there is something worth all the knowledge upon earth, — which is happiness and a genial nature. It is thus that the sunshine of happy faces is reflected upon our own. We may even find a beam of it in every thing that Heaven looks upon. The dullest minds do not vegetate for nothing, any more than the grass in a green lawn. We do not require the trees to talk with us, or get impatient at the monotonous quiet of the fields and hedges. We love them for their contrast to noise and bustle, for their presenting to us something native and elementary, for the peaceful thoughts they suggest to us, and the part they bear in the various beauty of creation.

Is a bird's feather exhibited in company, or a piece of sea-weed, or a shell that contained the stupidest of created beings, every one is happy to look at it, and the most fastidious pretender in the room will delight to expatiate on its beauty and contrivance. Let this teach him charity and good sense, and inform him that it is the grossest of all coxcombry to dwell with admiration on a piece of insensibility, however beautiful, and find nothing to excite pleasing or profitable reflections in the commonest of his fellow-men.

A POPULAR VIEW OF THE HEATHEN MYTHOLOGY.

THE divinities of the ancient mythology are of a very tangible order. They were personifications of the power of the external world, and of the operations of the intellect; and sometimes merged themselves into the particular providence of an eminent prince cr reformer. Mankind wishing to have distinct ideas of the unknown powers of the universe, naturally painted them at first in their own shapes; and not being able to conceive of them otherwise than by the light of their understanding, they as naturally gifted them with their own faculties, moral and intellectual. Hence, the heathen gods were reflections of the qualities most admired or feared during the times in which they originated; and to the same cause were owing the inconsistencies and the vices palmed upon them by the stories of different ages and nations, whose gods became lumped together; and hence the trouble that the philosopher had in endeavoring to reconcile the popular superstitions with a theology more becoming.* Plutarch, who was a priest at Delphi, and a regular devout pagan, but good-hearted and imbued with philosophy, is shocked at the popular stories of the rapes and quarrels of the gods; and Plato, on a similar account, was for banishing Homer from his republic. Plutarch will not allow that it was the real Apollo who fought a serpent and afterwards had to purify himself. He said it must have been a likeness of him, a demon. In other words the gods of Plutarch were to resemble the highest ideas which Plutarch could form of dignity and power. Hence, the greater philosophers whose ardor in the pursuit of truth rendered them still more desirous of departing from conventional degradations of it, came to agree that the nature of the deity was inconceivable; and that the most exalted being they

---

* Virtue or vice either if accompanied with power, will do to make a god of in barbarous times, and till mankind learn the perniciousness of that sort of apotheosis. An Eastern writer says that Pharaoh wished to pass for a divinity with his subjects, and had frequent conversation with the devil for that purpose. The devil put him off from time to time, till he told him one day that the hour was arrived. "How is that," cried Pharaoh, — "why is it time now, and was not before?" — "The reason is," replied the devil, "that you have not hitherto been quite bad enough: at length you have become intolerable, and there is no alternative between a revolt of your subjects, and their belief in your being a god. Once persuade them of that, and there is nothing so extravagant, either in word or deed, which they will not take from you with respect." *D'Herbelot*, article *Feraoun*.

could fancy was at an incalculable distance from it, — an emanation, a being deputed, a sort of spiritual incarnation of one of the divine thoughts ;— if we may so speak without absurdity and without blame. Plato, for instance, observing the moral imperfections of our planet, and not knowing how to account for them any more than we do (for the first cause of evil is always left in the dark), imagined that this world was created by what he called a Demiurgus, or inferior divine energy; just as an artist less than Raphael might paint a fine picture though not so good as what might have come from the hands of the greater one. If you asked him how he made out that the chief creator did not do the work himself, he would have referred you to the fact of the imperfection and to the existence of different degrees of skill and beauty in which we see all about us ; for he thought he had a right to argue from analogy, in default of more certain principles. This right he undoubtedly possessed, and it was natural and reasonable to exert it; but considering the imperfection of the human faculties and the false reports they make to us, even of things cognizable to the senses, it is, in truth, impossible to argue with any certainty from things human to things divine. The only service to all appearance, which our faculties can do for us in these questions, is to save us from the admission of gratuitous absurdities and dogmas dishonorable to the idea of a Divine Being, and to encourage us to guess handsomely and to good purpose. For sincerity at all events must not be gainsaid ; otherwise belief and probability and principle and natural love and the earth itself slide from under our feet. The mystery of the permission of evil still remained; the mystery of imperfection and of cause itself was only thrown back ; and in fact the invention of the Demiurgus was merely shifting the whole mystery of Deity from a first cause to a second. The old dilemma between omnipotence and omnibenevolence perplexed the understanding then, as it does now; and as this world was made the reflection of every other, or rather as evil was supposed to render all the operations of the Deity imperfect, except immediately in his own sphere; men seem to have overlooked among other guesses, the probability that evil may exist only in petty corners or minute portions of the universe, and even then be only the result of an experiment with certain elementary compounds to see whether *they* cannot be made planets of perfect happiness as well as the rest. For, after all, Plato's assumption of the innate and unconscious difficulty which matter presents in the working (or an inability of some sort, whatever it be, to render things perfect at once), is surely the best *assumption* among the hundreds that have been taken for granted on this point; seeing that it sets aside malignity, encourages hope, and stimulates us to an active and benign state of endeavor such as we may conceive to enlist us in the divine service. We must never take any thing on trust in order to make a handle of it for dictation or hypocrisy, or a selfish security, or an indolence which we may dignify with the title of resignation; but as we are compelled to assume or conjecture something or other, unless indeed we are deficient in the imaginative part of our nature, it is best to assume the best candidly, and acknowledge it to be an assumption in order that we may do the utmost we can. Happy opinions are the wine of the heart. What if this world be an experiment, part of which consists in our own co-operation, that is to say, in trying how far the inhabitants of it can acquire energy enough, and do credit enough, to the first cause, to add it finally to the number of blessed stars?

and what if more direct communication with us on the part of the operator, would of necessity put an end to the experiment? The petty human considerations of pride and modesty have nothing to do with the cordial magnitude of such guesses; and the beauty of them consists, we think, not merely in their cheerfulness and real piety, but in their adaptation to all experimental systems of utility, those of the most exclusive utilitarians not excepted. Such we confess is our own creed, which we boast at the same time to be emphatically Christian; and the good which our enthusiasm cannot help thinking such an opinion might do, will excuse us with the readers for this digression.*

The gods of Greece, taken in the popular view of them, were, upon the whole a jovial company, occasionally dispersed about the world, and assembling on Mount Olym-

---

* The hope of a happier state of things on earth, argues nothing against a life hereafter. The fitness of a human soul for immortality may be a part of the experiment. The divinest preacher of eternity that has appeared, expressly anticipated a happier period for mankind in their human state, though many who are called his followers are eager to load both themselves and the world they live in with contumely, — themselves as "innately vicious," and the world as "a vale of tears." Such are the compliments they think to pay their Creator! Yet these are the persons who talk with the greatest devotion of resigning themselves to God's will, and who pique themselves upon having the most exalted ideas of his nature! How much better to think it his will that they should bestir themselves to improve their own natures and the world! How much better to think it consonant with his nature that they should help to drain the "vale of tears," as they call it, just as they would any other valley, beauteous and full of resources! They do not think it necessary to be resigned when they can work for themselves; why should they when they can work for others? Resignation is always good, provided it means only patience in the midst of endeavor, or repose after it; but when it implies a mere folding of the hands, and a despair of making any thing good out of "God's own work," it is surely the lowest and most equivocal aspect under which piety could wish to be drawn.

pus. They dined and supped there, and made love like a party of gallants at a king's table. A pretty girl served instead of a butler; and the Muse played the part of a band.* When they came down to earth, they behaved like the party going home; made love again after their fashion; interfered in quarrels, frightened the old and the feeble; and next day joined a campaign, or presided at an orthodox meeting. In short, they did whatever the vulgar thought gallant and heroical, and were particularly famous for having their own way. If a god offended against all humanity, he had his reasons for it, and was a privileged person. He could do no wrong. But if humanity went counter to a god, the offender and all his generation were to suffer for it. A lady who had resisted the violence of his virtue, was not to be believed whenever she spoke the truth; or your brother became an owl or a flint-stone; or your son was to become a criminal, or a madman, because his grandfather unwittingly married against the god's consent. The vulgar thought how wilful and unjust they would be themselves if they had power; they saw how much kings were given to those kinds of peccadilloes; and therefore, if they could have become gods, how much more they would have been ungodly! It is true the philosopher refined upon all this: and agreeably to the way in which Nature works, there was a sort of cultivation of energy underneath it and an instinct of something beyond

---

* See the description in books and prints, the marriage of Cupid and Psyche. Raphael made a picture of it. Augustus is charged with having made an impious entertainment in imitation of these "charming noons and nights divine." Ben Jonson, we suppose in consideration of King James, who besides being a classical monarch, was devout as well as debauched, — has taken the liberty of misrepresenting the charge in his Poetaster, and making Augustus astonished at the impiety *in others*.

the common theories of right and wrong. Nature's character remained safe, and her good work proceeded. The divinity within us was superior to the ideas of him which we threw up.

Homer makes the gods of a mighty size. His Neptune goes a hundred miles at a stride. This grandeur is of a questionable sort. Homer's men become little in proportion as the gods become great; and Mars and Minerva lording it over a battle, are like giants "tempesting" among a parcel of mice. The less they were seen, the less the dignity on either side was compromised; for their effect might be as gigantic as possible.

The truest grandeur is moral. When there is a heavenquake because Jupiter has bent his brows; — when Apollo comes down in his wrath "like night-time," and a plague falls upon the people; when a fated man in a tragedy is described sleeping at the foot of an altar with three tremendous looking women (the furies) keeping an eye upon him; — when a doomed old man in a grove is called away by a voice, — after which he is never more seen; or to turn the brighter side of power, when Bacchus leaps out of his chariot in Titian's picture, looking (to our mortal eyes) with the fierce gravity of a wine-god's-energy, though he comes to comfort a mourner; or to sum up all that is sweet as well as powerful, when Juno goes to Venus to borrow her girdle, in order that she may appear irresistible in the eyes of Jupiter; it is then we feel all the force and beauty of the Greek fables; and an intimacy with their sculpture shows us the eternal youth of this beauty, and renders it a sort of personal acquaintance.

Milton wrote some fine verses on the cessation of heathen oracles, in which while he thinks he is triumphing over the dissolution of the gods like a proper Christian, he is evidently regretting and lingering over them, as was natural to a poet. He need not have lamented. A proper sense of universality knows how to reconcile the real beauty of all creeds; and the gods survive in the midst of his own epic, lifted by his own hand above the degradation to which he has thrust them. Vulcan, he says, was called Mammon in heaven, and was a fallen angel. But he has another name for him better than either. Hear how he rolls the harmony of his vowels.

> Nor was his name unheard, or unador'd
> In ancient Greece; and in Ausonian land
> Men call'd him Mulciber; and how he fell
> From heav'n, they fabled, thrown by angry Jove
> Sheer o'er the crystal battlements. From morn
> To noon he fell; — from noon to dewy eve, —
> A summer's day; and with the setting sun
> Dropt from the zenith like a falling star
> On Lemnos th' Ægean Isle. Thus they relate,
> Erring.
> PAR. LOST, *Book I.*

"Not more than you did," Homer might have said to him in Elysium, "when you called my divine architect a sordid archangel fond of gold, and made him fall from a state of perfect holiness and bliss, which was impossible."

"Brother, brother," Milton might have said, glancing at the author of the "Beggar's Opera," "we were both in the wrong; — except when you were painting Helen and Andromache, or sending your verses forward like a devouring fire."

"Or you," would the heroic ancient rejoin, "when you made us acquainted with the dignity of those two gentle creatures in Paradise, and wrote verses full of tranquil superiority, which make mine appear to me like the talking of Mars compared with that of Jupiter."

No heathen paradise, according to Milton, could compare with his; yet in saying so, he lingers so fondly among the illegal shades that it is doubtful which he prefers.

> Not that fair field
> Of Enna, where Proserpine, gathering flowers,
> Herself a fairer flow'r by gloomy Dis
> Was gather'd; which cost Ceres all that pain
> To seek her through the world; nor that sweet grove
> Of Daphne, by Orontes, and the inspir'd
> Castalian spring, might with this Paradise
> Of Eden strive; nor that Nyseian isle
> Girt with the river Triton, where old Cham,
> Whom gentiles Ammon call and Lybian Jove,
> Hid Amalthea, and her florid son,
> Young Bacchus, from his step-dame Rhea's eye.

Milton had, in fact, settled this question of the indestructibility of paganism in his youth. His college exercises showing that "nature could not grow old," showed also that the gods and goddesses must remain with her. The style of Milton's Latin verses is founded on Ovid; but his love of a conscious and sonorous music renders it his own, and perhaps there is nothing more like the elder English Milton than these young exercises of his in a classical language.

Dr. Johnson objects to Milton's Lycidas (which is an elegy on a lost companion of his studies), that "passion plucks no berries from the myrtle and ivy; nor calls upon Arethuse and Mincius; nor tells of *rough Satyrs and Fauns with cloven heel.*" To which Wharton very properly answers, "but poetry does this: and in the hands of Milton does it with a peculiar and irresistible charm. Subordinate poets exercise no invention when they tell how a shepherd has lost a companion, and must feed his flocks alone, without any judge of his skill in piping; but Milton dignifies and adorns these common artificial incidents with unexpected touches of picturesque beauty, with the graces of sentiment and with the novelties of original genius." Wharton says further, that "poetry is not always unconnected with passion," and then gives an instance out of the poem where Milton speaks of the body of his lost friend. But he might have added that poetry itself is a passion; that Fleet Street and "the Mitre," though very good things, are not the only ones; that these two young friends lived in the imaginative, as well as the every-day world; that the survivor most probably missed the companion of his studies more on the banks of the Arethuse and the Mincius, than he did in the college grounds; in short, that there is a state of poetical belief, in which the images of truth and beauty which are by their nature lasting, become visible and affecting to the mind in proportion to the truth and beauty of its own tact for universality. Bacon, though no poet, had it, and adorned his house with pagan sculptures; because, being a universal philosopher, he included a knowledge of what was poetical. All the poets have had it as a matter of course, more or less; but the greatest most of all. Shakespeare included it for the very reason that he left no part of the world unsympathized with; namely, that he was, of all poets, the most universal.

> Hyperion's curls; the front of Jove himself;
> An eye like Mars to threaten and command;
> A station like the herald Mercury,
> New-lighted on a heaven-kissing hill.

These Miltonic lines flowed from the same pen that recorded the vagaries of Falstaff and Mrs. Quickly. Dr. Johnson would have made a bad business of the heathen mythology. He did so when he made a Turk pull his enemy out of the "Pleiad's golden chariot."* He was conversant only with what is called real life; wonderfully well indeed, and with great wit and good sense; but there he stopped. He might have as soon undertaken to describe a real piece of old poetical beauty, or passion either, as clap his wig on the head of Apollo. He laughed with reason at Prior, for comparing his Chloes to Venus and Diana, and talking of their going out a hunting *with ivory quivers graceful at their side.* This was the French notion of using the Greek fables; and with the French, indeed, the heathen mythology became the most spurious and the most faded of drugs. They might as well have called a box of millinery the oracle of Delphi. The Germans understood it better, but we do not think it has ever been revived to more beautiful account than in the young poetry and remote haunts of imagination of the late Mr. Keats. He lamented that he could not do it justice. "Oh, how unlike," he cries, speaking of the style of his fine poem, Hyperion,

> To that large utterance of the early gods!

But this was the modesty of a real poet. Milton himself would have been happy to read his Hyperion aloud, and to have welcomed the new spirit among the choir of poets, with its

> Elysian beauty, melancholy grace.

Mr. Shelley beautifully applied to his young friend the distich of Plato upon Agathon, who having been, he says, a morning star among the living, was now an evening

---

* In his tragedy of Irene. Gibbon has noticed it somewhere in the Decline and Fall.

star in the shades. Here, also, was the true taste of the antique. Nay, it is possible that the melancholy of modern genius to the eyes of which a larger and obscurer world has been thrown open, may have discovered a more imaginative character in the mythology of the ancient poets, than accompanies our usual notion of it. The cheerfulness of all those poets, except the dramatic ones, and the everlasting and visible youth of their sculptures, come before us, and make us think of nothing but Pan and Pomona, of Bacchus, Apollo, and the Graces. Nor is it possible to deny that this is the general and perhaps the just impression, though exaggerated; and that the Pythian organ, with all its grandeur, does not roll such peals

>Of pomp and threatening harmony

as those of the old Gregorian chapels, and the mingling hierarchies of earth and heaven.* Unfortunately the grandest parts of all religions have hitherto appealed to the least respectable of our passions,—our fear. It is the beauty of the truly divine part of Christianity that it appeals to love; and if it then inspires melancholy, it is one of a nobler sort, animating us to endeavor and promising a state of things, to which the grandeur both of Paganism and Catholicism may become as the dreams of remembered sickness in infancy.

At all events, it is certain that some of the great modern poets in consequence of their remoteness from the age of pagan belief, and its every-day effect on the mind, often

---

* On the Feast of St. Michael and All Saints, the Catholic Church believes that the whole of the faithful on earth and *in heaven*, with all the angelical hierarchies, are lifting up their voices in unison! one of the sublimest and most beautiful fancies that ever entered into the heart of man.

write in a nobler manner upon the gods of antiquity than the ancients themselves. He that would run the whole round of the spirit of heathenism to perfection, must become intimate with the poetry of Milton and Spenser; of Ovid, Homer, Theocritus, and the Greek tragedians; with the novels of Wieland, the sculptures of Phidias and others, and the pictures of Raphael, and the Caraccis, and Nicholas Poussin. But *a single page of Spenser or one morning at the Angerstein Gallery*, will make him better acquainted with it than a dozen such folios as Spence's Polymetis, or all the mythologists and book-poets who have attempted to draw Greek inspiration from a Latin fount.

ON THE GENII OF THE GREEKS AND ROMANS, AND THE SPIRIT THAT WAS SAID TO HAVE WAITED ON SOCRATES.

THE angelical or middle beings of the Greeks and Romans are called by the common name of genii, though the term is not correct, for the Greeks were unacquainted with the word genius. Their spirit was called a demon; and we suspect that a further distinction is to be drawn between the two words, for a reason which will be seen by and by. The ill sense in which demon is now taken, originated with the Fathers of the Church, who, assuming that a pagan intelligence must be a bad one, caused the word to become synonymous with devil. But there are few things more remarkable than the abundant use which the Church made of the speculations of the Greek philosophers, and the contempt with which indiscreet members of it have treated them. Take away the subtleties of the Platonic theology from certain sects of Christians, and their very orthodoxy would tumble to pieces.

Demon, if it be derived, as most of the learned think, from a word signifying *to know by inquiry*, and the root of which signifies *a torch*, may be translated the enlightened, or, simply, a light or intelligence. A blessed spirit, eternally increasing in knowledge or illumination (which some think will be one of its beatitudes), gives an enlarged sense to the word demon.

Plato certainly had no ill opinion of his demon, even when the intelligence was acting in a manner which the vulgar pronounced to be evil, and upon which the philosopher has delivered a sentiment equally profound and humane. The following may be regarded as a summary of his notions about the spiritual world. Taking up the religion of his country, as proclaimed by Hesiod and others, and endeavoring to harmonize it with reason, he conceived that, agreeably to the ranks and gradations which we fancy in nature, there must be intermediate beings between men and gods, — the gods themselves being far from the top of spirituality. We have already stated his opinions on that subject. Next to the gods came the demons, who partook of their divinity mixed with what he called the soul of the world, and ministered round about them as well as on earth; in fact, were the angels of the Christian system but a little more allied to their superiors. "What other philosophers called demons," says the devout platonical Jew Philo, "Moses usually called angels." * Next to

---

* There is good reason to believe that Dionysius, the pretended Areopagite, who is the great authority with writers upon the angelical nature, was a Platon-

demons, but farther apart from them than demons were from the gods, and yet partaking of the angelical office, were heroes, or spirits clothed in a light ethereal body, and partaking still more of the soul of the world; perhaps the souls of men who had been heroical on earth, or sent down to embody them to that end. And lastly came the souls of men, which were the faintest emanation of the Deity, and clogged with earthly clothing in addition to the mundane nature of their spirits.*

The chiefs among these spiritual beings were very like the gods, and often mistaken for them, which is said to have given them great satisfaction. It is upon the strength of this fancy that attempts were made to account for the

---

izing Christian of the school of Alexandria. If so, there is no saying how far we are not indebted for our ordinary notions of angels themselves to Plato, nor indeed how far the Christian and Jewish angel and the demon of the Greeks are not one and the same spirit; for it is impossible to say how much of the Jewish Cabala is not Alexandrian. On the other hand, the Platonists of that city mixed up their dogmas with the Oriental philosophy, so that the angel comes round again to the East, and is traceable to Persia and India. Nothing of all this need shake him; for it is in the heart and hopes of man that his nest is found. Plato's angel, Pythagoras's, Philo's, Zoroaster's, and Jeremy Taylor's, are all the same spirit under different names; and those who would love him properly, must know as much, or they cannot. Henry Moore and others, who may be emphatically styled our angelical doctors, avowedly undertook to unite the Platonic, Pythagorean, and Cabalistic opinion. (See Enfield's Abridgment of Brucker.) It is true they derived them all from the Hebrew, — which is about as much as if they had said that the Egyptians were skilled in all the learning of Moses, instead of Moses in all the learning of the Egyptians.

* Demons and heroes were the angels and saints of the Catholic hierarchy. They had their chapels, altars, feasts, and domestic worship precisely in the same spirit; and the souls of the departed were from time to time added to the list. (See the Abbé Banier's "Mythology and Fables of the Ancients," explained from history, vol. iii. p. 434.) The heroines were the female saints. We make this remark in no ironical spirit, though the Abbé would not thank us for it.

stories of the gods, and their freaks upon earth; for demons, any more than angels, were not incapable of a little aberration. The supposed visits, for instance, of Jupiter down to earth, when he came —

> "Now, like a ram, fair Helle to pervert,
> Now, like a bull, Europa to withdraw,"

were the work of those spirits about him, who may truly be called the jovial, and who delighted in bearing his name, as a Scottish clan does that of its chieftain. We have already mentioned the pious indignation of Plutarch at the indiscreet tales of the poets. It is remarkable that, according to Plato, these satellites encircled their master precisely in the manner of the angelical hierarchies. "But how different," it may be said, "were their natures!" Not, perhaps, quite so much so as may be fancied. We have already hinted a resemblance in one point; and, in others, the advantage has not always been kept on the proper side. Milton's angels, when they let down the unascendable, heavenly staircase to imbitter the agonies of Satan, did a worse thing than any recorded of the Jupiters and Apollos. We must be cautious how, in attributing one or two virtues to a set of beings, we think we endow them with all the rest.

Demons were not, as some thought them, the souls of men. The latter had the honor of assisting demons, but were a separate class. Indeed, according to Plato, the word soul might as well have been put for man, in opposition to spirit; for he held that the human being was properly a soul, using the body only as an instrument. Nor was this soul the guardian angel or demon, though sometimes called a demon by reason of its superiority, but man himself. It was immortal, pre-existent; and the object of virtue was to restore it to its former state of beatitude in certain regions of light, from which it had fallen. This, among other doctrines of Plato, has been a favorite one with the poets, and would appear to have been seriously entertained by one of the present day.* What difficulty it clears, or what trouble it takes away, we cannot see. Progression is surely a better doctrine than recovery; especially if we look upon evil as partial, fugitive, and convertible, like a hard substance, to good. Besides, we should take the whole of our species with us, and not always be looking after our own lost perfections.

The guardian demons assigned to man, came out of the whole of these orders indiscriminately. Their rank was proportioned to the virtue and intelligence of the individual. Plotinus and others had guardian demons of a very high order. The demon of Socrates is said to have been called a god, because it was of the order that were taken for gods. It was the business of this spiritual attendant to be a kind of soul in addition. The soul, or real man, governed the animal part of us; and the demon governed the soul. He was a tutor accompanying the pupil. If the pupil did amiss, it was not the tutor's fault. He lamented, and tried to mend it, perhaps, by subjecting it to some misery, or even vice. The process in this case is not very clear. Good demons appear sometimes to be distinct from bad ones, sometimes to be confounded with them. The vulgar supposed, with the Jesuit who wrote the "Pantheon," that every person had two demons assigned to him: one a good demon who incited him to virtue; the other a bad one, who prompted him "to all manner of vice

---

* " Our life is but a dream and a forgetting."
WORDSWORTH.

and wickedness."* But the benign logic of Plato rejected a useless malignity. Evil when it came, was supposed to be for a good purpose: or rather not being of a nature to be immediately got rid of, was turned to good account; and man was ultimately the better for it. The demon did every thing he could to exalt the intellect of his charge, to regulate his passions, and perfect his nature throughout; in short, to teach his soul, as the soul aspired to teach the body; and what is remarkable, though he could not supply fate itself, he is said to have supplied things fortuitous; that is to say, "to give us a chance," as we phrase it, and put us in the way of shaping what we were to suppose was rough-hewn. This was reversing the Shakespearian order of Providence, or rather, perhaps, giving it a new meaning; for we, or the untaught part of us, and fate, might be supposed to go blindly to the same end, did not our intelligence keep on the alert.

> There's a *divinity* that shapes our ends,
> Rough-hew them how we will.†

---

* See the "Pantheon" attributed to Mr. Tooke. Tooke's "Pantheon" is a *rifacimento* of King's "Pantheon," which was a translation from a Jesuit of the name of Pomey. It contains "in every page, an elaborate calumny," says Mr. Baldwin, "upon the gods of the Greeks, and that in the coarsest thoughts and words that taverns could furnish. The author seems continually haunted by the fear that his pupil might prefer the religion of Jupiter to the religion of Christ." — Baldwin's "Pantheon," preface, p. 5. This philosophical mythologist is of opinion that there was no ground for fear of that sort. We have observed elsewhere how little the young readers of Tooke think of the abuse at all; but if they had any sense of it, undoubtedly it goes in Jupiter's favor. We believe there is one thing which is not lost upon them, and that is, the affected horror and secret delight with which the Jesuit dwells upon certain vagaries of the gayer deities. Besides, he paints sometimes in good, admiring earnest; and then the boys attend to him as gravely. See, for instance, the beginning of his chapter on Venus, which, if we read once at school, we read a thousand times, comparing it with the engraving.

† See Taylor's and Sydenham's "Translations of Plato," vol. i. p. 16, and vol. ii. p. 308.

If all this is not much clearer than attempts to explain such matters are apt to be, and if the parts of Plato's theology (which were derived from the national creed) do little honor sometimes to the general spirit of it, which was his own; there is something at all times extremely elevating in his aspirations after the good and beautiful. St. Augustin complained that the reading of Plato made him proud. We do believe that it is impossible for readers of any enthusiasm to sit long over some of his writings (the Banquet for instance) and not feel an unusual exaltation of spirit, — a love of the good and beautiful, for their own sakes, and in honor of human nature. But there is no danger, we conceive, provided we correct this poetical state of self-aspiration with a remembrance of the admonitions of Christianity, — the sympathy with our fellow-creatures. The more hope we have of ourselves under that correction, the more we shall have of others.

The great point is to elevate ourselves by elevating humanity at large.

It is difficult to know what to make of the demon of Socrates. It is clear that he laid claim to a special consciousness of this attendant spirit — a sort of revelation, that we believe had never before been vouchsafed. The spirit gave him intimations rather what to avoid than to do; for the Platonists tell us, that Socrates was led by his own nature to do what was right; but out of the fervor of his desire to do it, was liable to be mistaken in the season. For instance, he had a tendency to give the benefit of his wisdom to all men indiscriminately; and here the demon would sometimes warn him off, that he might not waste his philosophy upon a fool. This was at least an ingenious and mortifying satire. But the spirit interfered also on occasions that seem very trifling, though accordant with the office assigned to him by Plato of presiding over fortuitous events. Socrates was going one day to see a friend in company with some others, when he made a sudden halt, and told them that his demon had advised him not to go down that street, but to choose another. Some of them turned back, but others persisting in the path before them, "on purpose as 'twere, to confute Socrates his demon," encountered a herd of muddy swine, and came home with their clothes all over dirt. Charillus, a musician who had come to Athens to see the philosopher Cebes, got especially mudded, so that now and then, says Plutarch, "he and his friends would think in merriment on Socrates his demon, wondering that it never forsook the man, and that Heaven took such particular care of him."* It was particular enough in heaven, to be sure, to hinder a philosopher from having his drapery damaged; but we suppose matters would have been worse, had he gone the way of the inferior flesh. He would have made it worth the pigs' while to be more tragical.

This demon is the only doubtful thing about the character of Socrates, for as to the common misconceptions of him, they are but the natural conclusions of vulgar minds; and Aristophanes, who became a traitor to the graces he had learned at his table, and condescended to encourage the misconceptions in order to please the instinctive jealousy of the men of wit and pleasure about town, was but a splendid buffoon. But when we reflect that the wisdom inculcated by Socrates was of a nature particularly straightforward and practical; this supernatural twist in

---

* See the story as related by Plutarch, and translated by Creech, in the "Morals by several Hands." Vol. II. p. 287. The street preferred by the philosopher was "Trunkmakers Street," and the fatal one "Gravers Row," says Creech, "near the Guildhall."

his pretensions appears the more extraordinary. To be sure it has been well argued, that no men are more likely to be put out of their reckoning by a sudden incursion of fancy or demand upon their belief, than those who are the most mechanical and matter-of-fact on all other points. They are not used to it ; and have no grounds to go upon, the moment the hardest and dryest ones are taken from under them. Plato has rendered it difficult to believe this of Socrates ; but then we have the authority of Socrates for concluding that Plato put a great deal in his head that he never uttered ; and the Socrates of Xenophon, we think, the practical farmer and house-keeper, might not be supposed incapable of yielding to superstitious delusion out of a defect of imagination. Socrates sometimes reminds us of Dr. Johnson. He was a Johnson on a higher scale, healthier with more self-command ; and instead of being intemperate and repenting all his life, had conquered his passions, and turned them into graces becoming his reason. Johnson had a sturdy every-day good sense and wit and words to impress it ; but it was only persuasion in him: in Socrates it was persuasion and practice. Now Johnson had a strong tendency to be moved by superstitious impressions and perplexities from within. A sudden action of the bile, not well understood, or taken as a moral instead of a physical intimation, would give rise to some painful thoughts ; and this (which is a weakness that many temperaments given to reflection and not in perfect health, have found it necessary to guard against), would lead him into some superstitious practice, or avoidance. There is a circumstance related of him, very like this one of Socrates ; only the sedentary, diseased, dinner-loving Englishman made a gloomy business of it ; while the sturdy gymnastic Athenian, mastering the weakness of his stomach, turned the superstition on his side into an elegance and an exaltation. The fact we allude to is, that Johnson would never go down Cranbourne Alley, or some street thereabout. He always turned and went round about. Had he been gay and confident, not overwhelmed with scrofula, and with the more gloomy parts of his creed, he might have sworn as Socrates did, that it was his guardian angel that told him not to go that way. Had it been Jeremy Taylor — Jeremy the amiable and the handsome, the Sir Charles Grandison of Christianity, who, with equal comfort to his security, pronounced a panegyric upon a wedding ring, or a description of eternal torments (so much can superstition pervert a sweet nature) — he, if he had thought he had an intimation from within, would have infallibly laid it to the account of the prettiest angel of the skies. Was it something of a like vanity in Socrates (too superior to his fellows, not to fall into some disadvantage of that sort)? or was it an unhealthy movement within him happily turned? or was it a joke which was to be taken for serious, by those who liked? or did it arise from one of those perplexities of not knowing what to conclude, to which the greatest minds may be subject when they attain to the end of their experience, and stand between the known world and the unknown? or, lastly, was it owing (as we fear is most likely) partly to a superstition retained from his nurse, and partly to a determination to construe an occasional fancy, thus warranted, into a conscious certainty, and so turn his interest with heaven to the account of his effect among men? Such, we fear, is the most reasonable conjecture, and such we take to be the general impression; though with a delicacy, equally singular and creditable to them, mankind (with rare exceptions) seem to have agreed to say as little about the matter as possible, choosing rather to give so great a man the benefit of their ignorance, than lose any part of their reverence for his wisdom. One thing must not be forgotten; that this pretension to an unusual sense of his attendant spirit assisted in getting him into trouble. He was accused of introducing false gods, — a singular charge, which shows how much the opinion of a guardian deity had gone out of use. On the other hand, he argued (with a true look of feeling, and which must afterwards have had great effect), that it was not his fault if he beheld in omens and intimations the immediate influence of his guardian angel, and not merely the omens themselves. That he did believe in the latter somehow or other, is generally admitted.

It is not a little curious, that this is the only story of a good demon that has come down to us in the records of antiquity. Some philosophers had theirs long afterwards; but these were evident imitations. Stories of bad demons, according to the vulgar notion, are more numerous. Two are to be found in the life of Apollonius of Tyana. Another is in Pausanus, and a third is the famous one of Brutus. These injurious persons were seldom however bad by nature. They become so from ill usage, being in fact, the souls of men who had been ill treated when alive.

ON THE GENII OF ANTIQUITY AND THE POETS.

HE bad demon was thought to be of formidable shape, black, frowning, and brutal. A man, according to Pausanias, fought with one, and drove him into the sea. As we have told the story before (in the "Indicator"),* and it is little to tell, we shall proceed to give the noblest passage ever written about demons, in the scene out of Shakespeare. The spirit that appeared to Brutus has been variously represented. Some made it of the common order of malignant appearances; others have described it as resembling Cæsar. This was the light in which it was beheld by our great poet.

With what exquisite art; that is to say, with what exquisite nature, has he not introduced this scene, and made us love and admire the illustrious patriot, who having done what he could upon earth, and prepared for his last effort, is about to encounter the menaces of fate. How admirably, by the help of the little boy and the lute, has he painted him, who was only a dictator and a warrior because he was a great humanist, the Platonic philosopher in action, the ideal, yet not passionless, man, — such a one as Shakespeare loved, not because he loved only select human nature, but because he loved all that human nature contained!

We must confess, that in our opinion the address to the Ghost is not so good as in simple old Plutarch. There is too much astonishment and agitation in it; if not for na-

---

* In the article on the "Household Gods of the Ancients."— ED.

ture, at least for the superinduced and philosophic nature, that we are led to suppose was in Brutus; and the same objection might be made to what follows. The household are called up in too much alarm. It is Brutus's care for his servants, his bidding them take their rest, and what he says to the little lute-player, overcome with sleep, that render the scene so charming. The divine scene also between him and Cassius, where he tells him that "Portia is dead," has just preceded it.

> *Brutus.* Lucius, my gown. [*Exit* LUCIUS.] Farewell, good Messala;
> Good night, Titinius: — noble, noble Cassius,
> Good night, and good repose.
> *Cassius.* O, my dear brother!
> This was an ill beginning of the night:
> Never come such division 'tween our souls!
> Let it not, Brutus.
>   *Bru.* Every thing is well.
>   *Cas.* Good night, my lord.
>   *Bru.* Good night, good brother.
> *Titinius* and *Messala.* Good night, lord Brutus.
>   *Bru.*   Farewell, every one.
>   [*Exeunt Cas., Tit., and Mes.*
>
>   *Re-enter* LUCIUS *with the gown.*
>
> Give me the gown. Where is thy instrument?
>   *Lucius.* Here in the tent.
>   *Bru.*   What, thou speak'st drowsily?
> Poor knave, I blame thee not; thou art o'er-watched.
> Call Claudius, and some other of my men;
> I'll have them sleep on cushions in my tent.
>   *Luc.* Varro and Claudius.
>
>   *Enter* VARRO *and* CLAUDIUS.
>
>   *Varro.* Calls my lord?
>   *Bru.* I pray you, sirs, lie in my tent and sleep;
> It may be, I shall raise you by and by
> On business to my brother Cassius.
>   *Var.* So please you, we will stand, and watch your pleasure.
>   *Bru.* I will not have it so: lie down, good sirs;

It may be, I shall otherwise think me.
Look, Lucius, here's the book I sought for so;
I put it in the pocket of my gown. *[Servants lie down.*
   Luc. I was sure, your lordship did not give it me.
   Bru. Bear with me, good boy, I am much forgetful.
Canst thou hold up thy heavy eyes awhile,
And touch thy instrument a strain or two?
   Luc. Ay, my lord, an it please you.
   Bru.   It does, my boy.
I trouble thee too much, but thou art willing.
   Luc. It is my duty, sir.
   Bru. I should not urge thy duty past thy might;
I know young bloods look for a time of rest.
   Luc. I have slept, my lord, already.
   Bru. It is well done; and thou shalt sleep again;
I will not hold thee long: if I do live,
I will be good to thee. *[Music and a song.*
This is a sleepy tune: — O, murderous slumber!
Lay'st thou thy leaden mace upon my boy,
That plays thee music? — Gentle knave, good night;
I will not do thee so much wrong to wake thee.
If thou dost nod, thou break'st thy instrument;
I'll take it from thee; and good boy, good night.
Let me see, let me see; is not the leaf turn'd down,
Where I left reading? Here it is, I think. *[He sits down.*

        Enter the GHOST *of* CÆSAR.

How ill this taper burns! Ha! who comes here?
I think it is the weakness of mine eyes,
That shapes this monstrous apparition.
It comes upon me: — art thou any thing?
Art thou some god, some angel, or some devil,
That mak'st my blood cold, and my hair to stare?
Speak to me, what thou art.
   Ghost. Thy evil spirit, Brutus.
   Bru.   Why com'st thou?
   Ghost. To tell thee, thou shalt see me at Philippi.
   Bru. Well;
Then I shall see thee again?
   Ghost.   Ay, at Philippi. *[Ghost vanishes.*
   Bru. Why, I will see thee at Philippi then. —
Now I have taken heart, thou vanishest:
Ill spirit, I would hold more talk with thee. —

Boy! Lucius! Varro! Claudius! sirs awake!—
Claudius!
   Luc. The strings, my lord, are false.
   Bru. He thinks, he is still at his instrument.—
Lucius, awake.
   Luc. My lord?
   Bru. Didst thou dream that thou so cry'dst out?
   Luc. My lord, I do not know that I did cry.
   Bru. Yes, that thou didst; didst thou see any thing?
   Luc. Nothing, my lord.
   Bru. Sleep again, Lucius.—Sirrah, Claudius!
Fellow thou! awake.
   Var. My lord.
   Clau. My lord.
   Bru. Why did you so cry out, sirs, in your sleep?
   Var. and *Clau.* Did we, my lord?
   Bru.   Ay: saw you any thing?
   Var. No, my lord, I saw nothing.
   Clau.   Nor I, my lord.
   Bru. Go, and commend me to my brother Cassius;
Bid him set on his powers betimes before;
And we will follow.
   Var. and *Clau.* It shall be done, my lord.   *[Exeunt.*

The Roman genius appears to have been a very material sort of personage compared with the Greek demon, and altogether addicted to earth. We know not where it is found that he was first called *gerulus*, or a carrier on of affairs: perhaps in Varro; but whether as *gerulus*, or as genius (the spirit of things generated), the Romans made him after their own likeness, and gave him as little to do with the stars as possible. The Romans had not the fancy of the Greeks, and cared little for their ethereal pleasures. Accordingly, their attendant spirit was either fighting and conquering (on which occasion he took the wings of victory, as you may see in the imperial sculptures), or he was dining and enjoying himself: sitting under his plane-tree and drinking with his mistress. To gratify their appetites, was called "*indulging the genius;*" not to gratify them, was "*defrauding*" him. They seem to have forgotten that he had any thing to do with restraint. Ovid, the most poetical of their poets, in all his uses of the words genius or genii, never hints at the possibility of their having any meaning beyond something local and comfortable. There is the genius of the city, and the genius of one's father. The Sabine women were "a genial prey." Crowns of flowers are genial; a certain kind of musical instrument is particularly genial, and agrees with *dulcibus jocis*, — that is to say, with double meanings; Bacchus is the planter of the genial vine (genial indeed was a name of Bacchus); a popular holiday, pleasantly described in the Fasti, where every one is eating and drinking by the side of his lass, is a genial feast.*

Hence the acceptation of the word among ourselves, though we are fain to give it more grace and sentiment. The "genial bed" of Milton is not exactly Ovidian; though, by the way, the good-natured libertine was the favorite Latin poet of our great puritan.

We hear little of the bad genius among the Romans. They seem to have agreed to treat him as bad geniuses ought to be, and drop his acquaintance. But he was black, like his brother in Greece. Voltaire has a pleasant story of the black and white genius. Valerius Maximus, a servile writer, who had the luck to survive his betters and become a classic, tells a story (probably to please the men in power whom he deified) which appears to have been confounded with that of Brutus. "We are told by Valerius Maximus," says Mr. Tooke, "that when Cassius fled

---

* "Fastorum," lib. iii. v. 523. It is the description of a modern Florentine holiday.

to Athens, after Anthony was beaten at Actium, there appeared to him a man of long stature, of a black swarthy complexion, with large hair, and a *nasty* beard. Cassius asked him who he was; and the apparition answered, 'I am your evil genius.'" *

Spenser has placed an evil genius at the gate of his false bower of bliss, and old genius, or the fatherly principle of life and care, at the door of the great nursery-gardens of the universe.

> Old genius the porter of them was;
> Old genius, the which a double nature has.
>
> He letteth in, he letteth out to wend,
> All that to come into this world desire;
> A thousand thousand naked babes attend
> About him day and night, which do require
> That he with fleshly weeds would them attire.

What follows and precedes this passage is a true piece of Platonical coloring, founded upon the old Greek allegories. These nursery grounds, sprouting with infants and with the germs of all things, would make a very happy place if it were not for *Time*, who with his "flaggy wings," goes playing the devil among the beds, to the great regret of Venus. It is an old story, and a true; and the worst of it is, that Venus herself (though the poet does not here say so) joins with her enemies to assist him.

> ——— Were it not that Time their troubler is,
> All that in this delightful gardin growes
> Should happy been, and have immortal bliss:
> For here all plenty and all pleasure flowes;
> And swete Love gentle fitts among them throwes,
> Without fell rancour or fond gealosy:

---

* Tooke's "Pantheon," part 4, chap. iii. sect. 4. The genius speaks Greek, which was better bred of him than having a beard.

76 GENII OF ANTIQUITY AND THE POETS.

> Franckly each paramour his leman knowes;
> Each bird his mate; ne any does envy
> Their goodly meriment and gay felicity.
>
> There is continual spring, and harvest there
>   Continuall, both meeting at one tyme:
>   For both the boughes doe laughing blossoms beare,
>   And with fresh colours decke the wanton pryme,
>   And eke attonce the heavy trees they clyme,
>   Which seeme to labour under their fruites lode:
>   The whyles the joyous birdes make their pastyme
>   Emongst the shady leaves, their sweet abode,
>   And their trew loves without suspicion tell abrode.

We are then presented with one of his arbors, of which he was the cunningest builder in all fairy-land. The present one belongs to Venus and Adonis.

> Right in the middest of that Paradise
>   There stood a stately mount, on whose round top
>   A gloomy grove of mirtle trees did rise,
>   Whose shady boughes sharp steele did never lop,
>   Nor wicked beastes their tender buds did crop,
>   But like a girlond compassed the hight,
>   And from their fruitfull sydes sweet gum did drop,
>   That all the ground, with pretious deaw bedight,
>   Threw forth most dainty odours and most sweet delight.
>
> And in the thickest covert of that shade
>   There was a pleasant arber, not by art
>   But of the trees own inclination made,
>   Which knitting their rancke braunches part to part,
>   With wanton yvie-twine entrayled athwart,
>   And eglantine and caprifole emong,
>   Fashion'd above within their inmost part,
>   That neither Phœbus beams could through them throng,
>   Nor Æolus sharp blast could worke them any wrong.
>   FAIRY QUEENE, Book III. Canto vi.

Here Venus was wont to enjoy the company of Adonis; "Adonis," says Upton, "being matter, and Venus, form."

Ovid would have said, " he did not know how that might be, but that the allegory 'was genial.' "

The poets are a kind of eclectic philosophers, who pick out of theories whatever is suitable to the truth of natural feeling and the candor of experience ; and thus, with due allowances for what is taught them, may be looked upon as among the truest as well as most universal of philosophers. The most opinionate of them, Milton for one, are continually surrendering the notions induced upon them by their age or country, to the cause of their greater mother-country, the universe ; like beings deeply sympathizing with man, but impatient of wearing the clothes and customs of a particular generation. It is doubtful, considering the whole context of Milton's life, and taking away the excitements of personal feelings, whether he was a jot more in earnest when playing the polemic, than in giving himself up to the dreams of Plato ; whether he felt more, or so much, in common with Raphael and Michael, as with the genius of the groves of Harefield, listening at night-time to the music of the spheres. In one of his prose works (we quote from memory) he complains of being forced into public brawls and "hoarse seas of dispute ;" and asks, what but a sense of duty could have enabled him thus to have been " put off from beholding the bright countenance of Truth in the quiet and still air of delightful studies." This truth was truth universal ; this air, the same that haunted the room of Plato, and came breathing from Elysium. No man had a greater taste than he for the "religio loci," — the genius of a particular spot. The genius of a wood in particular, was a special friend of his, as indeed he has been of all poets. The following passage has been often quoted ; but we must not on that account pass it by. New beauties may be found in it every time. A passage in a wood has been often trod, but we tread it again. The pleasure is ever young, though the path is old. So —

> When the sun begins to fling
> His flaring beams, me, Goddess, bring
> To arched walks of twilight groves,
> And shadows brown, that Sylvan loves,
> Of pine or monumental oak,
> Where the rude axe with heaved stroke,
> Was never heard the nymphs to daunt,
> Or fright them from their hallow'd haunt.
> There in close covert by some brook,
> Where no profaner eye may look,
> Hide me from day's garish eye,
> While the bee with honied thigh,
> That at her flowery work doth sing,
> And the waters murmuring,
> With such consort as they keep,
> Entice the dewy-feather'd sleep;
> And let some strange mysterious dream
> Wave at his wings in aery stream
> Of lively portraiture display'd,
> Softly on my eye-lids laid.
> And as I wake, sweet music breathe
> Above, about, or underneath,
> Sent by some spirit to mortals good,
> Or the unseen genius of the wood.
>
> PENSEROSO.

In the Arcades, a Marque performed at Harefield before the Countess of Derby, one of these genii makes his appearance. Two noble shepherds coming forward are met by the "genius of the wood." We will close our article with him as a proper harmonious personage, who unites the spirit of the Greek and Roman demonology. He need not have troubled himself, perhaps, with "*curling*" the groves; and his "*tassel'd*" horn is a little fine and particular, — not remote enough or audible. But the

young poet was writing to please young patricians. The
"tassel" was for *their* nobility; the rest is for his own.

> Stay, gentle swains; for though in this disguise,
> I see bright honour sparkle through your eyes;
> Of famous Arcady ye are, and sprung
> Of that renowned flood, so often sung,
> Divine Alpheus, who by secret sluce
> Stole under seas to meet his Arethuse;
> And ye, the breathing roses of the wood,
> Fair silver-buskined nymphs, as great and good;
> I know, this quest of yours, and free intent,
> Was all in honour and devotion meant
> To the great mistress of yon princely shrine,
> Whom with low reverence I adore as mine;
> And, with all helpful service, will comply
> To further this night's glad solemnity;
> And lead ye, where ye may more near behold
> What shallow-searching fame hath left untold;
> Which I full oft, amidst these shades alone,
> Have sat to wonder at, and gaze upon;
> For know, by lot from Jove, I am the power
> Of this fair wood, and live in oaken bower,
> To nurse the saplings tall, and curl the grove
> With ringlets quaint, and wanton windings wove.
> And all my plants I save from nightly ill
> Of noisome winds, and blasting vapours chill;
> And from the boughs brush off the evil dew,
> And heal the harms of thwarting thunder blue,
> Or what the cross dire-looking planet smites,
> Or hurtful worm with canker'd venom bites.
> When evening gray doth rise, I fetch my round
> Over the mount and all this hallow'd ground;
> And early, ere the odorous breath of morn
> Awakes the slumbering leaves, or tassel'd horn
> Shakes the high thicket, haste I all about,
> Number my ranks, and visit every sprout
> With puissant words, and murmurs made to bless.
> But else in deep of night, when drowsiness
> Hath lock'd up mortal sense, then listen I
> To the celestial Syrens' harmony,
> That sit upon the nine infolded spheres,
> And sing to those that hold the vital shears,

> And turn the adamantine spindle round,
> On which the fate of gods and men is wound.
> Such sweet compulsion doth in musick lie,
> To lull the daughters of necessity.

This is a passage to read at twilight; or before putting out the candles, in some old country house. There is yet one more passage which we must quote from Milton, about a genius. It concerns also a very demoniacal circumstance, the cessation of the heathen oracles. See with what regret the poet breaks up the haunt of his winged beauties, and sends them floating away into dissolution with their white bodies out of the woods.

> The oracles are dumb,
> No voice or hideous hum
>   Runs through the arched roof in words deceiving.
> Apollo from his shrine
> Can no more divine,
>   With hollow shriek the steep of Delphos leaving.
> No nightly trance, or breathed spell,
> Inspires the pale-eyed priest from the prophetick cell.
>
> The lonely mountains o'er,
> And the resounding shore,
>   A voice of weeping heard and loud lament;
> From haunted spring and dale,
> Edg'd with poplar pale,
>   The parting Genius is with sighing sent:
> With flower-inwoven tresses torn
> The nymphs in twilight shade of tangled thickets mourn
>
> In consecrated earth,
> And on the holy hearth,
>   The Lars, and Lemures, mourn with midnight plaint;
> In urns, and altars round,
> A drear and dying sound
>   Affrights the Flamens at their service quaint;
> And the chill marble seems to sweat,
> While each peculiar Power foregoes his wonted seat.

He proceeds to dismiss the idols of Palestine, and the brute gods of Egypt,

Trampling the unshowered grass with lowings loud.

We do not feel for those, nor does he; but the little household gods of Rome, trembling like kittens on the hearth, and the nymphs of Greece mourning their flowery shades, he loses with an air of tenderness. He forgets that he and the other poets had gathered them into their own Elysium.

FAIRIES.

I.

HE word *fairy*, in the sense of a little miniature being, is peculiar to this country, and is a southern appellation applied to a northern idea. It is the *fee* and *fata* of the French and Italians; who mean by it an imaginary lady of any sort, not of necessity small and generally of the human size. With us, it is the *elf* of our northern ancestors, and means exclusively the little creature inhabiting the woods and caverns, and dancing on the grass.

The progress of knowledge, which humanizes everything, and enables our fancies to pick and choose, has long rendered the English fairy a harmless being, rarely seen of eye and known quite as much, if not more, through the pleasant fancies of the poets, than the earthier creed of the common people. In Germany, also, the fairy is said to have become a being almost entirely benevolent. But among our kinsmen of the North, the Swedes and Danes, and especially the insular races of Iceland and Rugen, the old opinions appear to be in force; and, generally speaking, the pigmy world may be divided into four classes.

First, the white or good fairies, who live above ground, dancing on the grass, or sitting on the leaves of trees — the fairy of our poets. They are fond of sunshine, and are ethereal little creatures.

Second, the dark or under-ground fairies (the dwarfs, trolls, and hill-folk of the continent), an irritable race, workers in mines and smithies, and doing good or evil offices, as it may happen.

Third, the house or homestead fairy, our Puck, Robin Goodfellow, Hobgoblin, &c. (the *Nis* of Denmark and Norway, the *kobold* of Germany, the *brownie* of Scotland, and *tomtegubbe*, or *old man of the house* in Sweden). He is of a similar temper, but good upon the whole, and fond of cleanliness, rewarding and helping the servants for being tidy, and punishing them for the reverse.

And fourth, the water fairy, the kelpie of Scotland, and Nick, Neck, Nickel, Nickar, and Nix, of other countries, the most dangerous of all, appearing like a horse, or a mermaid, or a beautiful girl, and enticing people to their destruction. He is supposed by some, however, not to do it out of ill will, but in order to procure companions in the spirits of those who are drowned.

All the fairies have qualities in common; and for the most part, eat, drink, marry, and are governed like human beings; and all without exception are thieves, and fond of power. In other words, they are like the human beings that invented them. They do the same good and ill offices, are subject to the same passions, and are called *guid folk* and *good neighbors*, out of the same feelings of fear or gratitude. The better sort dress in gay clothes of green, and are handsome; the more equivocal are ugly, big-nosed little knaves, round-eyed and humpbacked, like Punch, or the figures in caricatures. The latter dress in red or brown caps, which they have a great dread of losing, as they must not rest till they get another; and the *hill-folk* among them are great enemies to noise. They keep their promises, because if they did not, the Rugen people say they would be changed into reptiles, beetles, and other ugly creatures, and be obliged to wander in that shape many years. The ordinary German kobold, or house goblin, delights in a mess of grits or water-gruel, with a lump of butter in it. In other countries, as in England of old, he aspires to a cream bowl. Hear our great poet, who was as fond of a rustic supper as any man, and has recorded his roasting chestnuts with his friend Diodati.

> Then to the spicy nut-brown ale,
> With stories told of many a feat,
> How fairy Mab the junkets eat;
> She was pinch'd and pull'd, she sed;
> And he, by friar's lantern led;
> Tells how the drudging Goblin swet,
> To earn his cream-bowl duly set,
> When in one night, ere glimpse of morn,
> His shadowy flail hath thresh'd the corn,
> That ten day-laborers could not end;
> Then lies him down the lubbar fiend,
> And, stretch'd out all the chimney's length,
> Basks at the fire his hairy strength;
> And crop full out of doors he flings,
> Ere the first cock his matin rings.
> Thus done the tales, to bed they creep,
> By whispering winds soon lull'd asleep.

This *gigantifying* of Robin Goodfellow is a sin against the true fairy religion; but a poet's sins are apt to be too agreeable not to be forgiven.* The friar with his lantern, is the same Robin, whose pranks he delighted to record even amidst the stately solemnities of Paradise Lost,— philosophizing upon the nature of the ignis fatuus, that he might have an excuse for bringing him in.

> Lead then, said Eve. He, leading, swiftly roll'd
> In tangles, and made intricate seem straight,
> To mischief swift. Hope elevates, and joy
> Brightens his crest; as when a wandering fire,
> Compact of unctuous vapor, which the night
> Condenses, and the cold environs round,
> Kindled through agitation to a flame,
> Which oft, they say, some evil spirit attends,
> Hovering and blazing with delusive light,
> Misleads the amaz'd night-wanderer from his way
> To bogs and mires, and oft through pond or pool;
> There swallow'd up and lost, from succor far.
> So glister'd the dire Snake.

We have remarked more than once, that the belief in supernatural existences round about us is indigenous to every country, and as natural as fears and hopes. Cli-

---

* "Robin Goodfellow," says Warton, "who is here made a gigantic spirit, fond of lying before the fire, and called the lubbar fiend, seems to be confounded with the sleepy giant mentioned in Beaumont and Fletcher's 'Knight of the Burning Pestle,' Act iii, Sc. I. vol. vi. p. 411, edit. 1751." There is a pretty tale of a witch that had the devil's mark about her, God bless us, that had a giant to her son that was called "Lob-lye-by-the-fire." Todd's Milton, vol. vi. p. 96. Burton in a passage subsequently quoted, tells us in speaking of these fairies, that there is "a bigger kind of them, called with us Hobgoblins and Robin Goodfellows, that would in those superstitious times grinde corne for a messe of milke, cut wood, or do any manner of drudgery worke." Melanch. part i. sec. 2, p. 42, edit. 1632. The bigness arose probably out of the superhuman labor; but, though Milton has made fine use of the lubbar fiend with his "hairy strength," it is surprising he should have sacrificed the greater wonder of the *little* potent fairy to that of a giant.

mate and national character modify it; parts of it may be borrowed; a people may abound in it at one time, and outgrow the abuse of it in another: but wherever human nature is to be found, either in a state of superstitious ignorance, or imaginative knowledge, there the belief will be found with it, modified accordingly.

We shall not trouble ourselves, therefore, with attempting to confine the origin of the fairies to this or that region. A bird, a squirrel, a voice, a tree nodding and gesticulating in the wind, was sufficient to people every one of them with imaginary beings. But creeds may oust creeds or alter them, as invaders alter a people; and there are two circumstances in the nature of the popular fairy, assignable to that northern mythology, to which the belief itself has been traced; we mean the smallness of its stature, and the supposition at one time prevailing, that it was little better than a devil. It is remarkable, also, that inasmuch as the northern mythology is traceable to the Eastern invaders of Europe, our fairies may have issued out of those same mountains of Caucasus, the great Kaf, to which we are indebted for the Peries and Genii. The Pygmies were supposed by the ancients to people the two ends of the earth, northern and southern, where the growth of nature was faint and stunted. In the north they were inhabitants of India, the cranes their enemies being Scythians: in the other quarters, they were found by Hercules in the desert where they assailed him with their bows and arrows, as the Lilliputians did Gulliver, and were carried off by the smiling demigod, in the skin of his lion. Odin, the supposed Scythian or Tartar, is thought to have been the importer of the northern fables. His wandering countrymen of the crane region, may have a nigher personal acquaintance with the little people of the North, than is supposed. In the tales now extant among the Calmuc Tartars, and originating it seems in Thibet, mention is made of certain little children encountered by a wandering Khan in a wood, and quarrelling about "an invisible cup." The Khan tricks them of it in good swindling style; and proceeding onwards meets with certain *Tchadkurs* or evil spirits, quarrelling about some "boots of swiftness," of which he beguiles them in like manner.*

These may be chance coincidences; but these fictions are not of so universal a nature as most; and we cannot help regarding them as corroborations of the Eastern rise of our fablers of the North. We take this opportunity, before we proceed, of noticing another remarkable circumstance in the history of popular fictions; which is, that it is doubtful whether the Greeks had any little beings in their mythology. They regarded the Pygmies as a real people, and never seem to have thought of giving them a lift into the supernatural. And it may be observed, that although the Spaniards have a house-spirit which they call *Duende*, and Tasso, in the fever of his dungeon, was haunted with a *Folletto*, which is the *Follet* or *Lutin* of the French, it does not appear that these southern spirits are of necessity small; still less have those sunny nations any embodied system of fairyism. Their fairies are the

---

* See an excellent article in the "Quarterly Review," entitled "Antiquities of Nursery Literature." Of similar merit and probably by the same hand (which we presume to be that of Mr. Southey) is another on the popular mythology of the Middle Ages. We cannot refer to the volume, our copy happening to form part of a selection which we made some years ago from a bundle of the two reigning Reviews. [These articles are in volumes 21 and 22, of the "Quarterly Review." They were not written by Southey, at least they are not in the list of his contributions to the "Review" published in his biography. ED.]

enchantresses of romance. Little spirits appear to be of the country of little people, commented on by their larger neighbors. It is true that little shapes and shadows are seen in all countries; but the general tendency of fear is to magnify. Particular circumstances must have created a spirit at once petty and formidable.

We are of opinion with the author of the "Fairy Mythology," that the petty size of the haunted idols of antiquity argues nothing conclusive respecting the size of the beings they represented. Besides, they were often large as well as small, though the more domestic of them, or those that immediately presided over the hearth, were of a size suitable to convenience. The domestic idols of all nations have probably been small, for the like reason.

Whether the Lares were supposed to be of greater stature or not by the learned, it is not impossible that the constant sight of the little images generated a corresponding notion of the originals. The best argument against the smallness of these divinities is, that there is no mention of it in books; and yet the only passage we remember to have met with, implying any determinate notion of stature, is in favor of the little. We here give it out of an old and not very sage author.

"After the victory had and gotten against the Gethes, the Emperor Domitian caused many shewes and triumphs to be made, in signe and token of joy; and amongst others hee invited publickly to dine with him, all sorts of persons, both noble and unnoble, but especially the Senators and Knights of Rome, to whom he made a feast in this fashion. Hee had caused a certaine house of al sides to bee painted black, the pavement thereof was black, so likewise were the hangings, or seelings, the roofe and the wals also black; and within it hee had prepared a very low room, not unlike a hollow vault or cell, ful of emptie siedges or seats. Into this place he caused the Senators and Knights, his ghests, to be brought, without suffering any of their pages or attendants to enter in with them. And first of all he caused a little square piller to be set near to every one of them, upon the which was written the partie's name sitting next it; by which there hanged also a lamp burning before each seat, in such sort as is used in sepulchers. After this, there comes into this melancholicke and dark place a number of yong pages, with great joy and merriment, starke naked, and spotted or painted all over with a die or colour as blacke as inke : who, resembling these spirits called Manes, and such like idols, did leape and skip round about those Senators and Knights, who, at this unexpected accident, were not a little frighted and afraid. After which, those pages set them down at their feete, against each of them one, and there stayed, whilste certaine other persons (ordayned there of purpose) did execute with great solemnity all those ceremonies that were usually fit and requisit at the funeralls and exequies of the dead. This done, there came in others, who brought and served in, in black dishes and platters, divers meats and viands, all coloured black, in such sort that there was not any one in the place but was in great doubt what would become of him, and thought himself utterly undone, supposing he should have his throat cut, onely to give pleasure and content to the Emperour. Besides, there was kept the greatest silence that could be imagined. And Domitian himself being present, did nothing else but (without ceasing) speake and talke unto them of murthers, death and tragedies. In the end, the Emperour having taken his pleasure of them at the full, he caused their pages and lackies, which attended them without the gates, to come in unto them, and so sent them away home to their own houses, some in coches, others in horselitters, guided and conducted by strange and unknown persons, which gave them as great cause of fear as their former entertainment. And they were no sooner arrived everyone to his own house, and had scant taken breath from the feare they had conceived, but that one of their servants came to tell them, that there were at the gates certaine which came to speake with them from the Emperour. God knows how this message made them stirre, what excessive lamentations they made, and with how exceeding feares they were perplexed in their minds; there was not any, no, not the hardiest of them all, but thought that hee was sent for to be put to death. But to make short, those which were to speake with them from the Emperour, came to no other purpose but to bring them either a little piller of silver, or some such like vessel or piece of plate (which had beene set before them at the time of their entertainment); after which, everyone of them had also sent unto him, for a present from the Emperour, one of those pages that had counterfeyted those *Manes* or Spirits at the banquet, they being first washed and cleansed before they were presented unto them."

Spirits of old could become small; but we read of none that were essentially little except the fairies. It was a Rabbinical notion, that angelical beings could render themselves as small as they pleased; a fancy of which Milton has not scrupled to avail himself in his Pandemonium.* It was proper enough to the idea of a being

---

* Milton's reduction of the size of his angels is surely a superfluity, and diminishes the grandeur of their meeting. It was one of the rare instances (theology apart) in which his learning betrayed his judgment.

made of thought or fire; though one would think it was easier to make it expand like the genius when let loose, than be contracted into the jar or vial in the first instance. But if spirits went in and out of crevices, means, it was thought, must be taken to enable them to do so; and this may serve to account for the Fairies themselves, in countries where other circumstances disposed the fancy to create them: but all the attributes of the little northern being, its petty stature, its workmanship, its superiority to men in some things, its simplicity and inferiority in others, its supernatural practices, and the doubt entertained by its believers whether it is in the way of salvation, conspire, we think, to render the opinion of M. Mallet, in his "Northern Antiquities," extremely probable; viz., that the character of the fairy has been modified by the feelings entertained by our Gothic and Celtic ancestors respecting the little race of the Laplanders, a people whom they despised for their timid peacefulness, and yet could not help admiring for their industry, and fearing for their *magic*.

In the "Edda," or northern "Pantheon," the dwarfs are described as a species of beings bred in the dust of the earth, like maggots in a carcase. "It was indeed," says the Edda, "in the body of the Giant Ymer, that they were engendered and first began to move and live. At first they were only worms; but by order of the gods they at length partook both of human shape and reason; nevertheless, they always dwell in subterranean caverns and among rocks."

Upon this passage, M. Mallet says (under correction of his translator), "We may discover here one of the effects of that ignorant prejudice, which hath made us for so many years regard all arts and handicrafts as the occupation of mean people and slaves. Our Celtic and Gothic ancestors, whether Germans, Scandinavians, or Gauls, imagining there was something magical, and beyond the reach of man in mechanic skill and industry, could scarcely believe that an able artist was one of their own species, or descended from the same common origin. This, it must be granted, was a very foolish conceit; but let us consider what might possibly facilitate the entrance of it in their minds. There was perhaps some neighboring people, which bordered upon the Celtic or Gothic tribes; and which, although less warlike than themselves, and much inferior in strength and stature, might yet excel them in dexterity; and addicting themselves to the manual arts, might carry on commerce with them, sufficiently extensive to have the fame of it spread pretty far. All these circumstances will agree well enough with the Laplanders, who are still as famous for their magic, as remarkable for the lowness of their stature; pacific even to a degree of cowardice, but of a mechanic industry which formerly must have appeared very considerable. The stories that were invented concerning this people, passing through the mouths of so many ignorant relators, would soon acquire all the degrees of the marvellous of which they were susceptible. Thus the dwarfs soon became (as all know, who have dipped but a little into the ancient romances) the forgers of enchanted armor, upon which neither swords nor conjurations could make any impression. They were possessed of caverns full of treasure, entirely at their own disposal. This, to observe by the bye, hath given birth to one of the cabalistic doctrines, which is perhaps only one of the branches of the ancient northern theology. As the dwarfs were feeble, and but of small courage, they were supposed to be crafty, full of artifice and deceit. This, which in the old romances is called *disloyalty*, is the character always given of them in those fabulous narratives. All these fancies having received the seal of time and universal consent, could be no longer contested, and it was the business of the poets to assign a fit origin for such ungracious beings. This was done in their pretended rise from the dead carcase of a great giant. The dwarfs at first were only the maggots, engendered by its putrefaction: afterwards the gods bestowed upon them understanding and cunning. By this fiction the northern warriors justified their contempt of them; and at the same time accounted for their small stature, their industry, and for their supposed propensity for inhabiting caves and clefts of the rocks. After all, the notion is not everywhere exploded, that there are in the bowels of the earth Fairies, or a kind of dwarfish and tiny beings, of human shape, remarkable for their riches, their industry, and their malevolence. In many countries of the North, the people are still firmly persuaded of their existence. In Ireland, at this day, the good folks show the very rocks and hills, in which they maintain that there are swarms of these small subterranean men, of the most tiny size, but most delicate figures."

When Christianity came into the North, these little people, who had formed part of the national faith, were converted by the ordinary process into devils; but the converts could never heartily enter into the notion. Accordingly, in spite of the endeavors of the clergy (which it is said, have been more or less exerted in vain to this day), a sort of half-and-half case was made out for them ; and the inhabitants of several northern countries are still of opinion that elves may be saved, and that it is cruel to tell them otherwise. An author, quoted in the " Fairy Mythology" (vol. i. p. 136), has a touching theory on this subject. We are informed in that work, " that the common people of Sweden and thereabouts believe in an intermediate class of elves who, when they show themselves, have a handsome human form, and the idea of whom is connected with a deep feeling of melancholy, as if bewailing a half-quenched hope of redemption." — " Afzelius is of opinion," says a note on the passage, " that the superstition on this point is derived from the time of the introduction of Christianity into the North ; and expresses the sympathy of the first converts with their forefathers, who died without a knowledge of the Redeemer, and lay bound in heathen earth, and whose unhappy spirits were doomed to wander about these lower regions, or sigh within their mounds, till the great day of redemption."

Our old prose writers scarcely ever mention the Fairies without letting us see how they were confounded with devils, and yet distinguished from them. " Terrestrial devils," says Burton, " are those Lares, Genii, Faunes, Satyrs, Wood-nymphs, Foliots, Fairies, *Robin Goodfellows*, &c., which as they are most conversant with men, so they do them the most harm. Some think it was they alone that kept the heathen people in awe of old, and had so many idols and temples erected to them. Of this range was *Dagon* amongst the Philistines, Bel amongst the Babylonians, Astarte amongst the Sidonians, Baal amongst the Samaritans, Isis and Osiris amongst the Egyptians, &c. Some put our Fairies into this rank, which have been in former times adored with much superstition ; with sweeping their houses, and setting of a pail of water, good victuals, and the like ; and then they should not be pinched, but find money in their shoes, and be fortunate in their enterprises. These are they that dance on heaths and greens, as Lavater thinks with Tritemius, and as Olaus Magnus adds, leave that green circle which commonly we find in plains and fields, which others hold to proceed from a meteor falling, or some accidental rankness of the ground, so Nature sports herself; they are sometimes seen by old women and children. *Hierom Pauli* in his description of the city of *Bercino* (*in Spain*), relates how they have been familiarly seen near that town, about fountains and hills. *Giraldus Cambrensis* gives instance in a monk in Wales that was so deluded. *Paracelsus* reckons up many places in *Germany*, where they do usually walk in little courts some two feet long."

"Our mothers' maids have so frayed us," says gallant Reginald Scot, "with Bul-beggars, Spirits, Witches, Urchens, Elves, Hags, Fairies, Satyrs, Pans, Fauns, Syrens, Kit with the Canstick, Tritons, Centaurs, Dwarfs, Giants, Imps, Calcars, Conjurors, Nymphs, Changelings, *Incubus*, Robin Goodfellows, the Spoon, the Mare, the Man in the Oak, the Helwain, the Fire-drake, the Puckle, Tom Thumb, Hobgoblin, Tom Tumbler, Boneless,* and other such Bugs, that we are afraid of our own shadows: insomuch that some never fear the devil but in a dark night;

---

* There is a personage in Eastern history, who appears to have been of kin to this grim phenomenon. He was a sorcerer of the name of Setteiah. He is described as having his head in his bosom, and as being destitute of bone in every part of his body, with the exception of his skull and the ends of his fingers. It was only when he was in a rage that he could sit up, anger having the effect of swelling him; but he could at no time be made to stand on his feet. When it was necessary to move him from place to place, they folded him like a mantle; and when there was occasion to consult him in the exercise of his profession, it was the practice to roll him backwards and forwards on the floor, like a churning skin, till the answer was obtained. See Major Price's "Essay towards the History of Arabia, antecedent to the birth of Mohammed," p. 196.

and then a polled sheep is a perilous beast, and many times is taken for our father's soul, especially in a churchyard, where a right hardy man heretofore scant durst pass by night but his hair would stand upright." *

In consequence of this opinion in the popular Mythology, the merry and human-like Fairies during a degrading portion of the history of Europe, were made tools of, in common with all that was thought diabolical, to worry and destroy thousands of miserable people ; but it is more than pleasant, — it is deeply interesting to an observer, to see what an instinctive impulse there is in human beings to resist the growth of the worst part of superstition, and vindicate nature and natural piety. Do but save mankind from taking intolerance for God's will, and exalting the impatience of being differed with into a madness, and you may trust to the natural good humor of the best of their opinions, for as favorable a view as possible of all with which they can sympathize. Even their madness in that respect is but a perversion of their natural wish to be liked and agreed with. The first thing that men found out in behalf of the Fairies, was that they were a good deal like themselves ; the next was to think well of them upon the whole, rather than ill ; and when Reginald Scot and others helped us out of this cloud of folly about witchcraft, the Fairies became brighter than before. In England the darker notions of them almost entirely disappeared with the big-

---

* The list of the unclean spirits in Middleton's tragicomedy of the " Witch," is closely copied from the passage in Reginald Scot. — See the Speech of Hecate.

Urchins, elves, hags, satires, pans, fauns, silence.
Kit with the candlestick ; tritons, centaurs, dwarfs, imps.
The spoon, the mare, the man i' th' oak, the hellwain, the fire-drake, the puckle.

otries in Church and State ; and at the call of the poets, they came and adorned the books that had done them service, and became synonymous with pleasant fancies.

II.

 IT may be agreeable to follow up the growth of this good-humored light in something like chronological order. The old romances began it. Oberon, the beautiful and beneficent, afterwards king of the Fairies, made his appearance very early. He is the Elberich, or Rich Elf, of the Germans, and became Oberon, with a French termination, in the romance of "Huon de Bourdeaux." The general reader is well acquainted with him through the abridgment of the work by the Count de Tressan, and the Oberon of Wieland, translated by Mr. Sotheby. He is a tiny creature, in the likeness of a beautiful child, with a face of exceeding loveliness ; and wears a crown of jewels. His cap of invisibility, common to all the Fairies (which is the reason why they must not lose it), became famous as the Tarn-Kappe, or Daring Cap, otherwise called the Nebel or Mist-Cap, and the Tarn-hut, or Hat of Daring.* In the poem of the German Voltaire, he possesses the horn which sets everybody dancing. He and his brother dwarfs, of the Northern Mythology, are the undoubted

---

* " Tarn, from *taren*, to dare (says Dobenell), because they gave courage along with invisibility. Kappe is properly a cloak, though the tarn-kappe or nebel-kappe is generally represented as a cap or hat." — *Fairy Mythology*, vól. ii. p. 4. Perhaps the word *cape*, which may include something both of cap and cloak, might settle their apparent contradiction. Hood implies both : and the goblin is sometimes called Robin Hood, and Hoodekin.

ancestors of the fallen but illustrious family of the Tom Thumbs, who became sons of tailors and victims of cows. Of the same stock are the Tom Hickathrifts and Jack the Giant Killer, if, indeed, they be not the gods themselves, merged into the Christian children of their former worshippers. Their horrible coats, caps of knowledge, swords of sharpness, and shoes of swiftness, are, as the "Quarterly Reviewer" observes, "all out of the great heathen treasury." Thumb looks like an Avatarkin, or little incarnation of Thor. Thor was the stoutest of the gods, but then the gods were little fellows in stature, compared with the giants. In a chapter of the "Edda," from which the reviewer has given an amusing extract, the giant Skrymner rallies Thor upon his pretensions and size, and calls him "the little man."* As the god, nevertheless, was more than a match for these lubbers of the skies, his worshippers might have respected the name in honor of him; a panegyrical raillery not unknown to other mythologies, nor unpractised towards the "gods of the earth."† The

---

* In the agreeable learning which the reviewer has brought to bear on this subject, in the "Antiquities of Nursery Literature," he has deprived us of our old friend the Giant Cormoran, who turns out to be a mistake of the printer's devil for Corinoran, "the Corinæus, probably, of Jeffery of Monmouth and the Brut." However, a printer's devil has a right to speak to this point; and we cannot help thinking that Cormoran ought to be the word, both on account of the devouring magnitude of the sound, and its suitability to the brazen tromp of a Cornish mouth —

"Here's the valiant Cornish man,
Who slew the giant Cormoran."

Abraham Cann or Polkinghorn ought to speak it; or the descendants of the Danish hero Kolson, who have *ora rotunda* in that quarter.

† "Little Will, the scourge of France,
No godhead but the first of men;" —

West of England, it may be observed, is a great Fairy country, though even the miners and their natural darkness have not been able to obscure the sunnier notions of Fairy-land, now prevailing in that quarter as much as any. The Devonshire Pixies or Pucksies are the reigning elves, and are among the gayest and most good-humored to be met with. Mr. Coleridge, in his juvenile poems, has put some verses into their mouths, not among his best, but such as he may have been reasonably loth to part with. The sea-air which he breathed at a distance, and "the Pixies' Parlour" (a grotto of the roots of trees, in which he found his name carved by the hands of his childhood), were proper nurseries for the author of the "Ancient Mariner."

Chaucer's notion of Fairies was a confused mixture of elves and romance-ladies, and Ovid, and the Catholic *diablerie*. We had taken his fairies for the regular little dancers on the green (induced by a line of his to that effect in the following passage); but the author of the "Fairy Mythology" has led us to form a different opinion. The truth is, that a book in Chaucer's time was a book, and everything to be found in those rare authorities became a sort of equal religion in the eyes of the student. Chaucer, in one of his verses, has brought together three such names as never met, perhaps, before or since, — "Samson, Turnus, and Socrates." He calls Ovid's Epistles " The Saint's Legends of Cupid." Seneca and St. Paul are the same grave authorities in his eyes ; in short, whatever was written was a scripture : something clerkly, and what

---

says Prior, speaking of William the 3d, and rebuking, at the same time, Boileau's deifications of Louis. So Frederick or Napoleon, or both, were called by their soldiers "the Little Corporal."

a monk ought to have written if he could. His Lady Abbess wears a brooch exhibiting a motto out of Virgil. Elves, therefore, and Provençal Enchantresses, and the nymphs of the Metamorphoses, and the very devils of the Pope and St. Anthony, were all fellows well met, all supernatural beings, living in the same remote regions of fancy, and exciting the gratitude of the poet. He is angry with the friars for making more solemn distinctions, and displacing the little elves in their walks; and he runs a capital jest upon them, which has become famous.

> "In olde dayes of the kinge Artour,
> Of which that Britons speke gret honour,
> All was this land full filled of faerie;
> The Elf-quene, with hire joly compagnie,
> Danced ful oft in many a grene mede.
> This was the old opinion as I rede;
> I speke of many hundred yeres ago;
> But now can no man see non elves mo,
> For now the grete charitee and prayeres
> Of limitoures and other holy freres,
> That serchen every land and every streme,
> As thikke as motes in the sonne-beme,
> Blissing halles, chambres, kichenes, and boures,
> Citees and burghes, castles highe and toures,
> Thropes and bernes, shepeness and dairies,
> This maketh that ther ben no faeries;
> For ther as wont to walken was an elf,
> Ther walketh now the limitour himself,
> In undermeles and in morwenings,
> And sayth his matines and his holy thinges,
> As he goth in his limitation.
> Women may now go safely up and doun;
> In every bush and under every tree,
> Ther is non other incubus but he."

In another poem, we meet with Pluto and Proserpine as the King and Queen of Faerie; where they sing and dance about a well, enjoying themselves in a garden, and quoting Solomon. The "ladies" that wait upon them are the damsels that accompanied Proserpine in the vale of Enna, when she was taken away by his Majesty in his "griesly cart." This is a very different cart from a chariot made of the gristle of grasshoppers.

The national intellect, which had been maturing like an oak, from the time of Wickliffe, drawing up nutriment from every ground, and silently making the weakest things contribute to its strength, burst forth at last into flowers and fruit together, in the noonday of Shakespeare. A shower of fairy blossoms was the ornament of its might. Spenser's fairies are those of Romance, varied with the usual readings of his own fancy; but Shakespeare, the popular poet of the world, took the little elfin globe in his hand, as he had done the great one, and made it a thing of joy and prettiness for ever. Since then the fairies have become part of a poet's belief, and happy ideas of them have almost superseded what remains of a darker creed in the minds of the people. The profound playfulness of Shakespeare's wisdom, which humanized every thing it touched, and made it know its own value, found out the soul of an activity, convertible into good, in the restlessness of mischief; and Puck, or the elf malicious, became jester in the court of Oberon the Good Fairy,—his servant and his help. The "Elves" in the Tempest are rather the elemental spirits of the Rosicrucians, confounded both with classical and popular mythology. It is in the "Midsummer Night's Dream" that the true fairies are found, as they ought to be; and there amidst bowers and moonlight, will we indulge ourselves awhile with their company. We make no apology to the reader for our large quotations. They have been repeated many times and lately on the present subject; yet we should rather have to apologize for the omission, considering how excellent they are. To add what novelty we could, or rather to make our quotations as peculiar to our work as possible, we had made up our minds to bring together all the passages in question out of Shakespeare's drama, as far as they could be separated from other matter, and present them to our readers under the title of a Fairy Play; but we began to fear that the profane might have some color of reason for complaining of us, and accusing us of an intention to swell our pages. We have, therefore, confined ourselves to selections which are put under distinct heads, so as to form a kind of gallery of Fairy pictures. We shall take the liberty of commenting as we go, even if our remarks are called forth on points not immediately belonging to the subject. It is not easy to read a great poet, and not indulge in exclamations of fondness. Besides, there is something fairy-like in having one's way.

EMPLOYMENT OF A DAMSEL OF THE FAIRY COURT.

Fairy. Over hill, over dale,
    Thorough bush, thorough brier,
Over park, over pale,
    Thorough flood, thorough fire,
I do wander every where,
Swifter than the moon's sphere;
And I serve the fairy queen,
To dew her orbs upon the green:
The cowslips tall her pensioners be ;
In their gold coats spots you see ;
Those be rubies, fairy favours:
In those freckles live their savours ;
I must go seek some dew-drops here,
And hang a pearl in every cowslip's ear.

Flowers, in the proper fairy spirit, which plays betwixt sport and wisdom with the profoundest mysteries of nature, are here made alive, and turned into fantastic servants.

In fairy-land, whatever may be, is. We may gather from this and another passage in Cymbeline, that Shakespeare was fond of cowslips, and had observed their graces with delight. It is a delicate fancy to suppose that those ruby spots contain the essence of the flower's odor, and were presents from their ruling sprite. And the hanging a pearl in every cowslip's ear (besides the beauty of the line) seems to pull the head of the tall pensioner sideways, and make him quaintly conscious of his new favor.

BOWER OF QUEEN TITANIA.

I know a bank whereon the wild thyme blows,
Where ox-lips and the nodding violet grows;
Quite over-canopied with lush woodbine,
With sweet musk-roses, and with eglantine;
There sleeps Titania, some time of the night,
Lull'd in these flowers with dances and delight

What beautiful lines are these? Observe in the next the goggle-eyed owl, who is nightly astonished at the fairies, as if amazement were his business; and also the childlike warning to the snails and daddy longlegs to keep aloof.

THE QUEEN IN HER BOWER.

Tita. Come, now a roundel, and a fairy song;
Then, for the third part of a minute, hence;
Some to kill cankers in the musk-rose buds;
Some war with rear-mice for their leathern wings,
To make my small elves coats; and some keep back
The clamorous owl, that nightly hoots and wonders
At our quaint spirits: sing me now asleep;
Then to your offices, and let me rest.

SONG.

1st Fairy. You spotted snakes, with double tongue,
Thorny hedge-hogs, be not seen;

Newts and blind-worms do no wrong;
Come not near our fairy queen.

Chorus. Philomel, with melody,
Sing in our sweet lullaby:
Lulla, lulla, lullaby; lulla, lulla, lullaby;
Never harm, nor spell nor charm,
Come our lovely lady nigh,
So, good night, with lullaby.

2d Fairy. Weaving spiders, come not here;
Hence, you long-legged spinners, hence;
Beetles black, approach not near;
Worm, nor snail, do no offence.

Chorus. Philomel, with melody, &c.

1st Fairy. Hence, away! now all is well.
One, aloof, stand sentinel.

TRICKS OF THE FAIRY KING ON HIS QUEEN.

Titania, by practice of Oberon, falls in love with a weaver, on whom Puck has clapped an ass's head. Enter Puck with him and some others. Imagine the weaver to be Liston.

Quince. O monstrous! O strange! we are haunted. Pray, masters! fly, masters! help! [*Exeunt Clowns.*
Puck. I'll follow you, I'll lead you about, around,
Through bog, through bush, through brake, through brier;
Sometime a horse I'll be, sometime a hound,
A hog, a headless bear, sometime a fire,
And neigh, and bark, and grunt, and roar, and burn,
Like horse, hound, hog, bear, fire, at every turn. [*Exit.*
Bot. Why do they run away? this is a knavery of them to make me afeard.

Re-enter SNOUT.

Snout. O Bottom, thou art changed! What do I see on thee?
[*Exit Snout.*
Bot. What do you see? You see an ass's head of your own, do you?

Re-enter QUINCE.

Quin. Bless thee, Bottom! bless thee! thou art translated. [*Exit.*
Bot. I see their knavery: this is to make an ass of me, to fright me if they

could. But I will not stir from this place, do what they can: I will walk up and down here, and I will sing, that they shall hear I am not afraid.

> The ousel-cock, so black of hue,
>   With orange-tawny bill;
> The throstle with his note so true,
>   The wren with little quill.

Tita. What angel wakes me from my flowery bed?
Bot.
> The finch, the sparrow, and the lark,
>   The plain-song cuckoo gray,
> Whose note full many a man doth mark,
>   And dares not answer nay;

for, indeed, who would set his wit to so foolish a bird?—who would give a bird the lie, though he cry *cuckoo* never so?

Tita. I pray thee, gentle mortal, sing again:
Mine ear is much enamoured of thy note,
So is mine eye enthralled to thy shape;
And thy fair virtue's force perforce doth move me,
On the first view, to say, to swear, I love thee.

Bot. Methinks, mistress, you should have little reason for that: and yet, to say the truth, reason and love keep little company together now-a-days: the more the pity, that some honest neighbours will not make them friends. Nay, I can gleek upon the occasion.

Tita. Thou art as wise as thou art beautiful.

Bot. No so, neither: but if I had wit enough to get out of this wood, I have enough to serve mine own turn.

Tita. Out of this wood do not desire to go;
Thou shalt remain here whether thou wilt or no.
I am a spirit of no common rate;
The summer still doth tend upon my state,
And I do love thee: therefore, go with me;
I'll give thee fairies to attend on thee;
And they shall fetch thee jewels from the deep,
And sing, while thou on pressed flowers dost sleep.
And I will purge thy mortal grossness so,
That thou shalt like an airy spirit go.
Peas-blossom! Cobweb! Moth! and Mustard-seed!

1st Fairy. Ready.
2d Fairy.   And I.
3d Fairy.   And I.
4th Fairy.   Where shall we go?
Tita. Be kind and courteous to this gentleman;
Hop in his walks and gambol in his eyes;

>Feed him with apricocks, and dewberries;
>With purple grapes, green figs, and mulberries;
>The honey-bags steal from the humble-bees,
>And, for night-tapers, crop their waxen thighs,
>And light them at the fiery glow-worm's eyes,
>To have my love to bed, and to arise;
>And pluck the wings from painted butterflies,
>To fan the moonbeams from his sleeping eyes:
>Nod to him, elves, and do him courtesies.

1st Fairy. Hail mortal!
2d Fairy. Hail!
3d Fairy. Hail!
4th Fairy. Hail!
Bot. I cry your worship's mercy, heartily. I beseech your worship's name.
Cob. Cobweb.
Bot. I shall desire of you more acquaintance, good Master Cobweb: if I cut my finger I shall make bold with you. Your name, honest gentleman?
Peas. Peas-blossom.
Bot. I pray you to remember me to Mistress Squash, your mother, and to Master Peascod, your father. Good Master Peas-blossom, I shall desire of you more acquaintance too. Your name, I beseech you, sir?
Mus. Mustard-seed.
Bot. Good Master Mustard-seed, I know your patience well: that same cowardly, giant-like, ox-beef hath devoured many a gentleman of your house: I promise you, your kindred hath made my eyes water ere now. I desire of you more acquaintance, good Master Mustard-seed.
Tita. Come wait upon him; lead him to my bower.
>The moon, methinks, looks with a wat'ry eye;
>And when she weeps, weeps every little flower,
>Lamenting some enforced chastity.
>Tie up love's tongue, and bring him silently.

The luxurious reduplication of the rhyme in this exquisite passage, has been noticed by Mr. Hazlitt.
Again, in act the fourth:—

Tita. Come, sit thee down upon this flow'ry bed,
>While I thy amiable cheeks do coy,
>And stick musk-roses in thy sleek smooth head,
>And kiss thy fair large ears, my gentle joy.

Bot. Where's Peas-blossom?
Peas. Ready.

Bot. Scratch my head, Peas-blossom. Where's Monsieur Cobweb?
Cob. Ready.
Bot. Monsieur Cobweb; good Monsieur, get your weapons in your hands, and kill me a red-hipp'd humble-bee on the top of a thistle; and good Monsieur, bring me the honey-bag. Do not fret yourself too much in the action, Monsieur; and, good Monsieur, have a care the honey-bag break not; I would be loth to have you overflow with a honey-bag, Signor. Where's Monsieur Mustard-seed?
Mus. Ready.
Bot. Give me your neif, Monsieur Mustard-seed. Pray you, leave your courtesy, good Monsieur.
Mus. What's your will?
Bot. Nothing, good Monsieur, but to help Cavalero Peas-blossom to scratch. I must to the barber's, Monsieur; for methinks I am marvellous hairy about the face: and I am such a tender ass, if my hair do but tickle me, I must scratch.
Tita. What, wilt thou hear some music, my sweet love?
Bot. I have a reasonable good ear in music: let us have the tongs and the bones.
Tita. Or say, sweet love, what thou desir'st to eat.
Bot. Truly a peck of provender; I could munch your good dry oats. Methinks I have a great desire to a bottle of hay; good hay, sweet hay, hath no fellow.
Tita. I have a venturous fairy that shall seek
   The squirrel's hoard, and fetch thee new nuts.
Bot. I had rather have a handful or two of dried peas. But, I pray you, let none of your people stir me; I have an exposition of sleep come upon me.
Tita. Sleep thou, and I will wind thee in my arms.
   Fairies, begone, and be always away. [*Exeunt fairies.*
   So doth the wood-bine the sweet honey-suckle
   Gently entwist,—the female ivy so
   Enrings the barky fingers of the elm.
   O, how I love thee! how I dote on thee!

THE FAIRIES BLESS A HOUSE AT NIGHT-TIME.

Enter PUCK.

Puck. Now the hungry lion roars,
   And the wolf behowls the moon;
   Whilst the heavy ploughman snores,
      All with weary task fordone.
   Now the wasted brands do glow,
      Whilst the screech-owl, screeching loud,
   Puts the wretch, that lies in woe,
      In remembrance of a shroud.

Now it is the time of night,
   That the graves, all gaping wide,
Every one lets forth his sprite,
   In the church-way paths to glide:
And we fairies that do run
   By the triple Hecate's team,
From the presence of the sun,
   Following darkness like a dream,
Now are frolick; not a mouse
Shall disturb this hallow'd house;
I am sent, with broom, before,
To sweep the dust behind the door.

Enter OBERON *and* TITANIA *with their train.*

Oberon. Through this house give glimmering light,
   By the dead and drowsy fire:
Every elf, and fairy sprite,
   Hop as light as bird from brier;
And this ditty, after me,
Sing and dance it trippingly.

Tita. First, rehearse this song by rote,
To each word a warbling note,
Hand in hand, with fairy grace,
Will we sing, and bless this place.

SONG AND DANCE.

Oberon. Now, until the break of day,
Through this house each fairy stray.
To the best bride-bed will we,
Which by us shall blessed be;
And the issue, there create,
Ever shall be fortunate.
So shall all the couples three
Ever true in loving be:
And the blots of nature's hand
Shall not in their issue stand:
Never mole, hare-lip, nor scar,
Nor mark prodigious, such as are
Despised in nativity,
Shall upon their children be.
With this field-dew consecrate,
Every fairy take his gait!

> And each several chamber bless,
> Through this palace with sweet peace:
> E'er shall it in safety rest,
> And the owner of it be blest.
> Trip away;
> Make no stay;
> Meet me all by break of day.

It is with difficulty that in these, and indeed in all our quotations, we refrain from marking particular passages. One longs to vent one's feelings, like positive grappling with the lines; and besides, we have the temptation of the reader's company to express our admiration. But we fear to do injustice to what we should leave unmarked; and indeed to be thought impatient with the others. Luckily where all is beautiful, the choice would often be difficult, if we stopped to make any; and if we did not, we should be printing nothing but italics.

Queen Mab, as the author of the "Fairy Mythology" remarks, has certainly dethroned Titania; but we cannot help thinking that both he, and the poets who have helped to dethrone her, are in the wrong; and that Voss is right, when he rejects the royalty of both monosyllables. Queen or quean is old English for woman, and is still applied to females in an ill sense. Now Mab is the fairies' midwife, plebeian by office, indiscriminate in her visits, and descending so low as to make elf-locks, and plait the manes of horses. We have little doubt that she is styled *queen* in an equivocal sense, between a mimicry of state and something abusive; and that the word *Mab* comes from the same housewife origin as *Mop, Moppet,* and *Mob-Cap.* The *a* was most likely pronounced broad; as in Mall for Moll, Malkin for Maukin; and *Queen Mab* is perhaps the quean in the Mob-cap, — the midwife riding in her chariot, but still vulgar; and acting some such part with regard to fairies and to people's fancies, as one of Sir Walter Scott's fanciful personages (we forget her name) does to flesh and blood in the novel.*

The passages in Ben Jonson regarding fairies want merit enough to be quoted; not that he had not a fine fancy, but that in this instance, as in some others, he overlaid it with his book-reading, probably in despair of equalling Shakespeare. The passages quoted from him by the author of the " Fairy Mythology," rather out of respect than his usual good taste, are nothing better than so many commonplaces, in which the popular notions are set forth. There is, however, one striking exception, out of the " Sad Shepherd," —

> "There, in the stocks of trees, white fays do dwell,
> And span-long elves, that dance about a pool
> With each a little changeling in their arms."

This is very grim, and to the purpose. The changeling, supernaturally diminished, adds to the ghastliness, as if born and completed before its time.

For our next quotation, which is very pleasant, we are indebted, amongst our numerous obligations, to the same fairy historian. There is probably a good deal of treasure of the same sort in the rich mass of Old English Poetry; but the truth is, we dare not trust ourselves with the search. We have already a tendency to exceed the limits assigned us; and on subjects like these we should be tolled on from one search to another, as if Puck had taken the shape of a bee. The passage we speak of is in Randolph's pastoral of " Amyntas, or the Impossible Dowry." A young rogue of the name of Dorylas " makes a fool of

---

* The White Lady of Avenel, in the Monastery, was undoubtedly the personage Hunt had in his mind. — ED.

a 'fantastique sheapherd,' Jocastus, by pretending to be Oberon, King of Fairy." In this character, having provided a proper retinue (whom we are to suppose to be boys) he proposes a fairy husband for Jocastus's daughter, and obliges him by plundering his orchard. We take the former of these incidents for granted, from the context, for we have not seen the original. Dorylas appears sometimes to act in his own character, and sometimes in that of Oberon. In the former the following dialogue takes place between him and his wittol, descriptive of

A FAIRY'S JOINTURE.

Thestylis. But what estate shall he assure upon me ?
Jocastus. A royal jointure, all in Fairy land.

* * * * * * * * *

Dorylas knows it.
A curious park —
Dorylas. Paled round about with pickteeth.
Joc. Besides a house made all of mother of pearl.
An ivory tennis-court.
Dor. A nutmeg parlour.
Joc. A sapphire dairy-room.
Dor. A ginger hall.
Joc. Chambers of agate.
Dor. Kitchens all of crystal.
Am. O, admirable ! This it is for certain.
Joc. The jacks are gold.
Dor. The spits are Spanish needles.
Joc. Then there be walks —
Dor. Of amber.
Joc. Curious orchards —
Dor. That bear as well in winter as in summer.
Joc. 'Bove all, the fish-ponds, every pond is full —
Dor. Of nectar. Will this please you? Every grove
Stored with delightful birds.

Dorylas proceeds to help himself to the farmer's apples, his brother rogues assisting him. This license, it must be owned, is royal. But what is still pleasanter, we are

here presented for the first time with some fairy Latin,
and very good it is, quaint and pithy. The Neapolitan
Robin Goodfellow, who goes about in the shape of 'a little
monk, might have written it.

FAIRIES ROBBING AN ORCHARD, AND SINGING LATIN.

Dor. How like you now my grace? Is not my countenance
Royal and full of majesty? Walk not I
Like the young prince of pigmies? Ha! my knaves,
We'll fill our pockets. Look, look yonder, elves;
Would not yon apples tempt a better conscience
Than any we have, to rob an orchard? Ha!
Fairies, like nymphs with child, must have the things
They long for. You sing here a fairy catch
In that strange tongue I taught you, while ourself
Do climb the trees. Thus princely Oberon
Ascends his throne of state.
  Elves. Nos beata Fauni proles,
       Quibus non est magna moles,
       Quamvis lunam incolamus,
       Hortos sæpe frequentamus.

       Furto cuncta magis bella,
       Furto dulcior puella,
       Furto omnia decora,
       Furto poma dulciora.

       Cum mortales lecto jacent,
       Nobis poma noctu placent;
       Illa tamen sunt ingrata,
       Nisi furto sint parata.

       We the Fairies blithe and antic,
       Of dimensions not gigantic,
       Though the moonshine mostly keep us,
       Oft in orchards frisk and peep us.

       Stolen sweets are always sweeter;
       Stolen kisses much completer;
       Stolen looks are nice in chapels;
       Stolen, stolen be your apples.

> When to bed the world are bobbing,
> Then's the time for orchard robbing;
> Yet the fruit were scarce worth pealing,
> Were it not for stealing, stealing.

Jocastus's man Bromio prepares to thump these pretended elves, but the master is overwhelmed by the condescension of the princely Oberon in coming to his orchard, when —

> His Grace had orchards of his own more precious
> Than mortals can have any.

The elves therefore, by permission, pinched the officious servant, singing, —

> Quoniam per te violamur,
> Ungues hic experiamur;
> Statim dices tibi datam
> Cutem valde variatam.

> Since by thee comes profanation,
> Taste thee, lo! scarification.
> Noisy booby! in a twinkling
> Thou hast got a pretty crinkling.

Finally, when the coast is clear, Oberon cries, —

> So we are clean got off: come, noble peers
> Of Fairy, come, attend our royal Grace.
> Let's go and share our fruit with our Queen Mab
> And the other dairy-maids: where of this theme
> We will discourse amidst our capes and cream.

> Cum tot poma habeamus,
> Triumphos lœti jam canamus:
> Faunos ego credam ortos,
> Tantum ut frequentent hortos.

> I, domum, Oberon, ad illas,
> Quæ nos manent nunc ancillas,
> Quarem osculemur sinum,
> Inter poma, lac, et vinum.

Now for such a stock of apples,
Laud me with the voice of chapels.
Fays, methinks, were gotten solely
To keep orchard-robbing holy.

Hence then, hence, and let's delight us
With the maids whose creams invite us,
Kissing them, like proper fairies,
All amidst their fruits and dairies.

III.

NEXT comes Drayton, a proper fairy poet, with an infinite luxury of little fancies. Nor was he incapable of the greater; but he would not blot; and so took wisely to the little and capricious. His "Nymphidia," a story of fairy intrigue, is too long and too unequal to be given entire; but it cuts out into little pictures like a penny sheet. You might border a paper with his stanzas, and read them instead of grotesque. His fairy palace is roofed with the skins of bats, gilded with moonshine;—a fancy of exquisite fitness and gusto. There ought to be *type by itself*,—pin-points, or hieroglyphical dots,—in which to set forth the following

NAMES OF FAIRIES.

Hop, and Mop, and Drop so clear,
Pip, and Trip, and Skip, that were
To Mab, the sovereign lady dear,
    Her special maids of honour;
Fib, and Tib, and Pinch, and Pin,
Tick, and Quick, and Fill and Fin,
Tit, and Wit, and Wap, and Win,
    The train that wait upon her.

Oberon's queen (who is here called Mab) has made an assignation with Pigwiggen, a great fairy knight. The king, furious with jealousy, pursues her, and is as mad as Orlando. He grapples with a wasp whom he mistakes for the enemy; next plunges upon a glowworm, and thumps her for carrying fire: then runs into a hive of bees who daub him all over with their honey; then leaps upon an ant, and gallops her; then scours over a mole-hill, and plumps into a puddle up to his neck. The queen hears of his pursuit, and she and all her maids of honor secrete themselves in a nutshell. Pigwiggen goes out to meet the king, riding upon a *fiery earwig!*

A FAIRY'S ARMS AND WAR-HORSE.

His helmet was a beetle's head
Most horrible and full of dread,
That able was to strike one dead,
    Yet it did well become him.
And for his plume a horse's hair,
Which being tossed by the air,
Had force to strike his foe with fear,
    And turn his weapon from him.

Himself he on an earwig set,
Yet scarce he on his back could get,
So oft and high he did curvet
    Ere he himself could settle;
He made him turn, and stop, and bound,
To gallop and to trot the round,
He scarce could stand on any ground,*
    He was so full of mettle.

The queen, scandalized and alarmed at the height to which matters are now openly proceeding, applies to Proserpina for help. The goddess takes pity on her, and during a dreadful combat between the champions, comes up with a bag full of Stygian fog and a bottle of Lethe water. The contents of the bag being suddenly dis-

---

* Stare loco nescit, &c. — VIRGIL.

charged, the knights lose one another in the mist; and on the latter's clearing off, the goddess steps in as herald on behalf of Pluto to forbid further hostilities, adding that the ground of complaint shall be duly investigated, but first recommending to the parties to take a draught of the liquor she has brought with her, in order to enlighten their understandings. They drink and forget every thing; and the queen and her maids of honor, "closely smiling" at the jest, return with them to court, and have a grand dinner. Now this is "worshipful society," and a good plot. The "*machines*," as the French school used to call them, are in good keeping; and the divine interference worthy.

In the "Muses' Elysium" of the same poet is a description of a fairy wedding. The bride wears buskins made of the shells of the lady-bird, with a head-dress of rose-yellows and peacock-moons, &c.; but her bed is a thing to make one wish one's self only a span long, in order to lay one's cheek in it. The coverlid is of white and red rose-leaves; the curtains and tester of the flower-imperial, with a border of harebells; and the pillows are of lily, stuffed with butterfly-down.*

---

* From "The Recreations of Christopher North," we take this beautiful and very poetical description of a Fairy's Funeral: —

There it was, on a little river island, that once, whether sleeping or waking we know not, we saw celebrated a fairy's funeral. First we heard small pipes playing, as if no bigger than hollow rushes that whisper to the night winds; and more piteous than aught that trills from earthly instrument was the scarce audible dirge! It seemed to float over the stream, every foam-bell emitting a plaintive note, till the airy anthem came floating over our couch, and then alighted without footsteps among the heather. The pattering of little feet was then heard, as if living creatures were arranging themselves in order, and then there was nothing but a more ordered hymn. The harmony was like the melting of musical dew-drops, and song, without words, of sorrow and death. We opened our eyes, or rather sight came to them when closed, and dream was vision: Hundreds of creatures, no taller than the crest of the lap-

We think, with the author of the "Mythology," that Herrick's fairy poetry is inferior to that of Drayton. Herrick is indeed very inferior to the reputation which a few happy little poems have obtained for him; and the late reprint of his works has done him no good. For one delicacy there are twenty pages of coarseness and insipidity. His epigrams, for the most part, are ludicrous only for the total absence of wit; and inasmuch as he wanted sentiment, he was incapable of his own voluptuousness. His passion is cold, and his decencies impertinent. In his offerings at pagan altars, the Greek's simplicity becomes a literal nothing; though there is an innocence in the pedantry that is by no means the worst thing about him. His verses on his maid Prue are edifying. Herrick was a jovial country priest, a scholar, and a friend of Ben Jonson's, and we dare say had been a capital university-man. Scholarship and a certain quickness were his real inspirers, and he had a good sense, which in one instance has exhibited itself very remarkably; for it led him to speak of his being "too coarse to love." To be sure, he

---

wing, and all hanging down their veiled heads, stood in a circle on a green plat among the rocks; and in the midst was a bier, framed as it seemed of flowers unknown to the Highland hills; and on the bier a fairy, lying with uncovered face, pale as the lily, and motionless as the snow. The dirge grew fainter and fainter, and then died quite away; when two of the creatures came from the circle, and took their station, one at the head and the other at the foot of the bier. They sang alternate measures, not louder than the twittering of the awakened wood-lark before it goes up the dewy air, but dolorous and full of the desolation of death. The flower-bier stirred; for the spot on which it lay sank slowly down, and in a few moments the greensward was smooth as ever — the very dews glittering about the buried fairy. A cloud passed over the moon; and, with a choral lament, the funeral troop sailed duskily away, heard afar off, so still was the midnight solitude of the glen. Then the disenthralled Orchy began to rejoice as before through all her streams and falls; and at the sudden leaping of the waters and outbursting of the moon, we awoke. — ED.

has put the observation in the mouth of a lady, and probably he found it there. He well deserved it for the foolish things he has said. He made a good hit now and then, when fresh from reading his favorite authors; and among them, we must rank a fairy poem mentioned by the author of the "Legends of the South of Ireland." His office helped to inspire him in it, for it is a satire, and a bitter one, on the ceremonies of Catholic worship. We must own we have a regard for a Catholic chapel; but it is not to be denied that some of the duties performed in it are strange things, and open to quaint parodies. The names of the saints in Herrick are worthy of Drayton.

There is one thing in the fairies of Drayton which deserves mention. He does not shirk the miscellaneous, and, in some respects, anti-human nature of their tastes. The delicacies at their table are not always such as we should think pleasant, or even bearable. This is good; perhaps more so than he was aware, for he overdoes it.

Milton's "pert fairies and dapper-elves" are a little too sophistical. They are too much like fairies *acting* themselves; which is overdoing the quaint nicety of their consciousness. But in addition to the well-known passages we have quoted from him already, there is a very fine one in his First Book. He is speaking of the transformation of the devils into a crowd in miniature.

> As bees
> In spring-time, when the sun with Taurus rides,
> Pour forth their populous youth about the hive
> In clusters: they among fresh dews and flowers
> Fly to and fro, or on the smoothed plank,
> The suburb of their straw-built citadel,
> New rubb'd with balm, expatiate and confer
> Their state affairs. So thick the aery crowd
> Swarm'd and were straiten'd; till the signal given,
> Behold a wonder! They but now who seem'd

> In bigness to surpass earth's giant sons,
> Now less than smallest dwarfs in narrow room
> Throng numberless, like that Pygmean race,
> Beyond the Indian mount; or faery elves,
> Whose midnight revels, by a forest side,
> Or fountain, some belated peasant sees,
> Or dreams he sees, while overhead the moon
> Sits arbitress, and nearer to the earth
> Wheels her pale course; they, on their mirth and dance
> Intent, with jocund music charm his ear;
> At once with joy and fear his heart rebounds.

There is a pretty fairy tale in Parnell, where a young man, by dint of moral beauty, loses his hump. Perhaps it was this poem that suggested a large prose piece to the same effect, written, we believe, by a descendant of the poet's family, and well worthy the perusal of all who are not acquainted with it. It is entitled "Julietta, or the Triumph of Mental Acquirements over Bodily Defects;" and is found in most circulating libraries. But the most beautiful of all stories on the subject, and indeed one of the most beautiful stories in the world, is the celebrated fairy tale of "Beauty and the Beast." Of this, however, we may speak another time; for the fairies of the French books (however minute may be their dealings occasionally) are not the little elves of the North, but the Fates or enchantresses of Romance, paying visits to the nursery.

We shall conclude with a few goblin anecdotes, illustrative of the present state of fairy belief in its true northern region, that is to say, in the British and other islands, Scandinavia, and Germany; and, as the creed is, in fact, the same throughout the whole of that part of the world, though modified by the customs of the different people, we shall not stop to make literal or national distinctions, when the spirit of the thing is the same. Our authorities are the "Fairy Mythology," and the "Fairy

Legends of the South of Ireland;" but it is proper to state, as the authors of these works make a point of doing, that the great masters of Fairy lore now living are Messrs. Grimm, the German writers, with whose language (the language of Goethe) we are, to our regret, unacquainted. But we are zealous students at second hand.

A man who had a Nis, or goblin, in his house, could think of no other way of getting rid of him than by moving. He accordingly packed up his goods, and was preparing to set off with the cart, when the Nis put up his head from it, and cried out—"Eh! Well, we're moving to-day, you see."

A German, for a similar reason, set fire to his barn, hoping to burn the goblin with it.

Turning round to look at the blaze, as he was driving away, the goblin said, "It was time to move, wasn't it?"

There was a Nis that was plagued by a mischievous boy. He went one night to the boy, as he was sleeping in bed by the side of a tall man, and kept pulling him up and down, under the pretence of not being able to make him fit the other's stature. When he was down he was too short; and when up, not long enough. "Short and long don't match," said he; and kept pulling him up and down all night. Being tired by daylight, he went and sat on a wall, and as the dog barked, but could not get at him, the Nis kept plaguing him, by thrusting down first one leg and then the other, saying, "Look at my little leg! Look at my little leg!" By this time the boy got up dreadfully tired with his dream, and while the Nis was wrapt up in his amusement, the boy went behind him, and tumbled him into the yard, saying, "Look at him altogether."

Two Scotch lassies were eating a bowl of broth. They had but one spoon, and yet they scarcely seemed to have tasted their mess, but they had come to the bottom of it. "I hae got but three sups," cried the one, "and it's a' dune!" "It's a' dune, indeed," cried the other. "Ha! ha! ha!" cried a third voice, "Brownie has got the raist o't."

A husband going a journey, gave a Kobold the charge of his wife during his absence. The good man departed, and Kobold had nothing to do from that day forward but assume frightful shapes, fling people down, and crack ribs. At length the husband came back, and a figure at the door welcomed him with a face pale, but delighted. "Who are you?" cried the husband; for he did not know Kobold, he had grown so thin. "I am the keeper of our fair friend," said the elf, "but it is for the last time. Whew!" continued he, blowing, "what a time I've had of it!"

A Neck, or water spirit, was playing upon his harp, when two boys said to him, "What is the use, Neck, of your sitting and playing there? you will never be saved." Upon this the poor spirit began to weep bitterly. The boys ran home, and told their father, who rebuked them; so they came back again, and said, "Be of good cheer, Neck, father says you will be saved as well as us." The Neck then took his harp again, and played sweetly, *long after it was too dark to see him.* This is very beautiful.

The most ghastly, to our taste, of all the equivocal fairies, are the Elle-women, or Female Elves, of Denmark. The male is a little old man with a low-crowned hat; the female is young and fair, very womanly to all appearance, and with an attractive countenance, "but behind she is hollow, like a dough-trough. She has so many lures that people find it difficult to resist her; and they must always follow her about, if they once fondle her; otherwise they lose their senses. But she is apt to bring herself into suspicion by trying never to let her back be seen. If you make the sign of the cross, she is obliged to turn round. We know not whether the charm remains in spite of the dough-trough, provided you are once beguiled. A more unsatisfactory charm could not be found. Think of clasping her to your heart, and finding your hands come together within an ace of your breastbone!

> When lonely German clasps an Elle-maid,
> And finds too late a butcher's tray —

We may laugh at such horrors at this time of day, especially in England; but these darker parts of superstition are still mischievous sometimes to those who believe in them; and we have no doubt there are still believers, upon grounds which it would be found difficult to shake. To say the truth, we are among the number of those who, with all allowance for the lies that have been plentifully told on such matters, do yet believe that fairies have actually been seen; but then it was by people whose perceptions were disturbed. It is observable that the ordinary seers have been the old, the diseased, or the intoxicated; young people's aunts, or grandfathers, or peasants going home from the ale-house. When the young see them, their minds are prepared by a firm belief in what their elders have told them; so that terrors which should pass off for nothing, on closer inspection, become a real perception with these weaker heads; the ideas impressed upon the brain taking the usual morbid stand outside of it. We have no doubt that the case is precisely the same, in its degree, with the spectral illusion of faces and more horrid sights, experienced by opium-eaters, and others in a delicate state of health. We learn from a work of the late Mr. Bingley, that the metal known by the name of cobalt, is so called from the German word kobold, or goblin, so often mentioned in this article, the miners who dig for it appearing to be particularly subject to the vexations of the elf, in consequence of the poison which his namesake exhales.* If it should be asked how we can tell that any thing which is really seen does not really exist, we answer, that such a state of existence is, at all events, not a healthy one, and therefore its perceptions are not to be taken as proper to humanity. Not to mention that spectral illusions are of no use but to terrify, and are quite as likely, and more so, to happen to the conscientious and the delicately organized and considerate, as to those whose vices might be supposed to require them.

The consequence of these darker parts of the belief in fairies, is that deliriums have frequently been occasioned by them; fancied announcements and forebodings have preyed on the spirits in domestic life, and the popular mind kept in a state, which bigotry and worldliness have been enabled to turn to the worst account. But a countercharm was nevertheless growing up in secret against the witchcrafts of imagination, by dint of imagination itself, and the readiness with which it was prepared to enter into the thoughts of others, and sympathize with the great cause of knowledge and humanity. The cure for these and a hundred evils, is not the rooting out of imagination, which would be a proceeding, in fact, as impossible as undesirable, but the cultivation of its health and its cheerfulness. Good sense and fancy need never be separated. Imagination is no enemy to experience, nor can experience draw her from her last and best holds. She stands by,

---

* "Useful Knowledge," vol. i. p. 220.

willing to know every thing he can discover, and able to recommend it, by charms infinite, to the good will and sentiment of all men. What has been in the world is, perhaps, the best for what is to be, none of its worst evils excepted; but found out and known to be evils, the latter have lost even their doubtful advantages; imagination, in the finer excitements of sympathy and the beautiful creations of the poets, casts off these shades of uneasy slumber; and all that she says to knowledge is, " Discard me not, for your own sake as well as mine; lest with want of me, want of sympathy itself return, and utility be again mistaken for what it is not, as superstition has already mistaken it."

The sum of our creed in these matters is this: Spectral illusion, or the actual sight of spiritual appearances, takes place only with the unhealthy, and therefore is not desirable as a general condition: but spiritual or imaginative sight is consistent with the healthiest brain, and enriches our sources of enjoyment and reflection. The three things we have to take care of, on these and all other occasions, are health, knowledge, and imagination.

GENII AND FAIRIES OF THE EAST, THE ARABIAN NIGHTS, &c.

HAIL, gorgeous East! Hail, regions of the colored morning! Hail, Araby and Persia! — not the Araby and Persia of the geographer, dull to the dull, and governed by the foolish, — but the Araby and Persia of books, of the other and more real East, which thousands visit every day, — the Orient of poets, the magic land of the child, the uneffaceable recollection of the man.

To us, the "Arabian Nights" is one of the most beautiful books in the world: not because there is nothing but pleasure in it, but because the pain has infinite chances of vicissitude, and because the pleasure is within the reach of all who have body and soul and imagination. The poor man there sleeps in a doorway with his love, and is richer than a king. The sultan is dethroned to-morrow, and has a finer throne the next day. The pauper touches a ring, and spirits wait upon him. You ride in the air; you are rich in solitude; you long for somebody to return your love, and an Eden encloses you in its arms. You have this world, and you have another. Fairies are in your moonlight. Hope and imagination have their fair play, as well as the rest of us. There is action heroical, and passion too: people can suffer, as well as enjoy, for love; you have bravery, luxury, fortitude, self-devotion, comedy as good as Moliere's, tragedy, Eastern manners, the wonderful that is in a commonplace, and the verisimilitude that is in the wonderful calendars, cadis, robbers, enchanted palaces, paintings full of color and drapery, warmth for the senses, desert in arms and exercises to keep it manly, cautions to the rich, humanity for the more happy, and hope for the miserable. Whenever we see the "Arabian Nights" they strike a light upon our thoughts, as though they were a talisman incrusted with gems; and we fancy we have only to open the book for the magic casket to expand, and enclose us with solitude and a garden.

This wonderful work is still better for the West than for the East; because it is a thing remoter, with none of our commonplaces; and because, our real opinions not being concerned in it, we have all the benefit of its genius without being endangered by its prejudices. The utility of a work of imagination indeed must outweigh the drawbacks upon it in any country. It makes people go out of themselves, even in pursuit of their own good; and is thus opposed to the worst kind of selfishness. These stories of vicissitude and natural justice must do good even to sultans, and help to keep them in order, though it is doubtful how far they may not also serve to keep them in possession. With us the good is unequivocal. The cultivation of hope comes in aid of the progress of society; and he may safely retreat into the luxuries and rewards of the perusal of an Eastern tale, whom its passion for the beautiful helps to keep in heart with his species, and by whom the behavior of its arbitrary kings is seen in all its regal absurdity, as well as its human excuses.

Like all matters on which the poets have exercised their fancy, the opinions respecting the nature of the supernatural beings of the East have been rendered inconsistent even among the best authorities. Sir John Malcolm says that *Deev* means a magician, whereas, in the Persian Dictionary of Richardson, it is rendered spirit and giant;

by custom, a devil: and Sir John uses it, in the same sense in general. D'Herbelot uses it in the sense of demon, and yet in his article on "Solomon" it is opposed to it, or simply means giant. Richardson tells us, that Peri means a beautiful creature of no sex ; whereas according to Sir William Ouseley, it is always female ; and Richardson himself gives us to understand as much another time. Upon the whole we think the following may be taken as the ordinary opinion, especially among authors of the greatest taste and genius.

The Persians (for all these supernatural tales originated with the Persians, Indians, and Chaldeans, and not with the Arabs, except in as far as the latter became united with the Persians), are of opinion, that many kings reigned, and many races of creatures existed, before the time of Adam.* The geologists ought to have a regard for this notion, which has an air of old knowledge beyond ours, and falls in with what has been conjectured respecting the diluvial strata. According to the Persians, a time may have existed, when mammoths, not men, were lords of the creation ; when a gigantic half-human phenomenon of a beast put his crown on with what was only a hand by courtesy ; and elephants and leviathans conversed under a sky in which it was always twilight. Very grand fictions might be founded on imaginations of this sort ; — a Preadamite epic : and knowledge and sensibility might be represented as gradually displacing successive states of beings, till man and woman rose with the full orb of the morning, — themselves to be displaced by a finer stock,

---

* Giafar the Just, sixth Imam, or Pontiff of the Mussulmans, was of opinion, that there had been three Adams before the one mentioned in Scripture, and that there were to be seventeen more. — D'Herbelot, in the article " Giafar."

if the efforts of cultivation cannot persuade them to be the stock themselves.

The race immediately preceding that of human kind resembled them partly in appearance, but were of gigantic stature, various-headed, and were composed of the element of fire. These were the Genii, Deevs, or race of *gigantic spirits* (*the Jann or Jinn* of the Arabs, — Pers. Jannian or Jinniàn).* They lived three thousand years each, and had many contests with other spirits, of whose nature we are left in the dark; but the heavens appear to have warred with them, among other enemies. A dynasty of forty, or according to others of seventy-two Solimans, reigned over them in succession, the last of whom was the renowned Soliman Jan-ben-Jan. His buckler, says D'Herbelot, is as famous among the Orien-

---

* Pronounced Jaun and Jinni*aun*. So Ispahaùn, Goolistaun, &c. It is a pleasure, we think, to know how to pronounce these Eastern words, and therefore we give the reader the benefit of our A B C learning. There is a couplet in Sir William Ouseley's "Travels" which *haunted* us for a month, purely because we had found out how to pronounce it, and liked the spirit of it. We repeat it from memory —

    Haùn sheer khaùn !
    Bèlkeh sheer dendaùn !

(Written — Han shir khan
    Belkeh shir dendan.)

The real spelling ought to be kept, for many reasons; but it is agreeable to find out the sound. The above couplet was an extempore of a Persian boy at an inn, who was struck with the dandy assumptions and enormous appetite of a native gentleman of the party. This person had been commissioned to show Sir William the country, and upon the strength of his having the name of khan (as if one of us were a Mr. Lord), gave himself the airs of the title. The jest of the little mimic (who gives us an advantageous idea of the Persian vivacity), would run something in this way in English, a lion being a common term of exaltation : —

    A lion-lord, indeed !
    You may know him by his feed.

tals, as that of Achilles among the Greeks. He possessed, also, in common with other Solimans, the cuirass called the Gebeh, and the Tig-atesch, or smouldering sword, which rendered them invisible in their wars with the demons.* In his time the race had become so proud and so incorrigible to the various lessons given to them and their ancestors from above, that Heaven sent down the angel Hareth to reduce them to obedience. Hareth did his work, and took the government of the world into his hands, but became so proud in his turn, that the deity in order to punish him created a new species of beings to possess the earth, and bade the angels fall down and worship it. Hareth refused, as being of a nobler nature, and was thrust, together with the chiefs of those who adhered to him, into hell, the whole race of the Genii being dismissed at the same time into the mountains of Kaf, and man left in possession of his inheritance. The Genii, however, did not leave him alone. They made war upon him occasionally till the time of the greatest of all the Solimans, Soliman ben Daoud (Solomon the son of David) who having finally conquered and driven them back, was allowed to retain power over them, to give peace of mind to such as had yielded in good time, and to compel the rest to succumb to him whenever he thought fit, as angels overcame the devils. These last are the rebellious Genii of the "Arabian Nights." They are the *Deevs*, in the diabolical and now the only sense of the word, — Deev signifying a gigantic evil spirit ; and are all monsters, more or less, and generally black ; though the most famous of them is the *Deev-Sifeed*, or great *white* devil, whose conquest was the crowning glory of Rustam, the Eastern Hercules.

---

* D'Herbelot, in the article "Soliman Ben Daoud."

They appear to be of different classes, and to have different names, except the latter be provincial. Some are called Ishreels, others Afreets, and another is our old acquaintance the Ghoul (pronounced ghool). They are permitted to wander from Kaf, and roam about the world, "as a security," says Richardson, "for the future obedience of man." They tempt and do mischief in the style of the Western devil, the lowest of them infesting old buildings, haunting church-yards, and feeding on dead bodies. The reader will recollect the lady who supped with one of them, and who used to pick rice with a bodkin. These are the Ghouls above mentioned. They sometimes inhabit waste places, moaning in the wind, and waylaying the traveller. A Deev is generally painted with horns, tail, and saucer eyes, like our devil; but an author now and then lavishes on a description of him all the fondness of his antipathy. The following is a powerful portrait of one of them, called an Afreet, in the Bahar Danush,— or "Garden of Knowledge" (translated from the Persian by Mr. Gladwin) : —

"On his entrance, he beheld a black demon, heaped on the ground like a mountain, with two large horns on his head, and a long proboscis, fast asleep. In his head the divine Creator had joined the likenesses of the elephant and the wild bull. His teeth grew out like the tusks of the wild boar, and all over his monstrous carcase hung shaggy hairs, like those of the bear. The eye of the mortal-born was dimmed at his appearance, and the mind, at his horrible form and frightful figure, was confounded.

"He was an Afreet created from mouth to foot by the wrath of God.

"His hair like a bear's, his teeth like a boar's. No one ever beheld such a monster.

"Crooked-backed and crab-faced; he might be scented at the distance of a thousand furlongs.

"His nostrils were like the ovens of brick-burners, and his mouth resembled the vat of a dyer.

"When his breath came forth, from its vehemence the dust rose up as in a whirlwind, so as to leave a chasm in the earth; and when he drew it in, chaff, sand, and pebbles, from the distance of some yards, were attracted to his nostrils."

Some of these wanderers about the world appear nevertheless to be of a milder nature than others, and undertake to be amiable on the subject of love and beauty: though this indeed is a mansuetude of which most devils are rendered capable. In the story of Prince Camaralzaman and the Princess of China, a "cursed genie" makes common cause with a good fairy in behalf of the two lovers. The fairy makes no scruple of chatting and comparing notes with him on their beauty, at the same time addressing him by his title of "cursed," and wondering how he can have the face to differ with her. The devil, on the other hand, is very polite, calling her his "dear lady" and "agreeable Maimoune," and tremblingly exacting from her a promise to do him no harm, in return for his telling her no lies. The question demands an umpire; and, at a stamp of Maimoune's foot, out comes from the earth "a hideous, humpbacked, squinting, and lame genie, with six horns on his head, and claws on his hands and feet." Caschcasch (this new monster) behaves like a well-bred arbiter; and the fairy thanks him for his trouble. In the "Arabian Tales; or, sequel to the Arabian Nights,"* is an evil

---

* The "Arabian Tales" are unquestionably of genuine Eastern groundwork, and amidst a great deal of pantomimic extravagance, far inferior to the

genius resembling the Asmodeus of the Devil on Two
Sticks. Asmodeus is evidently Eastern, the Asmadai of
the "Paradise Lost."

There is a world of literature in the East, of which we
possess but a little corner; though, indeed, that corner is
exquisite, and probably the finest of all.*

"Nights," have some capital stories. Il Bondocani, for instance, and Maugraby. But till we have the express authority of a scholar to the contrary, it is difficult to say that a French hand has not interfered in it, beyond what is stated by the translator of the reformed edition. There are fine things in the story of Maugraby.

* Doubts have been gratuitously and not very modestly expressed of the value of the celebrated Eastern poets; but surely a few names could not have risen eminently above myriads of others, and become the delight and reverence of nations, without possessing something in common with the great attractions of humanity in all countries. Sir John Malcolm pronounces Ferdoosi, the epic poet of Persia, to be a great and pathetic genius; and he gives some evidence of what he says, even in a prose sketch of one of his stories, which, says the original, is a story "full of the waters of the eye." There is a couplet, translated by Sir William Jones, from the same author, which shows he had reflected upon a point of humanity that appears obvious enough, and yet which was never openly noticed by an Englishman till the time of Shakespeare. Sir William's couplet is in the modern fashion, and probably not in the original simplicity, but it is well done, and fit to remember. It is upon crushing an insect.

> Ah! spare yon emmet, rich in hoarded grain:
> He lives with pleasure, and he dies with pain.

Do the gratuitous critics recollect, that the stories of Ruth and Joseph, and the sublime book of Job, are from the East? or that the religion of simplicity itself comes from that quarter? the religion that set children on its knee, and bade the orthodox Pharisee retire? It appears to us highly probable, that even our Eastern scholars are liable to be mistaken respecting the pompous language of the Orientals. We talk of their highflown metaphors, and eternal substitution of images for words; but how far would not our own language be liable to similar misconception, if translated in the same literal spirit? What should we think of Persians, who instead of overlooking *the every-day nature* of our colloquial imagery should arrest it at every turn, and wonder how we can talk of standing in other people's shoes, taking false steps, throwing light on a subject, stopping the mouths of our enemies, &c.? There are bad and florid

So much for the rebellious or evil Jinn.

The Jinns obedient seldom make their appearance in a male shape; the Orientals, with singular gallantry of imagination, almost always making them females, as we shall see presently. The best of the males are of equivocal character, and retain much of the fiery and capricious natures of the genii of old. They may be good and kind enough, if they have their way; but do not willingly come in contact with men, except to carry off their wives or daughters; still resenting, it would seem, the ascendancy of human kind, and choosing to serve their own princes and genii, rather than be compelled to appear before masters of an inferior species, — for magicians have power over them, as our astrologers had over the spirits of Plato and the Cabala. They come frightfully, as well as against the grain, — in claps of thunder, and with severe faces. Furthermore, they have a taste for deformity, if we are to judge from the description of Pāri Banou's brother. He was not above a foot and a half high, had a beard thirty feet long, and carried upon his shoulders a bar of iron of five hundred weight, which he used as a quarter-staff. But we will indulge ourselves (and we hope the reader) with an extract about him. Prince Ahmed, who has had the good luck to marry the gentle Pari, which has excited a great deal of jealousy and a wish to destroy him, is requested by his father (into whose dull head the thought has been put) to bring him a little monster of a man of the above description.

"'It is my brother Schaibar,' said the fairy; 'he is

---

writers in all countries, perhaps more in Persia, because the people there are more fervent; but we should judge of a literature by its best specimens, not its worst.

of so violent a nature, though we had both the same father, *that nothing prevents his giving bloody marks of his resentment for a slight offence; yet on the other hand, so good as to oblige any one in what they desire.* He is made exactly as the sultan, your father, described him, and has no other arms than a bar of iron of five hundred pounds weight, without which he never stirs, and which makes him respected. I will send for him, and you shall judge of the truth of what I tell you; but be sure you prepare yourself not to be frightened at his extraordinary figure, when you see him.' — 'What! my queen,' replied Prince Ahmed, 'do you say Schaibar is your brother? Let him be ever so ugly or deformed, I shall be so far from being frightened at the sight of him, that I shall love and honor him, and consider him as my nearest relation.'

" The fairy ordered a gold chafing-dish, with fire in it, to be set under the porch of her palace, with a box of the same metal, which was a present to her, out of which taking some incense, and throwing it into the fire, there arose a thick smoke.

" Some moments after, the fairy said to Prince Ahmed : ' Prince, there comes my brother, do you see him? do you see him?' The Prince immediately perceived Schaibar, who was but a foot and a half high, coming gravely, with his bar on his shoulder; his beard thirty feet long, which supported itself before him, and a pair of thick moustaches in proportion, tucked up to his ears and almost covering his face. His eyes were very small, like a pig's, and deep sunk in his head, which was of enormous size, and on which he wore a pointed cap; besides all this, he had a hump behind and before.

" If Prince Ahmed had not known that Schaibar was Pari Banou's brother, he would not have been able to look at him without fear; but knowing who he was, he waited for him with the fairy, and received him without the least concern.

"Schaibar, as he came forwards, looked at the prince with an eye that would have chilled his soul in his body, and asked Pari Banou, when he first accosted her, 'who that man was?' To which she replied, 'He is my husband, brother; his name is Ahmed; he is son to the Sultan of the Indies. The reason why I did not invite you to my wedding was, I was unwilling to divert you from the expedition you were engaged in, and from which I heard, with pleasure, you returned victorious; on his account I have taken the liberty now to call for you.'

"At these words, Schaibar, looking on Prince Ahmed with a favorable eye, which however diminished neither his fierceness nor savage look, said, 'Is there any thing, sister, wherein I can serve him?'"

We must have one more extract on this part of our subject from the same delightful work. The King of the Genii, in the beautiful story of Zeyn Alasnam (which ends with a piece of dramatic surprise equally unexpected and satisfactory), is a good genius, and yet but a grim sort of personage. Our extract includes a boatman very awkward to sit with, an enchanted island, and a very princely Jinn.

Zeyn, Prince of Balsora, is in search of a ninth statue, which is necessary to complete a number bequeathed to him by his father. Agreeably to a direction found by him among the statues, he seeks an old servant of his father's, at Cairo, of the name of Morabec; and the latter undertakes to forward his wishes, but advertises him there is great peril in the adventure. The prince determines to proceed, and Morabec directs his servants to make ready for a journey.

"Then the prince and he performed the ablution of washing, and the prayer enjoined, which is called farz; and that done they set out. By the way they took notice of abundance of strange and wonderful things, and travelled many days; at the end whereof, being come to a delightful spot, they alighted from their horses. Then Morabec said to all the servants that attended upon them, 'Do you all stay in this place, and take care of our equipage till we return.' Then he said to Zeyn, 'Now, sir, let us go on by ourselves. We are near the dreadful place where the ninth statue is kept; you will stand in need of all your courage.'

"They soon came to a lake: Morabec sat down on the brink of it, saying to the Prince: 'We must cross this sea.' 'How can we cross it,' said Zeyn, 'when we have no boat?' 'You will see one in a moment,' replied Morabec; 'the enchanted boat of the King of the Genii will come for us. But do not forget what I am going to say to you; you must observe a profound silence; do not speak to the boatman, though his figure seem ever so strange to you; whatsoever extraordinary circumstances you may observe, say nothing; for I tell you beforehand, that if you utter the least word when we are embarked the boat will sink down.' 'I shall take care to hold my peace,' said the prince; 'you need only tell me what to do, and I will strictly observe it.'

"While they were talking, he espied on a sudden a boat in the lake, and it was made of red sandal-wood. It had a mast of fine amber, and a blue satin flag: there was only one boatman in it, whose head was like an elephant's, and his body like a tiger's. When the boat was come up to the prince and Morabec, the monstrous boatman took them up one after the other with his trunk, and put them into his boat, and carried them over the lake in a moment. He then again took them up with his trunk, set them on shore, and immediately vanished with his boat.

"'Now we may talk,' said Morabec: 'the island we are on belongs to the King of the Genii; there are no more such in the world. Look round you, prince; can there be a more delightful place? It is certainly a lovely representation of the charming place God has appointed for the faithful observers of our law. Behold the fields, adorned with all sorts of flowers and odoriferous plants; admire these beautiful trees, whose delicious fruit makes the branches bend down to the ground; enjoy the pleasure of these harmonious songs, formed in the air by a thousand birds of as many various sorts, unknown in other countries!' Zeyn could not sufficiently admire those with which he was surrounded, and still found something new as he advanced farther into the island.

"At length they came to a palace made of fine emeralds, encompassed with a ditch, on the banks whereof, at certain distances, were planted such tall trees, that they shaded the whole palace.

"Before the gate, which was of massy gold, was a bridge, made of one single shell of a fish, though it was at least six fathoms long, and three in breadth. At the head of the bridge stood a company of Genii, of a prodigious height, who guarded the entrance into the castle with great clubs of China steel.

"'Let us go no farther,' said Morabec; 'these Genii will knock us down; and, in order to prevent their coming to us, we must perform a magical ceremony.' He then drew out of a purse he had under his garment four long slips of yellow taffety; one he put about his middle, and laid the other on his back, giving the other two to the prince, who did the like. Then Morabec laid on the ground two large table-cloths, on the edges whereof he scattered some precious stones, musk, and amber. Then he sat down on one of these cloths, and Zeyn on the other; and Morabec said to the prince, 'I shall now, sir, conjure the King of the Genii, who lives in the palace that is before us: may he come in a peaceable mood to us! I confess I am not without apprehension about the reception he may give us. If our coming into the island is displeasing to him, he will appear in the shape of a dreadful monster; but if he approve of your design, he will show himself in the shape of a handsome man. As soon as he appears before us, you must rise and salute him, without going off your cloth; for you would certainly perish, should you stir off it. You must say to him, " Sovereign Lord of the Genii, my father, who was your servant, has been taken away by the angel of death; I wish your majesty may protect me as you always did my father." If the King of the Genii,' added Morabec, 'ask you what favor you desire of him, you must answer, "Sir, I most humbly beg of you to give me the ninth statue."'

"Morabec having thus instructed Zeyn, began his conjurations. Immediately their eyes were dazzled with a long flash of lightning, which was followed by a clap of thunder. The whole island was covered with a thick darkness; a furious storm of wind blew, a dreadful cry was heard, the island felt a shock, and there was such an earthquake as that which Asrayel is to cause on the day of judgment.

"Zeyn was startled, and began to look upon that noise as a very ill omen; when Morabec, who knew better than he what to think of it, began to smile, and said, 'Take courage, my prince, all goes well.' In short, that very moment the King of the Genii appeared in the shape of a handsome man, yet there was something of a sternness in his air."

The king promises to comply with the prince's request, but upon one condition — that he shall bring him a damsel of fifteen: a virgin beautiful and perfectly chaste; and that her conductor shall behave himself on the road with perfect propriety towards her, both in deed and thought. "Zeyn," says the story, "took the rash oath that was required of him;" but naturally asks, how he is to be sure of the lady? The Genius gives him a looking-glass on which she is to breathe, and which will be sullied or unsullied accordingly. The consequences among the ladies are such as Western romancers have told in a similar way; but at length success crowns the prince's endeavors, and he conducts the Genius's damsel to the enchanted island, not without falling in love, and being tempted to break his word and carry her away to Balsora. The king is pleased with his self-denial, and tells him that on his return home he will find the statue. He goes, and on the pedestal where it was to have stood, finds the lady! The behavior of the lady is in very good taste, and completes the charm of the discovery.

"'Prince,' said the young maid, 'you are surprised to to see me here: you expected to have found something more precious than me, and I question not but that you now repent having taken so much trouble: you expected a better reward.'

"'Madam,' answered Zeyn, 'Heaven is my witness that I more than once was like to have broken my word with the King of the Genii, to keep you to myself. Whatsoever be the value of a diamond statue, is it worthy the satisfaction of enjoying you? I love you above all the diamonds and wealth in the world.'"

GENII AND FAIRIES OF THE EAST. 139

All this to us is extremely delightful. We can say with the greatest truth, that at the age of fifty we repeat these passages with a pleasure little short of what we experienced at fifteen. We even doubt whether it is less. We come round to the same delight by another road. The genius is as grand to us, if not so frightful as of old; the boatman is peculiar; and the lady is charming. Such ladies may really be found on pedestals, for aught we know, in another life (one life out of a million). In short, we refuse to be a bit older than we were, having, in fact, lived such a little while, and the youth of eternity being before us.

So now, in youth and good faith, to come to our last and best genius, the peri! We call her so from custom, but pari is the proper word; and in the story above-mentioned, it is so spelled. We shall here observe, that the French have often misled us by their mode of spelling Eastern words. The translation of the "Arabian Nights" (which came to us through the French) has palmed upon our childhood the *genie*, or French word, for the genius of the Latins, instead of the proper word jinn. The French pronunciation of *peri* is *pari;* and in Richardson's Dictionary the latter is the spelling. It would have looked affected, some years ago, to write pari for peri; though, in the story just alluded to, an exception is made in favor of it: but in these times, when the growth of general learning has rendered such knowledge common, and when Boccaccio has got rid among us of his old French misnomer of Boccace (which a friend of ours very properly called bookcase), we might as well write *pari* and *jinn*, instead of *peri* and *genie*, loth, as we confess we are, to give up the latter barbarism — the belief of our childhood. But, somehow, we love any truth when we can get it, fond as we are of fiction.

Pari, then, in future, we will venture to write it, and jinn shall be said instead of genie or even genius; with which it is said to have nothing to do. This may be true; and yet it is curious to see the coincidence between the words, and for our part we are not sure, if the etymology could be well traced, that something in common might not be found between the words as well as the things. There might have been no collusion between the countries, and yet a similarity of sound might have risen out of the same ideas. This circumstance in the philosophy of the human history is, we think, not sufficiently attended to on many occasions. Fictions, for example, of all sorts have been traced to this and that country, as if what gave rise to them with one people might not have produced them out of the same chances and faculties with another; obvious mixtures and modifications may be allowed, and yet every national mind throw up its own fancies, as well as the soil its own flowers. The Persians may have a particular sort of fancy as they have of lilac or roses; but fairies, or spirits in general, are of necessity as common to all nations as the grass or the earth, or the shadows among the trees.

Thus out of similar grounds of feeling may issue the roots of the same words. It is curious that *jinn, jinnian,* and *geni*-us, should so resemble one another; for *us* is only the nominative termination of the Latin word, and has nothing to do with the root of it. The Eastern word pari, and our fairy, are still more nearly allied, especially by the Arabic pronunciation, which changes *p* into *f.* It has been justly argued, that fairy is but a modern word, and meant formerly the region in which the Fay lived, and not the inhabitant. This is true; but the root may still be the same, and the Italian word fata, from which it has been reasonably derived, says nothing to the contrary, but the reverse ; for *ta* or *tum* is but a variety of inflection. *Fata* is the Latin *fatum*, or fate, whence come the words *fatua, fama*, and *fanum ;* words implying something *spoken* or *said*, —

<blockquote>Aery tongues that syllable men's names.</blockquote>

Fari is the Latin *to speak*. All these words come from the Greek phaton, phatis, phao, to say, which signifies also to express, to bring to light, and to appear ; and phaos signifies light. Here is the union of speech and appearance, and thus from the single root *pha* or *fay* may have originated the words peri or fari, the English fairy, the old English fay, which is the fée of our neighbors, the Latin fatum or fate, even the *parcæ* (another Latin word for the Fates), the Greek phatis, the old Persian *ferooer* (a soul, a blessed spirit, which is the etymology of the author of the " Fairy Mythology "), and the word fable itself, together with fancy, fair, famous, and what not. We do not wish to lay more stress on this matter than it is worth. There is no end to probabilities, and any thing may be deduced from any thing else. Horne Tooke derived King Pepin from the Greek pronoun osper, and King Jeremiah from pickled cucumber,* — a sort of sport which we recommend as an addition to the stock at Christmas. But the extremes of probability have their use as well as abuse. The spirit of words, truly studied, involves a deep philosophy and important consequences ; and any thing is

---

* As thus, "Osper, eper, oper, — diaper, napkin, pipkin, pippin-king, King Pepin." And going the reverse way, " King Jeremiah, Jeremiah King, jerkin, *gerkin*, pickled cucumber." *Fohi* and *Noah*, says Goldsmith, are evidently the same ; for change *fo* into *no*, and *hi* into *ah*, and there you have it.

good which tends to make out a common case for mankind.

Pari is the female genius, beautiful and beneficent. D'Herbelot says there are male Paries, and he gives the names of two of them, Dal Peri and Milan Schah Peri, who were brothers of Merjan Peri, supposed to be the same as the Western Fairy, Morgana. The truth seems to be, that originally the Paries were of no sex: the poets first distinguished them into male and female; and their exceeding beauty at last confined them to the female kind. We doubt, after all that we see in the writings of Sir William Ousely and others, whether any poet, Western or Eastern, would now talk of a male Pari. At any rate, it would appear as absurd to us of the West, as if anybody were to discover that the three Graces were not all female. The Pari is the female Fairy, the lady of the solitudes, the fair enchantress who enamors all who behold her, and is mightily inclined to be enamored herself, but also to be constant as well as kind. She is the being "that youthful poets dream of when they love." She includes the magic of the enchantress, the supernaturalness of the fairy, the beauty of the angel, and the lovability of the woman; in short, is the perfection of female sweetness.*

Pari has been derived from a word meaning winged, and from another signifying beauty. But enough has been said on this point. We are not aware of any story in which Paries are represented with wings: but they

---

* Where we say *angel-faced*, the Persians say *pari-faced*, *pari-peyker*, *pari-cheker*, *pari-rokhsar*, *pari-roy*, are all terms to that effect. The *Parysatis* of the Greeks is justly supposed to be the *pari-zade*, or *pari-born*, of the Persians.

have the power of flight. In an Eastern poem, mentioned by D'Herbelot, the evil Jinns in their war with the good take some Paries captive, and hang them up in cages, in the highest trees they can find. Here they are from time to time visited by their companions, who bring them precious odors, which serve a double purpose; for the Paries not only feed upon odors, but are preserved by them from the approach of the Deevs, to whom a sweet scent is intolerable. Perfume gives an evil spirit a melancholy, more than he is in the habit of enduring: he suffers because there is a taste of heaven in it. It is beautiful to fancy the Paries among the tops of the trees, bearing their imprisonment with a sweet patience, and watching for their companions. Now and then comes a flight of these human doves, gleaming out of the foliage; or some good genius of the other sex dares a peril in behalf of his Pari love, and turns her patience into joy.

Paries feed upon odors; but if we are to judge from our sweet acquaintance, Pari Banou, they are not incapable of sitting down to dinner with an earthly lover. The gods lived upon odors, but they had wine in heaven, nectar and ambrosia, and furthermore could eat beef and pudding, when they looked in upon their friends on earth, — see the story of Baucis and Philemon, of Lycaon, Tantalus, &c. It is true Prince Ahmed was helped by his fair hostess to delicious meats, which he had never before heard of; odors, perhaps, taking the shape of venison or pilau; but he found the same excellence in the wines; and the fairy partook both of those and the dessert, which consisted of the choicest sweetmeats and fruits. The reader will allow us to read over with him the part of the story thereabouts. Such quarters of an hour are not to be had always, especially in good company; and we presume all the readers of these papers are well met, and of good faith. If any one of a different sort trespasses on our premises, and does not see the beauties we deal with, all we can say is, that he is in the usual condition of those profane persons who are punished when they venture into Fairy-land, by that very inability of sight, which he, poor fellow, would fain consider a mark of his discernment. — So now to our dinner with a Fairy.

The reader will recollect, that Prince Ahmed shot an arrow a great way among some rocks, and, upon finding it was astonished to see how far it had gone. The arrow was also lying flat, which looked as if it had rebounded from one of the rocks. This increased his surprise, and made him think there was some mystery in the circumstance. On looking about, he discovered an iron door. He pushed it open and went down a passage in the earth. On a sudden, " a different light succeeded to that which he came out of; " he entered a square, and perceived a magnificent palace, out of whieh a lady of exceeding beauty made her appearance at the door, attended by a troop of others.

"As soon as Prince Ahmed perceived the lady, he hastened to pay his respects ; and the lady on her part, seeing him coming, prevented him. Addressing her discourse to him first, and raising her voice, she said to him, 'Come near, Prince Ahmed; you are welcome.'

"It was no small surprise to the prince to hear himself named in a palace he never heard of, though so nigh his father's capital; and he could not comprehend how he should be known to a lady who was a stranger to him."

By the way, who knows what our geologists may come to, provided they dig far enough, and are worthy ? Strange things are surmised of the interior of the earth; and

Burnet, now-a-days, would have rubbed his hands to think what phenomenon may turn up.*

"After the proper interchanging of amenities on either side, the prince is led into a hall, over which is a dome of gold and onyx. He is seated on a sofa; the lady seats herself by him, and addresses him in the following words: 'You are surprised, you say, that I should know you and not be known by you; but you will be no longer surprised when I inform you who I am. You cannot be ignorant that your religion teaches you to believe that the world is inhabited by Genii as well as men; I am the daughter of one of the most powerful and distinguished of these Genii, and my name is Pari Banou; therefore you ought not to wonder that I know you, the sultan your father, and the Princess Nouronnihar. I am no stranger to your loves or your travels, of which I could tell you all the circumstances, since it was I myself who exposed to sale the artificial apple which you bought at Samarcande, the carpet which Prince Houssain met with at Bisnagar, and the tube which Prince Ali brought from Schiraz. This is sufficient to let you know that I am not unacquainted with any thing that relates to you. The only thing I have to add is, that you seemed to me worthy of a more happy fate than that of possessing the Princess Nouronnihar; and, that you might

---

* The author of the "Sacred Theory of the Earth,"—a book as good as a romance, and containing passages of great beauty. We speak of the Latin original. Burnet somewhere has expressed a desire *to know more* about Satan—what he is doing at present, and how he lives. There is a subterraneous Fairy-land, to which King Arthur is supposed to have been withdrawn, and whence he is expected to come again and re-establish his throne. Milton has a fine allusion to this circumstance in his Latin poem, "Mansus," v. 81. A poetical traveller in Wales might look at the mouth of a cavern, and expect to see the great king with his chivalry coming up, blowing their trumpets, into the daylight.

attain to it, I was present when you drew your arrow, and foresaw it would not go beyond Prince Houssain's. I took it in the air, and gave it the necessary motion to strike against the rocks near which you found it. It is in your power to avail yourself of the favorable opportunity which it presents to make you happy.' As the fairy, Pari Banou, pronounced these last words with a different tone, and looked at the same time tenderly on Prince Ahmed, with downcast eyes and a modest blush on her cheeks, it was not difficult for the prince to comprehend what happiness she meant. He presently considered that the Princess Nouronnihar could never be his, and that the fairy, Pari Banou, excelled her infinitely in beauty, attractions, agreeableness, transcendent wit, and as far as he could conjecture by the magnificence of the palace where she resided, in immense riches. He blessed the moment that he thought of seeking after his arrow a second time, and yielding to his inclination, which drew him towards the new object which had fired his heart, 'Madam,' replied he, 'should I, all my life, have had the happiness of being your slave, and the admirer of the many charms which ravish my soul, I should think myself the happiest of men. Pardon me the boldness which inspires me to ask you this favor, and do not refuse to admit into your court a prince who is entirely devoted to you.'

"'Prince,' answered the fairy, 'as I have been a long time my own mistress, and have no dependence on my parents' consent, it is not as a slave I would admit you into my court, but as master of my person, and all that belongs to me, by pledging your faith to me and taking me to be your wife. I hope you will not take it amiss that I anticipate you in making this proposal. I am, as I said, mistress of my will; and must add, that the same customs are not observed among fairies as among other ladies, in whom it would not have been decent to have made such advances : but it is what we do ; we suppose we confer obligation by it.'

"Prince Ahmed made no answer to this discourse, but was so penetrated with gratitude, that he thought he could not express it better than by coming to kiss the hem of her garment, which she would not give him time to do, but presented her hand, which he kissed a thousand times, and kept fast locked in his. 'Well, Prince Ahmed,' said she, 'will you not pledge your faith to me, as I do mine to you?'—'Yes, madam,' replied the prince, in an ecstasy of joy, 'what can I do better, and with greater pleasure? Yes, my sultaness, my queen, I will give it you with my heart, without the least reserve.' 'Then,' answered the fairy, 'you are my husband, and I am your wife. Our marriages are contracted with no other ceremonies, and yet are more firm and indissoluble than those among men, with all their formalities. But, as I suppose,' pursued she, 'that you have eaten nothing to-day, a slight repast shall be served up for you while preparations are making for our nuptial-feast this evening, and then I will show you the apartments of my palace, and you shall judge if this hall is the smallest part of it.'

"Some of the fairy's women who came into the hall with them, and guessed her intention, went immediately out, and returned presently with some excellent meats and wines.

"When the prince had eaten and drank as much as he cared for, the fairy, Pari Banou, carried him through all the apartments, where he saw diamonds, rubies, emeralds, and all sorts of fine jewels, intermixed with pearls, agate, jasper, porphyry, and all kinds of the most precious marbles ; not to mention the richness of the furniture, which was inestimable ; the whole disposed with such profusion, that the prince, instead of ever having seen any thing like it, acknowledged that there could not be any thing in the world that could come up to it.

"'Prince,' said the fairy, 'if you admire my palace so much, which is indeed very beautiful, what would you say to the palaces of the chief of our Genii, which are made much more beautiful, spacious, and magnificent? I could also charm you with my garden; but we will leave that till another time. Night draws near, and it will be time to go to supper.'

"The next hall which the fairy led the prince into, and where the cloth was laid for the feast, was the only apartment the prince had not seen, and it was not in the least inferior to the others. At his entrance into it he admired the infinite number of wax candles, perfumed with amber, the multitude of which, instead of being confused, were placed with so just a symmetry, as formed an agreeable and pleasant sight. A large beaufet was set out with all sorts of gold plate, so finely wrought, that the workmanship was much more valuable than the weight of the gold. Several choruses of beautiful women, richly dressed, and whose voices were ravishing, began a concert, accompanied with all kinds of the most harmonious instruments he had ever heard. When they were set down to table, the fairy, Pari Banou, took care to help Prince Ahmed to the most delicious meats, which she named as she invited him to eat of them, and which the prince had never heard of, but found so exquisite and nice, that he commended them in the highest terms, saying, that the entertainment which she gave him far surpassed those among men. He found also the same excellence in the wines, which neither he nor the fairy tasted till the dessert was served up, which consisted of the choicest sweetmeats and fruits.

"After the dessert, the Fairy, Pari Banou, and Prince Ahmed, rose from the table, which was immediately carried away, and sat on a sofa, at their ease, with cushions of fine silk, curiously embroidered with all sorts of large flowers, laid at their backs. Presently after, a great number of genii and fairies danced before them to the door of the chamber where the nuptial bed was made, and when they came there, they divided themselves into two rows, to let them pass, and after that retired, leaving them to go to bed.

"The nuptial feast was continued the next day; or rather, the days following the celebration were a continual feast, which the fairy, Pari Banou, who could do it with the utmost ease, knew how to diversify, by new dishes, new meats, new concerts, new dances, new shows, and new diversions; which were all so extraordinary, that Prince Ahmed, if he had lived a thousand years among men could not have imagined.

"The fairy's intention was not only to give the prince essential proofs of the sincerity of her love, and the violence of her passion, by so many ways; but to let him see, that as he had no pretensions at his father's court, he could meet with nothing comparable to the happiness he enjoyed with her; independent of her beauty and her charms, and to attach him entirely to herself, that he might never leave her. In this scheme she succeeded so well, that Prince Ahmed's passion was not in the least diminished by possession; but increased so much, that, if he had been so inclined, it was not in his power to forbear loving her."

This is a pretty satisfaction to the imagination, and good

only can come of it. They are under a great mistake who think that romances and pictures of perfection do harm. They may produce mounting impatience and partial neglect of duties here and there, but in the sum total they give a distaste to the sordid, elevate our anger above trifles, incline us to assist intellectual advancement of all sorts, and keep a region of solitude and sweetness for us, in which the mind may retreat and recreate itself, so as to return with hope and gracefulness to its labors. Imagination is the breathing room of the heart. The whole world of possibility is thrown open to it, and the air mixes with that of heaven.

Ulysses did not the less yearn to go back to the wife of his bosom, because a goddess had lain there. Affectionate habit is a luxury long drawn out; and constancy, made sweet by desert, is a sort of essence of immortality distilled.

To conclude the remarks on our story: Prince Ahmed, to be sure, had every reason to be faithful; but we feel it was because a sweet, sincere, and intelligent woman loved him, rather than a wonder-working fairy. She is a Cleopatra in what is pleasing, but she is also as unlike her as possible in what is the reverse; being very different as she says, from her brother Schaibar, who was resentful and violent. Such is the fairy of the East, the sweetest of all fairies, and fit kinswoman, by humanity, to the only creature we like better, which is the Flying Woman of our friend Peter Wilkins. With the former, we could live for ever, if disengaged and immortal; but with the latter, somehow, like Ulysses, we would rather die.

There remains one more supernatural being, the Arabian fairy, who lives in a well; for so she has been distinguished from her more elegant sister of the palace.

The Arabs, leading a hard and unsettled life, seem not to have had time, even in imagination, for the more luxurious pictures of Persia. They had all the imagination of home feeling, were devoted patriots and intense lovers, and have poured forth some of the most heart-felt poetry in the world. A volume of poems might be collected out of the romance of Antar, unsurpassed as effusions of passion. But the total absence of airy and preternatural fiction in their works is remarkable. When the two nations became united, and the successors of Mahomet shifted their throne from their old barren sands to the luxurious halls of Bagdad, the mythologies of their poets gradually became confounded; and it is difficult to pronounce, after all, how far the supposed Arabian fairy differs from the Pari, her sister; how many wonders she might have drawn out of her well, or how far the Pari could not inhabit a hole in the well on occasion, as the fairies of Italy do in the old stones of Fiesole. She was, no doubt, distinct originally, a coarser breed, like the gnome of the desert compared with the ladies of the court of Darius; but the distinction seems hardly to have survived. If Maimoune lives in a well, we have seen that Denhasch pronounced her charming; and though we might regard this as the flattery of a devil, the Fairy herself gives us to understand that she was a good spirit, one of those who submitted to Solomon; therefore charming by implication, and at all events mixed up with the spirits of Persia. The Jinns, male and female, are all capital architects, who can make a palace in a twinkling for others. We can hardly doubt they can do as much for themselves; and that Maimoune, if she had wished to please a lover, could have raised as splendid a house of reception for him as Banou.

The spiritual beings of the East then may, perhaps,

safely be classed as follows, according to the most received ideas: —

The Deev, or evil genius.

The Jinn, or good genius, if not otherwise qualified.

The Pari, or good female genius, always beneficent and beautiful.

Individuals of all these classes are permitted to roam about the world, and reside in particular places; but their chief residence, or Fairy-land, is understood to be in Jinnistan, or the place of the Genii, which is situated on the Greek mountain of Kaf, and divided into what may be called Good-land and Bad-land, or the domains of the good, and the domains of the rebellious Genii. In the former is the province of the good Genii, the land of *Shadukam*, or pleasure and desire: — and the Cities Juharbad, or the City of Jewels; — and Amberhabad, the City of Ambergris. In the latter stands Ahermanhabad, the City of Aherman, or the Evil Principle, over which reigns the bad King Arzhenk, a personage with a half-human body and the head of a bull. He is a connoisseur, and has a gallery of pictures containing portraits of all the different sorts of creatures before Adam.

All Genii, bad and good, being subjected in some sort to the human race, whom they all in the first instance agreed not to worship, are compellable by the invocations of magic, and forced to appear in the service of particular rings and talismans. In this they resemble the Genii of the Alexandrian Platonists and the Cabala. Sometimes a man possesses a ring without knowing its value, and happening to give it a rub, is shocked by the apparition of a giant, who in a tone of thunder tells him he is his humble servant, and wants to know his pleasure. Invocations must be practised after their particular form and letter, or the

Genius becomes riotous instead of obedient, and is perhaps the death of you ; and at least gives you a cuff of the ear, enough to fell a dromedary. They transport people whithersoever they please ; make nothing of building a house, full of pictures and furniture, in the course of a night ; and will put a sultan in their pockets for you, if you desire it. But if not your servants, they are dangerous acquaintances, and it is difficult to be on one's guard against them. You must take care, for instance, how you throw the shells about when you are eating nuts, otherwise an unfortunate husk to put out the eye of one of their invisible children, and for this you will suffer death unless you can repeat poems or fine stories. Numbers of Genii have remained imprisoned in brazen vessels ever since the time of Solomon, and it is not always safe to deliver them. It is a moot point whether they will make a king of you for it, or kick you into the sea. The Genius whom the fisherman sets free in the "Arabian Nights," gives an account of his feelings on this matter, highly characteristic of the nature of these fairy personages : —

"' During the first hundred years' imprisonment,' says he, ' I swore, that if any one should deliver me before the hundred years expired, I would make him rich, even after his death, but the century ran out, and nobody did me that good office. During the second, I made an oath that I would open all the treasures of the earth to any one that should set me at liberty, but with no better success. In the third, I promised to make my deliverer a potent monarch, to grant him every day three requests, of whatever nature they might be ; but this century ran out as the two former, and I continued in prison ; at last, being angry, or rather mad, to find myself a prisoner so long, I swore that, if afterwards any one should deliver me, I would kill him without mercy, and grant him no other favor but to choose what kind of death he would have; and, therefore, since you have delivered me to-day, I give you that choice.'"

The mode in which the Genii emerge from these brazen vessels is very striking. The spirit into which they have been condensed expands as it issues forth, and makes an enormous smoke, which again compresses into a body, black and gigantic; and the Genius is before you. He is in general a smoke of a weaker turn than our friend just alluded to. If we are to believe the story of the Brazen City in the "New Arabian Nights," whole beds of vessels, containing genuine condensed spirits of Jinn, were to be found in a certain bay on the coast of Africa. Deevs were as plenty as oysters. A sultan had a few brought him, and opening one after the other, the giant vapor issued forth, crying out, "Pardon, pardon, great Solomon; I will never rebel more."

Kaf is Caucasus, the "great stony girdle." The Persians supposed it, and do so still, to run round the earth, enclosing it like a ring. The earth itself stands on a great sapphire, the reflection of which causes the blue of the sky; and when the sapphire moves there is an earthquake, or some other convulsion of nature. On this mountain the Jinns reign and revel after their respective fashions; and there is eternal war between the good and the bad. Formerly the good Genii, when hard pressed, used to apply to an earthly hero to assist them. The exploits of Rustam, before mentioned, and of the ancient Tahmuras, surnamed *Deev-Bend* or the *Deev-Binder*, form the most popular subjects of Persian heroic poetry.

Kaf will gradually be undone, and the place of sapphire be not found; but the blue of the sky will remain; and till the Persian can expound the mystery of the cheek he loves, and know the first cause of the roses which make a bower for it, he will still, if he is wise, retain his Pari and his enchanted palace, and encourage his mistress to resemble the kind faces that may be looking at her.

———◆———

THE SATYR OF MYTHOLOGY AND THE POETS.

E lay before our readers the portrait of a very eminent half or *four-fifths* man, an old friend of the poets, particularly of the sequestered and descriptive order, and constantly alluded to in all modern as well as ancient quarters poetical. He is alive, not only in Virgil, and Theocritus, and Spenser, but in Wordsworth, in Keats, and Shelley, and in the pages of "Blackwood" and the "London Journal."

We keep the public in mind, from time to time, that one of the objects of the "London Journal" is to bring uneducated readers of taste and capacity acquainted with the pleasures of those who are educated; and we write articles of this description accordingly, in a spirit intended to be not unacceptable to either. Enter, therefore, the Satyr, — as in one of the Prologues to an old play. By and by, we shall give a Triton, a Nymph, &c., &c., and so on through all the gentle populace of fiction —*plebe degli, dei*, as Tasso calls them, — the "common people of the gods."

Such, we hope, in future times, — or worthy, rather, of such appellation, — will be all the people of the earth, — their poetry in common, their education in common, knowledge and its divine pleasures being as cheap as daisies in the mead.

The Satyr (not always, but generally) is a goat below the waist, and a man above, with a head in which the two beings are united. He has horns, pointed ears, and a beard; and there is just enough humanity in his face to make the look of the inferior being more observable. The expression is drawn up to the height of the salient and wilful. He is a merry brute of a demigod; and when not sleeping in the grass, is for ever in motion, dancing, after his quaint fashion, and butting when he fights. He goes in herds, though he is often found straying. His haunt is in the woods, where he makes love to the Dryads and other nymphs, not always with their good-will.

When he gets old he takes to drinking, grows fat, and is called a Silenus, after the most eminent gorbelly of his race: and then he becomes oracular in his drink, and disburses the material philosophy which his way of life has taught him. He is not immortal, but has a long life as well as a merry; some say a thousand years: others, many thousand. A thousand years, according to Aristotle, is the duration both of the Satyr and the Nymph.

The Faun, though often confounded with the Satyr, and supposed by some to be nothing but a Latin version of him, is generally taken by the moderns for a Satyr mitigated and more human. Goat's feet are not necessary to him. He can be content with a tail, and two little budding horns, like a kid.

"How the Satyrs originated," quoth the "serious" but not very "sage" Natalis Comes, "or of what parents they were begotten, or where or when they began to exist, or for what reason they were held to be gods by antiquity; neither have I happed upon any creditable ancient who can inform me, nor can I make it out myself." He says he takes no heed of the opinion of those who suppose them to have been the children of Saturn or Faunus. Pliny, he tells us, speaks of Satyrs, as certain animals in the Indian Mountains, of great swiftness, going on all-fours, but with a human aspect, and running upright. Furthermore, Pausanias mentions one Euphemus of Caria, who coming upon a cluster of "desert" islands in the extreme parts of the sea, and being forced by a tempest to alight on one of them called Satyras, found it inhabited by people of a red color, with tails not much inferior to those of horses. These gentlemen invaded the ships of their new acquaintance, and without saying a word, began helping themselves to what they liked. Finally, Pomponius Mela speaks of certain islands beyond Mount Atlas, in which lights were seen at night, and a great sound was heard of drums and cymbals and pipes, though nobody was to be seen by day; and these islands were said to be inhabited by Satyrs. To which beareth testimony the famous Hanno the Carthaginian.*

Boccaccio, in his treatise "De Montibus," appears to have transferred these islands to Mount Atlas itself; of which he says (dwelling upon the subject with his usual romantic fondness) that, " such a depth of silence is reported to prevail there by day, that none approach it without a certain horror, and a feeling of some divine presence; but at night-time, like heaven, it is lit up with many lights, and resounds with the songs and

---

* See all these authorities in Natalis Comes' " Mythologia," p. 304.

cymbals, the pipes and whistling reeds of Ægipans and Satyrs." *

The same writer, speaking of the opinion that Satyrs were goat-footed *homunciones*, or little men, tells the story of St. Anthony: "who searching through the deserts of the Thebais for the most holy eremite Paul, did behold one of them, and question him: the which made answer, that he was mortal; and that he was one of the people, bordering thereabouts, whom the Gentiles led away by a vain error, did worship as Fauns and Satyrs." "Other authors," he says, "esteemed them to be men of the woods, and called them Incubi, or Ficarii (Fig-eaters)." We here see who had the merit of it when figs were stolen.

Chaucer takes the Satyr for an incubus, probably from this passage of his favorite author. Speaking of the friar, whose office it was to go about blessing people's grounds and houses (which was the reason, he says, why there were no longer any fairies), he adds, in his pleasant manner: —

"Women may now go safely up and doun: —
In every bush, and under every tree,
There is non other Incubus but he."
WIFE OF BATH'S TALE.

But the most "particular fellow" on this subject is Philostratus; who, among the wild stories which he relates with such gravity of Apollonius the Tyanæan, has this, the wildest of them all, and, in his opinion the most weighty. As the account is amusing, we will extract nearly the whole of it: —

"After visiting," says he, "the cataracts (of the Nile),

---

* At the end of his " Genealogia Deorum."

Apollonius and his companions stopped in a small village in Ethiopia, where, whilst they were at supper, they amused themselves with a variety of conversation, both grave and gay. On a sudden was heard a confused uproar, as if from the women of the village exhorting one another to seize and pursue. They called to the men for assistance, who immediately sallied forth, snatching up sticks and stones, with whatever other weapons they chanced to find. ... All this hubbub arose from a Satyr having made his appearance, who for ten months past had infested the village. ... The moment Apollonius perceived his friends were alarmed at this, he said, 'Don't be terrified. ... There is but one remedy to be used in cases of such kind of insolence, and is what Midas had recourse to. He was himself of the race of Satyrs, as appeared plainly by his ears. A Satyr once invited himself to his house, on the ground of consanguinity, and whilst he was his guest, libelled his ears in a copy of verses, which he set to music, and played on his harp. Midas, who was instructed, I think, by his mother, learnt from her that if a Satyr was made drunk with wine and fell asleep, he recovered his senses and became quite a new creature. A fountain happening to be near his palace, he mixed it with wine, to which he sent the Satyr, who drank it till he was quite overcome with it. Now to show you that this is not all mere fable, let us go to the governor of the village, and if the inhabitants have any wine, let us make the Satyr drink, and I will be answerable for what happened in the case of the Satyr of Midas.' All were willing to try the experiment; and immediately four Egyptian amphoras of wine were poured into the pond, in which the cattle of the village were accustomed to drink. Apollonius invited the Satyr to drink, and added, along with the invitation, *some* *private menaces*, in case of refusal. The Satyr did not appear, *nevertheless the wine sank, as if it was drank*. When the pond was emptied, Apollonius said, 'Let us offer libations to the Satyr, who is now fast asleep.' After saying this, he carried the men of the village to the cave of the Nymphs, which was not more than the distance of a plethron from the hamlet, where, after showing them the Satyr asleep, he ordered them to give him no ill-usage, either by beating or abusing him : 'For,' said he, 'I will answer for his good behavior for the time to come.' This is the action of Apollonius, which, by Jupiter, I consider as what gave greatest lustre to his travels, and which was, in truth, their greatest feat. Any one who has perused the letter which he wrote to a dissipated young man, wherein he tells him he had tamed a Satyr in Ethiopia, must call to mind this story. *Consequently, no doubt* can now remain of the existence of Satyrs. . . . When I was myself in Lemnos, I remember one of my contemporaries, whose mother, they said, was visited by a Satyr, formed according to the traditional accounts we have of that race of beings. He wore a deerskin on his shoulders, *which exactly fitted him*, the forefeet of which, encircling his neck, were fastened to his breast. But of this I shall say no more, as I am sensible credit is due to *experience*, as well as to me." *

It is clear, from all these authorities, that various circumstances might have given rise to the idea of Satyrs. The Great Ape species alone, which, like the monkeys in Africa, might easily be supposed to be a race of men too idle to work, and holding their tongues to avoid it, would

---

* "Life of Apollonius of Tyana," translated from the Greek of Philostratus, by the Rev. Edward Berwick. p. 348.

be sufficient to suggest the fancy to an imaginative people. The Satyr Islands of Pausanias are evidently islands frequented by apes, or rather baboons; unless, indeed, we are to believe with Monboddo, that men once had tails; which is hardly a greater distinction from some men without them, than a philosopher is from a savage. Orang Outang signifies a wild man; and Linnæus has called the Great Ape the Ape Satyr (Simia Satyrus). Again, there have been real wild men; and a single one of these, such as Peter the Wild Boy, would people a country like Greece with Satyrs.

But it is not necessary to recur to palpable beings for a poetical stock. A sound, a shadow, a look of something in the dark, was enough to make them; and if this had not been found, they would still have been fancied. Satyrs, in an allegorical sense, are the animal spirits of the creation, its exuberance, its natural health and vigor, its headlong tendency to reproduction. In a superstitious and popular point of view, they were the spirits of the woods, a branch of the universal family of genii and fairies. Finally, in the great world of poetry, they partake, on both these accounts, of whatever has been said or done for them, that remains interesting to the imagination; and are still to be found there, immortal as their poets. As long as there is a mystery in the world, and men are unable to affirm what beings may *not* exist, so long poetry will have what existence it pleases, and the mind will have a corner in which to entertain them. Therefore, "the sage and serious Spenser" tells us wisely of

"The wood-god's breed which must for ever last."

In no part of the world of poetry were they ever more alive or lasting, than in the woods of his "Faerie Queene."

You have, indeed, a stronger sense of them in his pages, than in the works of antiquity. The ancient poets appear to have been too close at hand with them. The familiarity, though of a religious sort, had in it something of contempt. Spenser is always remote, — in the uttermost parts of poetry ; and thither shall he take us to meet them. Here they are, on a bright morning, in the thick of their glades. Una is in distress, and has cried out, so that her voice is heard throughout the woods.

> " A troope of Faunes and Satyres, far away
> Within the wood, were dancing in a rownd,
> Whiles old Sylvanus slept in shady arber sownd:
>
> Who when they heard that pitteous, strained voice,
> In haste forsooke their rurall merriment,
> And ran towards the far rebownded noyce,
> To weet what wight so loudly did lament.
> Unto the place they came incontinent:
> Whom when the raging Sarazin espyde,
> A rude, mishappen, monstrous rablement,
> Whose like he never saw, he durst not byde ;
> But got his ready steed, and fast away gan ryde.
>
> Such fearefull fitt assaid her trembling hart,
> Ne word to speake, ne joynt to move, she had.
> The salvage nation feele her secret smart,
> And read her sorrow in her count'nance sad ;
> Their frowning forheades, with rough hornes yclad
> And rustick horror, all asyde doe lay ;
> And, gently grenning, shew a semblance glad
> To comfort her ; and, feare to put away,
> Their backward-bent knees teach her humbly to obay.
>
> The doubtfull damzell dare not yet committ
> Her single person to their barbarous truth ;
> But still twixt feare and hope amazd does sitt,
> Late learnd what harme to hasty truth ensu'th ;
> They in compassion of her tender youth
> And wonder of her beautie soverayne,
> Are wonne with pitty and unwonted ruth ;

And, all prostráte upon the lowly playne,
Doe kisse her feete, and fawne on her with count'nance fayne.

Their harts she ghesseth by their humble guise,
And yieldes her to extremitie of time:
So from the ground she fearelesse doth arise,
And walketh forth without suspect of crime:
They, all as glad as birdes of joyous pryme,
Thence lead her forth, about her dauncing round,
Shouting, and singing all a shepheard's ryme;
And, with greene branches strowing all the ground,
Do worship her as queene, with olive girlond cround.

And all the way their merry pipes they sound,
That all the woods with doubled eccho ring;
And with their horned feet doe weare the ground,
Leaping like wanton kids in pleasant spring.
So towards old Sylvanus her they bring;
Who, with the noyse awaked, commeth out
To weet the cause, his weake steps governing
And aged limbs on cypresse stadle stout;
And with an yvie twyne his waste is girt about.

The wood-borne people fall before her flat,
And worship her as goddesse of the wood;
And old Sylvanus self bethinkes not, what
To think of wight so fayre; but gazing stood
In doubt to deeme her born of earthly brood.

The wooddy nymphes, faire Hamadryades,
Her to behold doe thether runne apace;
And all the troupe of light-foot Naiades
Flocke all about to see her lovely face."

Book I. canto 6.

Spenser has a knight among his chivalry, who was the son of a Satyr by the wife of a country gentleman, one Therion (or Brute) by name,—a severe insinuation on the part of the gentle poet:—

"A loose unruly swayne,
Who had more joy to raunge the forrest wyde,
And chase the salvage beast with busie payne,
Then serve his ladie's love."

Perhaps the poet intended a hint to the squires of his time. He tells us of another wife, who had a considerable acquaintance among the wood-gods. It is not so easy to relate her story; but she would be a charming person by the time she was thirty, and make a delicate heart content! His account of her is certainly intended as a lesson to old gentlemen.

> " The gentle lady, loose at random lefte,
> The greene-wood long did walke, and wander wide
> At wilde adventure, like a forlorne wefte;
> Till on a daye the Satyres her espide
> Straying alone withouten groome or guide:
> Her up they tooke, and with them home her ledd,
> With them as housewife ever to abide,
> To milk their goats, and make them cheese and bredd."

She forgets her old husband Malbecco, who has just arrived at the spot where she lives, —

> " And eke Sir Paridell, all were he deare,
> Who from her went to seek another lott,
> And now by fortune was arrived here.
>
> *   *   *   *   *   *
>
> Soone as the old man saw Sir Paridell,

(who was the person that had taken his wife from him).

> He fainted, and was almost dead with feare,
> Ne word he had to speake, his griefe to tell,
> But to him louted low, and greeted goodly well;
>
> And, after, asked him for Hellenore.
> ' I take no keepe of her,' sayd Paridell,
> ' She wonneth in the forest, there before.'
> So forth he rode as his adventure fell."

A great noise is afterwards heard in the woods, of bagpipes and "shrieking hubbubs;" the old man hides in a bush; and after awhile

> "The jolly Satyres full of fresh delight
> Came dauncing forth, and with them nimbly ledd
> Faire Hellenore, with girlonds all bespredd,
> Whom their May-lady they had newly made:
>
> She, proude of that new honour which they redd,
> And of their lovely fellowship full glade,
> Daunst lively, *and her face did with a lawrell shade.*"

What a sunny picture is in this line!

> "The silly man, that in the thickett lay
> Saw all this goodly sport, and grieved sore;
> Yet durst he not against it do or say,
> But did his hart with bitter thoughts engore,
> To see th' unkindness of his Hellenore.
> All day they daunced with great lustyhedd,
> And with their horned feet the greene grass wore;
> The wiles their gotes upon the brouzes fedd,
> Till drouping Phœbus gan to hyde his golden hedd.
>
> Tho up they gan their merry pypes to trusse,
> And all their goodly heardes did gather rownd."

The old gentleman creeps to his wife's bed's-head at night, and endeavors to persuade her to go away with him; but she is deaf to all he can say; so in the passion of his misery, and supernatural strength of his very weakness, he runs away, — "runs with *himself away*," — till, under the most appalling circumstances, he undergoes a transformation into Jealousy itself! a poetical flight, the daringness of which can only be equalled (and vindicated, as it is) by the mastery of its execution. See the passage; which, though a half-allegory, is calculated to affect the feelings of the poetical reader, almost as much as Burley and his cavern in "Old Mortality" do readers in general. It is at the end of Canto X. book 3.

Spenser has a story of "Foolish God Faunus," who comes on Diana when she is bathing; for which he is put into a deerskin, and she and her nymphs hunt him through wood and dale. Fauns and Satyrs, it is to be observed, are represented as wise or foolish, according as the poet allegorizes the elements of a country life, and the reflections, or clownish impulses, of sequestered people. The Faun, in particular, who was the more oracular of the two, might be supposed either to speak from his own knowledge, or to be merely the channel of a higher one, and so to partake of that reverend character of fatuity, which is ascribed in some countries to idiots. The Satyr was more conscious and petulant: he waited more especially upon Bacchus; was loud and saucy; may easily be supposed to have been noisiest and most abusive at the time of grapes; and it is to him, we think, and him alone (whatever learned distinctions have been made between *satyri* and *saturæ*, or the fruit which he got together, and him who got them), that the origin of the word satire is to be traced; that is to say, satire was such free and abusive speech, as the vintagers pelted people with, just as they might with the contents of their baskets.

To make Satyr, therefore, clever or clownish, or both, just as it suits the writer's purpose, is in good keeping. To make him revengeful for not having his will, is equally good, as Tasso has done in the "Aminta." To make him old, and scorned by a young mistress, is warrantable, as Guarini has done in the "Pastor Fido;" and even a touch of sentiment may not be refused him, if visited by a painful sense of the difference of his shape; which is an imitation of the beautiful Polyphemic invention of Theocritus, and was introduced into modern poetry by the precursor of those poets, the inventor of the sylvan drama "Beccari." But we cannot say so much for another great poet of ours, Fletcher, who, spoilt by his town breeding, and thinking he could not make out a case for chastity, and the admiration of it, but by carrying it to a pitch of the improbable, introduces into his "Faithful Shepherdess" a Satyr thoroughly divested of his nature, the most sentimental and Platonical of lovers, and absolute guardian of what he exists only to oppose. The clipping of hedges into peacocks was nothing to this. It was like changing warmth into cold, and taking the fertility out of the earth. Elegance was another affair. The rudest things natural contain a principle of that. You may show even a Satyr in his graces, as you may a goat in a graceful attitude, or the turns and blossoms of a thorn. But to make the shaggy and impetuous wood-god, with his veins full of the sap of the vine, a polished and retiring lover, all for the metaphysics of the passion, and bowing and backing himself out of doors like a "sweet signior," was to strike barrenness into the spring, and make the "swift and fiery sun," which the poet so finely speaks of, halt and become a thing deliberate. Pan, at the sight, should have cut off his universal beard. Certainly, the Satyr ought to have clipped his coat, and withdrawn into the urbanities of a suit of clothes. He should have "walked gowned."

However, there is a ruddy and rough side of the apple still left; and with this we proceed to indulge ourselves, cutting away the rest. Fletcher is a true poet, and could not speak of woods and wood-gods without finding means to give us a proper taste of them. His Satyr comes in well.

ENTER A SATYR WITH A BASKET OF FRUIT.

Satyr. Through yon same bending plain,
That flings his arms down to the main,
And through these thick woods have I run,
Whose bottom never kiss'd the sun

> Since the lusty spring began;
> All to please my master Pan
> Have I trotted without rest
> To get him fruit; for at a feast
> He entertains, this coming night,
> His paramour, the Syrinx bright.
>
> Here be grapes, whose lusty blood
> Is the learned poet's good,
> Sweeter yet did never crown
> The head of Bacchus; nuts more brown
> Than the squirrel's teeth, that crack them;
> Deign, oh, fairest fair, to take them.
> For these, black-eyed Dryope
> Hath oftentimes commanded me
> With my clasped knee to climb:
> See how well the lusty time
> Hath deck'd their rising cheeks in red,
> Such as on your lips is spread.
> Here be berries for a queen;
> *Some* be red, *some* be green."

(How much better than if he had said "some be red *and* some be green." He is like a great boy, poking over the basket, and pointing out the finest things in it with rustic fervor.)

> "These are of that luscious meat,
> The great god Pan himself doth eat:
> All these, and what the woods can yield,
> The hanging mountain or the field,
> I freely offer; and ere long
> Will bring you more, more sweet and strong:
> Till when humbly leave I take,
> Lest the great Pan do awake,
> That sleeping lies in a deep glade,
> Under a broad beech's shade.
> I must go, I must run,
> Swifter than the fiery sun."

In this passage, Mr. Seward, in his edition of "Beaumont and Fletcher," has a note containing an extract from Theocritus, so happily rendered that, as it suits our purpose, we will repeat it. It is seldom that a writer not professedly a poet, and an eminent one too, has struck forth so masterly a bit of translation. The verb in the last line even surpasses the original. We will put the Greek first, both in justice to it, and because (to own a whim of ours) the glimmering and thorny look of the Greek characters gives, in our eyes, something of a boskiness to one's pages. A page of a Greek pastoral is the next thing with us to a wood-side, or a landscape of Gasper Poussin : —

> Ου θεμις, ω ποιμαν, το μεσαμβρινον, ου θεμις αμμιν
> Συρισδεν· τον Πανα δεδοικαμες· η γαρ απ' αγρας
> Τανικα κεκμακως αμπανεται, εντι γε πικρος,
> Και οι αει δριμεια χολα ποτι ρινι καθηται.

> "Shepherd, forbear: no song at noon's dread hour;
> Tir'd with the chase, Pan sleeps in yonder bower;
> Churlish he is; and, stirr'd in his repose,
> The snappish choler quivers on his nose."

We must quote the Satyr's concluding speech, though it is not so much in character. The poet might have defended his straying in the air, but it must have been upon very abstract and ethereal grounds, foreign to the substantial part which he plays in this drama; and the fine allusion to Orpheus' lute is equally learned and out of its place. However, the whole passage is so beautiful, that we cannot help repeating it. Our Platonical friend is taking leave of the lady : —

> "*Satyr.* Thou divinest, fairest, brightest,
> Thou most pow'rful maid, and whitest,
> Thou most virtuous and most blessed,
> Eyes of stars, and golden tressed
> Like Apollo! tell me, sweetest,
> What new service now is meetest

> For the Satyr? Shall I stray
> In the middle air, and stay
> The sailing rack, or nimbly take
> Hold by the moon, and gently make
> Suit to the pale queen of night
> For a beam to give thee light?
> Shall I dive into the sea,
> And bring thee coral, making way
> Through the rising waves, that fall
> In snowy fleeces? Dearest, shall
> I catch thee wanton fawns, or flies,
> Whose woven wings the summer dyes
> Of many colours? Get thee fruit?
> Or steal from heav'n old Orpheus' lute!"

What a relic! The lute of Orpheus! and laid up in some corner of heaven! Doubtless in the thick of one of its grassiest nooks of asphodel; and the winds play upon it, of evenings, to the ear of Proserpine when she visits her mother, — giving her trembling memories to carry back to Eurydice.

THE NYMPHS OF ANTIQUITY AND OF THE POETS.

THE Nymphs of antiquity are the gentle powers of the earth, and therefore figured under the shape of beautiful females. A large or violent river had a god to it: — the nymph is ever gentle and sweet. The word signifies a marriageable female. It is traced to a word signifying moisture; and all the Nymphs, as a body, are said to have derived their origin from Neptune, or water — the first principle of all things.

Every fountain, every wood, many a single tree, had a nymph to it. An ancient could not stir out of doors, if he was religious, without being conscious that he was surrounded with things supernatural; and thus his religion, though full of beautiful forms, was a different thing to him from what it is to us. The nymph was lovely and beneficent; she took care of her brook or her grove for the agriculturist, and he humbly assisted her in his turn and presented her with flowers; and yet a sight of her was supposed to occasion a particular species of madness, thence called Nympholepsy. A living writer,* who has a young heart, has founded a pastoral drama upon it. We are informed, by a native of the Ionian Isles,† that to this day a peasant there cannot be persuaded to venture out of his cottage at noonday during the month of July, on account of the fairies whom he calls Aneraides, *i.e.*, Nereids. The truth is, that in this instance, as in that of the modern fairies, he who thought he beheld any thing supernatural was in a fair way of being delirious beforehand.

It was otherwise with the great or "initiated." Poets talked of seeing the nymphs, and the gods too, without any harm, not excepting Bacchus, the most awful vision of them all; ‡ and multitudes of heroes were descended and received favors from enamoured Dryads and Naiads. The old poets have a favorite phrase to denote these condescending amours. § The use of the fiction was obvious; nor was it confined to the maternal side of ancient heraldry. There is a story of a girl, who, having been honored with

---

* See "Amarynthus, or the Nympholept." By Mr. Horace Smith.

† Ugo Foscolo, in his criticism in the "Quarterly Review," upon the "Narrative and Romantic Poems of the Italians," vol. 21, p. 514.

‡ *Cospetto di Bacco* (Face of Bacchus) is still an oath among the Italians.

§ In the Homeric account of Venus's amours with Anchises, the goddess enjoins the hero, in case he is asked questions about their child, to say that a nymph was his mother; but on no account was he to dare to say it was Venus.

the attentions of the river Scamander, observed him one day standing in a crowd at a public festival; upon which the divinity was taken up and carried before the magistrate.

We shall give a list of the principal nymphs and their names; partly, because the genuine reader, who does not happen to be learned, will be glad of it, and partly on account of the beauty of the nomenclature. These were the Nereids, or nymphs of the sea, daughters of Nereus: Oreads, or nymphs of the mountains; Naiads, or nymphs of the streams; Dryads, or nymphs of the woods; and Hamadryads, or nymphs of trees by themselves; nymphs who were born and died each with her particular tree.

Those were the principal; but we also hear of the Limnads or Limniads, nymphs of the lakes; Potamèdes, or nymphs of the rivers; Ephydriads, or nymphs of the fountains; Napèæ, nymphs of the woody glens and meadows; and Mèliæ, nymphs of the honey-making.

But these specific appellations, we suppose, were given at will. There are furthermore the Bacchantes, or nymphs of Bacchus; the Hesperides, or daughters of Hesperus,

"Who sing about the Golden Tree,"

the nymphs who waited upon the deities in general; the celestial Sirens, who sat upon the spheres; and some reckon among them, the Graces and the Muses.

Aristophanes, in one of his plays, has introduced a chorus of clouds; and, though the singers appear to be the clouds themselves and not deities conducting them, it seems remarkable that an incarnation of those fair and benignant travellers through heaven escaped the fertile imagination of the Greeks.

All these nymphs passed a happy and graceful life of

mingled duty and pleasure, and evinced their benignity to mankind after their respective fashions : — the Nereids in assisting men at sea, and allaying the billows ; the Oreads in assisting hunters ; the Naiads or Dryads in taking care of the streams and woods ; and so on of the rest. They danced and bathed, and made love and played among the trees, and sat tying up their hair by the waters. As they were kind, they expected kindness, and were grateful for it. If their worshippers represented them as severe in their resentments, it was in punishment of what was thought impious ; and there is always some inconsistency in those personifications of the natural reaction of error.

Such was the life led by the nymphs of old, and such is the one they lead still, even in quarters where they would not be expected ; so native are they to the regions of poetry, that they will divide them with other mythologies rather than remove. It is as well to keep the latter distinct, though our old poets, in the interior of their philosophy, would have had much to say for uniting them. At all events, there they are all together in the pages of Spenser, as we shall presently see. Even Milton contrived not to let them go ; and Camoens, like a right sailor, finds them in every port.

We proceed to the different classes separately, and to touch upon what the poets have said of them. And, in the first place, as personal matters are as important to them as to other ladies, and the sea-nymphs got Neptune to send a whale against Queen Cassiopeia for pretending to be their equal in beauty, it is to be observed, as a caution to men at sea, that nobody must speak ill of green hair — such being the tresses of the Nereids. For our part, who are great readers of the poets, we make no scruple to say that we can fancy green mossy locks well enough, provided there is a sweet face under them. The painters have seldom ventured upon these anomalies; but the poets, whose especial business it is to have an universal sympathy, can fancy the sea-nymphs with their verdant locks, and even in the midst of their faint-smelling and storm-echoing bowers, and love them no less. Good offices and a robust power of enjoyment make the Nereid beautiful. She grapples with the waves and flings aside her hair from her soused cheeks; and the poet is willing to be a Triton for her sake. The most beautiful figure ever made by the nymphs as a body, is by these very sisters, in the Prometheus of Æschylus, where they come to console the stern demi-god in his sufferings. But as the scene is rather characteristic of them as cordial and pious females, than creatures of their particular class, it is here (with great unwillingness) omitted. A late admirable writer thought his contemporaries defective in imagination for not making the nymphs partake thoroughly of the nature of the element they lived in. He would have had a Dryad, for instance, as rugged and fantastic in her aspect as an old oak-tree, and divested of all human beauty. The ancients did not go so far as this. Beauty, in a human shape, was a *sine quâ non* with those cultivators of physical grace, in their most supernatural fancies; and the world have approved their taste, and retained the charming population with which they filled the woods and waters; but the poet, whenever he chooses, can still know how to make a " difference discreet." The Nereids lived in grottos on the sea-shore, as well as in bowers under water. They were fond of feeding the Halcyon; and sported and revelled, says the old poet, like so many joyous fish about the chariot of the sea-god. We are to suppose them diving underneath it from one another, and careering about it as it ran; splashing each other and their lovers with the sunny waters. Ben Jonson has painted them and their father in a jovial line: —

"——— Old Nereus and his fifty girls."

Homer, Hesiod, and Spenser have given lists of their names. The list of the English poet seems the best, because he has added descriptive epithets; — but these were unnecessary in the Greek, the names themselves being descriptions. This reconciles us to the dry look of the lists in the Greek poet, and explains the apparent arbitrariness of those in the English one; though even if the epithets of the latter had not been translations, or taken from other epithets bestowed upon them by his authorities, they would have had a good effect. They give a distinction to the individuals, — a character, as they pass by, to their faces and bearing.

> "Swift Proto, mild Eucrate, Thetis faire,
> Soft Spio, sweet Eudorè, Sao sad,
> Light Doto, wanton Glancè, and Galenè glad:
> White-handed Eunica, proud Dynamene,
> Joyous Thalia, goodly Amphitrite,
> Lovely Pasithee, kinde Eulimene,
> Light-foote Cymothoe, and sweet Melitè;
> Fairest Pherusa, Phao lilly white," &c.

Among the rest are " milke-white Galathæa, large Lisianassa, stout Autonoe, —

> "And, seeming still to smile, Glauconome;
> Fresh Alimeda, deckt with girlond greene;
> Hyponoe, with salt-bedewed wrests;
> Laomedia, like the christall sheene;
> Liagore, much praised for wise behests;
> And Psamathe for her brode snowy brests."

The intellectual and moral epithets do not seem so

natural as the material ones. The old fathers of the sea are the philosophers of those "watery shades." * The nymphs are the dancing billows.

In the hymn to Venus, above quoted, which is attributed to Homer, the mountain Hamadryads are represented as contending with the gods for the prize of dancing : —

> " Nymphs that haunt the height
> Of hills, and breasts have of most deep receipt."
>
> CHAPMAN'S TRANSLATION.

The favorite Greek beauty (deep-bosom'd) of which our reverend old poet here contrives to express so profound a sense by unloosening the compound epithet, was not in the way of their dancing, any more than the bosoms of the gypsies.

> "The light Sileni mix in love with these,
> And, of all spies the prince, Argicides."

Their lives have the same date with those

> "Of odorous fir-trees and high-foreheaded oaks ; "

but their decease is gently managed; unless, indeed, we are to fancy them partaking gradually of the decay; which is not likely, for the ancients never tell us of decrepid nymphs.

> "The fair trees still before the fair nymphs die;
> The bole about them grows corrupt and dry: "

and not till the boughs are fallen, do the lingering tenants

> "Leave the lovely light."

One of the speakers in Plutarch's essay on the " Ces-

---

* The God of the sea,
Sophist and sage, from no Athenian grove,
But cogitation in his watery shades."
HYPERION, Book ii.

sation of Oracles," has undertaken to compute the life of a nymph; which, by a process that would have been more satisfactory to Sir Kenelm Digby than to an oak-insurance office, he reckons at 9720 years. It is to be considered, however, as we have just noticed, that they looked young to the last. Spenser is the only poet that has ventured to speak of an "old nymph." He says that Proteus had one to keep his bower clean.

> "There was his wonne; ne living wight was seene,
> Save one old nymph, hight Panope, to keepe it cleane."

This is one of the liberties which he takes sometimes, especially when his rhyme is burnt out, and he seems between sleep and waking. His Panope is very different from Milton's: —

> "The air was calm, and on the level brine
> Sleek Panope with all her sisters play'd."

But these vagaries of Spenser do not hinder him from being a poet as elegant as he is great. There is to be found in them even a germ of the old epic impartiality. Indeed, none but a great poet, with a childlike simplicity, could venture upon them. We smile, but retain our respect; and are prepared to resume all our admiration for the next thing he utters.

In the Homeric hymn to Pan, for instance, the mountain-nymphs are described beautifully, as joining in with their songs when they hear the pipe of the sylvan god. Yet we see them to most advantage in the works of the great painters, and of Spenser himself. Poussin or Raphael never painted a set of nymphs more distinctly than our poet has done in his description of a bath of Diana, — a match for Titian's. The natural action of Diana, gath-

ering her drapery against her bosom, seems copied from
some painting or piece of sculpture, —

> Soon, her garments loose
> Upgath'ring, in her bosom she *compriz'd*,
> Well as she might, *and to the goddesse rose*,
> *Whiles all her nymphes did like a garland her enclose.*

And the enclosure of her by her nymphs is from Ovid:
but not the beautiful simile of the garland, nor the relish
with which every word comes from the poet's pencil. We
cannot pass by a couplet in the Latin poet without noticing it : —

> Fons sonat a dextra, tenui perlucidus unda,
> Margine gramineo patulos incinctus hiatus.
>
> METAM. Lib. iii., v. 161.

which has been well turned by Sandys : —

> A bubbling spring, with streams as clear as glass
> Ran chiding by, inlaid with matted grass.

In Ovid are the names of some of these Oreads. They
are remarkable for their fairy-like appearance in English,
and for being all derived from moisture; which would
lead us to suppose that the idea of nymphs dancing on the
mountains was suggested by the leaping of springs and
torrents. The names are Crocale, Nephele, Phiale, Hyale,
Psecas, and Rhanis ; that is to say, Pebble, Cloud, Phial,
Glassy, Dew-drop, and Rain. Pebble is no exception.
The philosophy that derived every thing from water, was
not likely to think sand and gravel the farthest off from
their original. There is reason to suppose that the
ancients took all clear-looking stones for a petrifaction of
water. When we are told, indeed, that "this element is
found in the driest of solid bodies, whatever be their description," and that, "a piece of hartshorn kept for forty
years, and thereby become as hard and dry as metal (so

that if struck against a flint it would give sparks of fire), upon being distilled, was found to yield an eighth part of its weight in water," we begin to think that, in this, as in so many other instances, the ancient philosophers anticipated the discoveries of the moderns, and that experiment only establishes the profundity of their guesses. It is probable that Akenside has something to this purpose in his hymn to the Naiads; but, as we have not the poem by us, and have as cold a recollection of it as of a morning in November, or one of old Panope's washing days, we return to our sunnier haunt. According to the ancients, the Oreads invented honey; the nymph Melissa, who discovered it, giving her name to the bee. And they are said to have been the first suggestors of the impropriety of eating flesh, making use of this new and sweet argument of honey, to turn mankind from those evil courses of the table.

The prettiest story told of the Naiads is their pulling Hylas into the water; and Theocritus has related it in the most beautiful manner. The Argonauts, he tells us, had landed on the shores of the Propontis to sup. They busied themselves with their preparations; and Hylas was despatched to fetch water for Alcides and Telamon, who were table-companions. The blooming boy, accordingly, took his way with his jug. See the passage in the thirteenth Idyl, v. 39, beginning

$$\mathrm{T}\alpha\chi\alpha\ \delta\varepsilon\ \chi\rho\alpha\nu\alpha\nu\ \varepsilon\nu\sigma\eta\sigma\alpha\nu.$$

The English reader must be content with a version:—

> And straight he was aware
> Of water in a hollow place, low down,
> Where the thick sward shone with blue celandine,
> And bright green maiden-hair, still dry in dew,
> And parsley rich. And at that hour it chanced

> The nymphs unseen were dancing in the fount, —
> The sleepless nymphs, reverenced of housing men ; —
> Winning Eunica ; Malis, apple-cheek'd ;
> And, like a night-bedewed rose, Nychèa.
>
> Down stepp'd the boy, in haste to give his urn
> Its fill, and push'd it in the fount; when lo!
> Fair hands were on him — fair, and very fast;
> For all the gentle souls that haunted there
> Were wrapt in love's sweet gathering tow'rds the boy;
> And so he dropp'd within the darksome well, —
> Dropp'd like a star, that, on a summer eve,
> Slides in ethereal beauty to the sea.

These nymphs, however, are rather the Ephydriads than the Naiads ; that is to say, nymphs of the fountain or wellspring, and not of the river. Shakespeare has painted the faces of the Naiads in a very pleasing manner : —

> "You nymphs call'd Naiads of the wandering brooks,
> With your sedge crowns, and ever harmless looks : "

but these were English Naiads, always gliding calmly through the meadows.

The Greek and Italian Naiads were equally benignant at heart, but, having torrents and dry summers to think of, their look was now and then a little more troubled. Virgil's epithet, "the white Naiad," eminently belongs to this order of nymphs, the silver body of whose stream is seen glistening in the landscape ; and he has made a pretty contrast of color in the flowers he has given her to pluck.

> "Tibi candida Nais
> Pallentes violas et summa papavera carpens."
> The white Naiad
> Pale violets plucks for thee, and tops of poppies.

The Nymph Arethusa was originally an Oread, whom Diana changed into a stream to help her to fly from the river-god Alpheus. Alpheus, nothing hindered, turned the course of his river to pursue her. The nymph prayed again, and was conveyed under ground, but the god was still after her. She was hurried even under the sea, but he still pursued; when she rose again in the island of Sicily for breath, there he was beside her. We are left to suppose that his pertinacity prevailed; for whatever present was bestowed upon his waters in Arcady is said to have made its appearance in the Sicilian fountain. Among all the names to be found in poetry, perhaps there is not a more beautiful one than this of Arethusa; and it turns well into English. Hear Milton, who speaking of Alpheus says that he

"Stole under seas to meet his Arethuse."

The modern Sicilian name is Retusa, which, pronounced in the soft manner of the Italians, and with something of z in the s (as we read the other), is not destitute of the beauty of the original.*

We were admiring, at this part of our article, that the ancients, among the less philosophical companions of their mythology, had not chosen sometimes to mingle the two species of Naiads and Dryads, considering that trees have so much to do with moisture, and with the origin of streams. Our attention was drawn at the same moment to a passage in Ovid; where he speaks of the Nymph Syrinx, a Naiad, as being "among the Hamadryads of Arcady." Perhaps he only meant to say, that she lived among them, as a Naiad, for the reason just mentioned,

---

* In Italy, among its strange union of things, ancient and modern, we saw one day upon a mantel-piece a card of a *Marquis de Retuse*. This was the designation, Frenchified, of the district in Sicily including the ancient fountain. Here was the Marquis of Arethusa!

might be supposed to do ; but the turn of the words and custom of the language both seem in favor of the other supposition. Sandys, however, clearly takes the passage in the former sense. Ovid says, "On the cold mountains of Arcady, and among the Arcadian Hamadryads, *there was* a Naiad," and according to his translator, she only lived amongst them. "Then thus the god" (Mercury who is singing and telling stories to Argus to get him to sleep) —

> "Then thus the god his charmed ears inclines:
> Amongst the Hamadryad Nonacrines,
> On cold Arcadian hills, for beauty famed,
> A Nais dwelt." *

The Dryads and Hamadryads are often confounded with one another; nor is the difference between them, when it is made, always justly discerned. Menage tells of somebody, who, on being asked by a lady what the difference was between a Dryad and a Hamadryad, said, the same as between an archbishop and a bishop. If every solitary tree had its Hamadryad, the woodman could not have approached it without impiety. The truth is, that as old trees of this kind became sanctified, either by the mere desire of keeping them alive, or by some votive circumstances attached to them as objects of religion, they were gifted with the care of a nymph. She was, in consequence, to die when they did ; and the sacrilegious peasant, while he was heaving his axe at the old trunk, would have to strike at the fair limbs which it enclosed.

A story has come down to us in Apollonius of the vengeance that overtook criminals of this sort, and of

---

* "Tam deus, Arcadia gelidis in montinis," inquit,
"Inter Hamadryades celeberrima Nonacrinas
Nais una fuit."

dreadful denouncements against their posterity; which, however, were not inexpiable by a little worship and sacrifice. But the gratitude of the nymph, when her tree was preserved from destruction, and the preserver turned out otherwise not insensible, was boundless. Charon of Lampsacus, an old commentator upon the writer just mentioned, tells us that, when Arcas the son of Calisto was hunting, he met a nymph in the woods, who requested his aid for an old oak-tree on the banks of a river, which the river was undermining. He rescued it from its threatened fate, and out of gratitude the nymph bore him two children. In another story, related by the same author, the hero was not so lucky. This person, whose name was Rhœcus, was applied to on a similar account; and having evinced a like humanity, showed a due taste in the first instance, when requested to ask his reward. The nymph promised to meet him; adding, that she would send a bee to let him know the time. The bee came accordingly, but Rhœcus, who was occupied with a game of dice, was impatient at being interrupted, and hurt the wings of the little messenger in brushing him away. The nymph, offended at this proof of the superficial nature of his feelings, not only would have nothing to say to him, but deprived him of the use of his limbs.*

It remains only to speak of the Bacchantes, the Hesperides, and certain solitary nymphs who lived apart, and

---

* We are obliged, as the historian of these our fictitious truths, to relate them in all their circumstances; otherwise the lady might have stopped short of giving Rhœcus a palsy. It is a remarkable instance of the natural dulness of Natalis Comes (for which Scaliger gives him a knock), that in relating this story of Rhœcus and the Nymph, he leaves off with her sending him the bee. [The story of the Hamadryad is told very minutely and beautifully in the " Indicator," and is the subject of one of Landor's " Hellenics."— ED.]

held a state like goddesses. The rest are not sufficiently identified with the class, or are too little distinguished from the former varieties, to need particular mention.

The Bacchantes, or Nymphs of Bacchus, are of a very different character from their sisters. They are equally remarkable for the turbulence of their movements, and the rigidness of their chastity; though as to the latter, "Juvenal," says an Italian Mythology, "is of another opinion;"* and Lycophron gives the title of Bacchantes to dissolute women. How the followers of the god of wine came to be thought so austere we know not. The delicacy of the moral, if it existed, has escaped us. If it were meant to insinuate that a drunken female repelled every thing amatory by the force of disgust, no case could be clearer: but ancient mythology abounds with the loves of wood-gods for these ladies, who on the other hand struggled plentifully to resist them. According to the authority just mentioned, Nonnus, a Greek author of the fifth century, who wrote a poem on Bacchus as big as a tun, represents them as so jealous of their virgin honor, that they went to bed with a live serpent round their waists, to guard against surprise. The perplexity in this matter originated, perhaps, in the chastity that was expected from the ordained priestesses of Bacchus, who are often confounded with his nymphs. But so little had the nature of the latter to do with chastity, that those who undertook to represent them, gave rise to the greatest scandal that ever took place in the heathen world, and such as the Romans were obliged to suppress by a regular state interference.

The Hesperides, so called because they were the granddaughters (Milton says the daughters) of Hesperus, and

---

* Dizionario d'ogni Mitologia. art. "Baccanti."

otherwise Atlantides, or daughters of Atlas, were three nymphs, who were commissioned, in company with a dragon, to guard the tree from which Juno produced the golden apples that she gave to Jupiter on her marriage day. The nymphs sang, and the dragon never slept; and so, in the melancholy beauty of that charm, the tree ever stood secure, and the apples " hung amiable." It was one of the labors of Hercules to undo this custody, and carry away the apples. The nymphs could only weep, while he killed the dragon. Various interpretations have been given to this story. Some say the apples meant sheep, from a word which signifies both; and that the sheep were called golden, because they were beautiful; the common metaphorical sense of that epithet among the ancients. Others discover in it an allegory on one of the signs of the Zodiac, on the sin of avarice, the discovery of a gold mine, &c.; but we shall be forgetting the spirit of our subject for the letter. Milton, in his "Comus," has touched upon the gardens of Hesperus, but not in his happiest manner. There is something in it too finical and perfumed. We have quoted the best lines when making out our list of the nymphs. Lucan makes you feel the massiveness of the golden boughs, and has touched beautifully on the rest.

> Fuit aurea silva,
> Divitiis graves et fulvo germine rami;
> Virgineusque chorus, nitidi custodia luci,
> Et nunquam somno damnatus lumina serpens. *

> A golden grove, it was, in a rich glade,
> Heavy with fruit that struck a burnish'd shade;
> A virgin choir the sacred treasure kept,
> And a sad serpent's eyes, that never slept.

---

* Quoted by Warton in his notes to Milton.

Mention of the Hesperides is made in the Argonautics of Apollonius, where the voyagers come upon the golden garden after Hercules had rifled it. The nymphs are observed lamenting over the slain dragon, but vanish at sight of the intruders. The latter, however, Orpheus being their spokesman, venture to implore them for water; and the nymphs, with the usual good-nature of their race, indulge the petition. They become visible, each in a tree, and tell them that the dreadful stranger, who had been there, had stamped in a rage of thirst on the ground, and struck up a fountain.

For accounts of the manners and conversation of nymphs the curious reader may consult the sixth book of Spenser, Drayton's "Muses' Elysium," the "Arcadia" of Sannazaro, Cintio Giraldi's sylvan drama, entitled "Egle," and the "Endymion" of Keats; to which may be added the bass-relief of ancient sculpture, and the works of the great painters. (Egle *brightness*) is a celebrated name in nymphology; so is Galatea (*milky*) and Œnone (*winy*). Cydippe (*Proud horse*) seems rather the name of a lady-centaur; but the Greeks were singularly fond of names compounded from horses. *Best-horse*, and *Golden-horse*, and *Haste-horse* were among their philosophers (Aristippus, Chrysippus, and Speusippus); and *Horse-mistress* and *Horse-tamer*, among their ladies (Hipparchia and Hippodamia) Of solitary nymphs, or rather such as lived apart, sometimes in state like goddesses, with nymphs of their own, the most celebrated are Circe, Calypso, and Egeria. The most beautiful mention of Egeria (*the Watchful?*) is in Milton's Latin poems, at least to the best of our recollection. See his lines addressed to Salsilli, a Roman poet, on his sickness. We regret we have not time to indulge ourselves in attempting a version of the passage.* Circe (*the Encircler*) is clearly the original of the modern enchantress.

"Pale, wan,
And tyrannizing was the lady's look,"

says Keats, describing her. (How beautiful!) Calypso (the *Secret*, or *Lying-hid*) though no magician, was a nobler enchantress after her fashion, as we see in Homer. Boccaccio, speaking of Circe, Calisto, and Clymene, says, that nymphs of their distinguished class were no other than young ladies, delicately brought up, and living in retirement, — "thalamorum colentes umbras," — cultivators of their boudoirs. "Impressions," he says, "of every sort, were easily made on creatures of this tender sort, as on things allied to the element of water; whereas, rustic women laboring out of doors, and exposed to the sun,

---

* From Cowper's translation of the poem, we extract the passage referred to: —

"Health, Hebe's sister, sent us from the skies,
And thou, Apollo, whom all sickness flies,
Pythius, or Pæan, or what name divine
Soe'er thou choose, haste, heal a priest of thine!
Ye groves of Faunus, and ye hills that melt
With vinous dews, where meek Evander dwelt!
If aught salubrious in your confines grow,
Strive which shall soonest heal your poet's woe,
That, render'd to the Muse he loves, again
He may enchant the meadows with his strain.
Numa, reclined in everlasting ease
Amid the shade of dark embowering trees,
Viewing with eyes of unabated fire
His loved Ægeria, shall that strain admire:
So soothed, the tumid Tiber shall revere
The tombs of kings, nor desolate the year,
Shall curb his waters with a friendly rein,
And guide them harmless, till they meet the main." — ED.

became "hispid" and case-hardened, and therefore deservedly lost the name of nymphs.*

THE SIRENS AND MERMAIDS OF THE POETS.

" EAVING Æaca on their homeward voyage," says Mr. Keightley, in his excellent " Mythology," " Odysseus (Ulysses) and his companions came first to the islands of the Sirens. These were two maidens, who sat in a mead close to the sea, and with their melodious voices so charmed those who were sailing by that they forgot home, and every thing relating to it, and abode there till their bones lay whitening on the strand. By the directions of Circe, Odysseus stopped the ears of his companions with wax, and had himself tied to the mast; and thus he was the only person who heard the song of the Sirens, and escaped.

" Hesiod † describes the mead of the Sirens as blooming with flowers, and says that their voice stilled the winds. Their names were said to be Aglaiophéme (*Clear-voice*), and Thelxiepeia (*Magic-speech*). It was feigned that they threw themselves into the sea with vexation at the escape of Odysseus; but the author of the " Orphic Argonautics " places them on a rock near the shore of Ætna, and makes the song of Orpheus end their enchantment, and cause them to fling themselves into the sea.

---

* Sunt præterea, &c. — " Genealogia Deorum," lib. vii. cap. 14.
† Frag. xxvii.

"It was afterwards fabled * that they were the daughters of the river-god Achelous, by one of the Muses. Some said that they sprang from the blood which ran from him when his horn was torn off by Hercules. Sophocles calls them the daughters of Phorcys.

"Contrary to the usual process, the mischievous part of the character of the Sirens was, in process of time, left out, and they were regarded as purely musical beings, with entrancing voices. Hence Plato, in his 'Republic,' places one of them on each side of the eight celestial spheres, where their voices form what is called the music of the spheres; and when the Lacedæmonians invaded Attica, Dionysius, it is said, appeared in a dream to their general, ordering him to pay all funeral honors to the new Siren, which was at once understood to be Sophocles, then just dead.†

"Eventually, however, the artists laid hold on the Sirêns, and furnished them with the feathers, feet, wings, and tails of birds."‡

According to this statement of our best English mythologist, the Sirens were but two. It is not a little surprising, however, that so careful a writer has omitted to notice the various accounts of their number, and the prevailing opinion of its having been three. "Fulgentius and Servius affirm," says Boccaccio, "that the Sirens were three,— one of them singing with the voice alone, another to the lyre, and a third playing on the flute. Leontius, however," he continues, "says there were four, and that the fourth sang to the timbrel." And a little further on, our Italian

---

* Apollod. i. 3.   † Pausan. i. 21.
‡ "Mythology of Ancient Greece and Italy. By Thomas Keightley, p. 246.

brings them up to five;* and this is the number (as we shall see), which is assigned them by Spenser.

Mr. Keightley, who has a just reverence for the oldest Greek authorities, and as proper a suspicion of Latin sources of fable, will stick to his Hesiod, and not care what is said by the later poets. His caution becomes a teacher; but as mythologies may, with others, be reasonably looked upon as of a more large and inclusive character, even to the admission of modern inventions, provided they be the work of great poets, the popular number of three may ordinarily be allowed to the Sirens; and when we come to Spenser, I, for one, must take the freedom of believing in five. Any true poet, not only after his death, like Sophocles, but before, is himself a Siren, who makes me believe what he pleases while he is about it.

The Sirens, then, are more particularly taken for three sisters, monstrous in figure, but charming in face and voice, who used to stand upon a place near the coast of Naples, and with alluring songs enticed wayfarers to their destruction. Some say the victims perished for want of food, pining and dying away, unable to do any thing but listen; others, that the three sisters devoured them; others, that they tumbled them out of their ships. The whole place was strewn with bones, and shone afar off with the whiteness, like cliffs; and yet neither this, nor their monstrous figure, visible on nearer approach, hindered the infatuated men from doting on their faces and sweet sounds; till, getting closer and closer, they glided headlong into the snare.

Ulysses had a permission, of which he availed himself,

---

* "Della Genealogia degli Dei," p. 123. (A translation of his Latin work. I quote from both these books in the present article, not having the latter by me when I wrote the above passage.)

to hear their song; but it cost him a desperate struggle. He ordered himself to be chained, and then to be unchained; but the sailors would only stand by the better orders, and put more chains upon him. So, the vessel shooting away, the sounds gradually died off, and he was saved. Upon this, the Sirens threw themselves into the sea, and perished. The only man (according to some) who had passed them before, was Orpheus, who, raising a hymn to the gods, in counterpart to their profaner warble, sailed along with his Argonauts, harping and triumphant. To one who has read the life of Alfieri, it is impossible not to be reminded of him by this story of Ulysses; how he had himself bound down in his chair, to avoid going to see his mistress; and how he struggled and raved to no purpose; imitating Orpheus at intervals, by going on with his verses. The reader will have seen, however, that the destruction of the Sirens has been attributed to Orpheus; so that, according to the writer of those Argonautics, the story of Ulysses is a fiction, even in the regions of fiction!

The song of the Sirens in Homer is not worthy of the great poet, being, indeed, rather the promise of one, than the song itself. It is true, the subject is adapted to the hearer; and we must not forget that this adaptation of themselves to the person who was to be tempted, was one among the artifices of the Sirens, and none of their least seductive. But they say little or nothing to the hero, in point of fact. The temptation must have lain in the promise and the sound. William Browne, a disciple of Spenser, and not unworthy of him, has given a song of the Sirens in his "Inner Temple Masque," which a modern Ulysses would at least reckon more tempting to his sailors: —

"Steer, hither steer your winged pines,
　　All beaten mariners;
　Here lie love's undiscover'd mines,
　　A prey to passengers;
　Perfumes far sweeter than the best
　Which make the phœnix' urn and nest.
　　Fear not your ships,
　Nor any to oppose you, save our lips;
　　But come on shore,
　Where no joy dies till love hath gotten more.

[These two last lines are repeated, as chorus, from a grove.]

"For swelling waves our panting breasts,
　　Where never storms arise,
　Exchange, and be awhile our guests;
　　For stars gaze on our eyes.
　The compass love shall hourly sing;
　And as he goes about the ring,
　　We will not miss
　To tell each point he nameth with a kiss.
Chorus. Then come on shore,
　Where no joy dies till love hath gotten more."

The shape of the Sirens has been variously represented. Some say (and this, we believe, is held to be the most orthodox description)* that they were entire birds, with the exception of a beautiful human face. Others, that they were half birds and half women, the female being the upper part.† Others, that they were half women and half fish; that is to say, mermaids;‡ and this figure has again been varied by wings, and the feet of a hen.§ If they

---

* "Lemprière," Art. "Sirenes."　† "Natalis Comes," lib. vii. cap. 13.

‡ "Vossius and Pontanus." (See Todd's "Spenser," vol. iv. p. 196, and Sandys's "Ovid," p. 101.

§ "Boccaccio, Geneal. Deor.," p. 56　Browne has taken his Sirens "as they are described by Hyginus and Servius, with their upper parts like women to the navel, and the rest like a hen."

were only human-faced birds, they must have confined their attractions to singing; for hands are required to play the musical instruments which are sometimes given them. But there were three of them, which is more than enough for harmony; and if, in addition to their harmony, they had beautiful faces, it is no matter how monstrously they terminated: the more monstrous the charmer, the more ghastly and complete the fiction.

These appalling seducers, according to some, were originally sea-nymphs of the proper shape, till Ceres punished them for not assisting her daughter when carried away by Pluto; though Ovid says that they took that adventure so much to heart, as to beg the gods to bestow wings on them, that they might search for her by sea as well as by land. It is added by others, that Juno (jealous, we suppose, after the usual fashion of that very uncomfortable and sublime busybody) encouraged them to challenge the Muses to a trial of song; upon which, being conquered, their kinswoman plucked them, and made crowns of their feathers. This is said to have taken place in Crete. If so, they must have migrated; for they are generally supposed to have inhabited certain islands on the coast of Naples, thence called Sirenusæ, where an oracle informed them that, unless they could entice and destroy every one who passed within hearing, they should perish themselves. When their fatal hour came, they are reported by some to have been changed into rocks, a fit ending for the hardness of sensuality.*

---

* But this, it seems, was not the last of the Sirens. "Their crimes," says W. J. Broderip, "were not sufficiently expiated. Years rolled on their ceaseless course. Greece was swallowed up by Rome, who in her turn fell at the feet of the Goth; and in the fulness of time there arose a wizard from the great northern hive, he of the polar star, who waved his wand, aroused the

Various names have been given to the Sirens, expressive of their attractions. The most received are Leucosia, Parthenope, and Ligeia; or

"The Fair, the Tuneful, and the Maiden-faced."

(It is impossible, on such an occasion, to resist giving the aspect of a verse, to words naturally tempting us to fall into one.)* Ligeia, however, may perhaps be rather translated the *shrill* and *high-sounding;* expressive of the triumphant nature of the female voice, — which rises above all others, in a very peculiar and consummate manner, as any one may have noticed in a theatre. Parthenope had a famous tomb at Naples, and gave her appellation to the old city. The mention of these two names in Milton is not introduced with the poet's usual learning; otherwise, he would have designated the bearers by the meanings of them. He has given Ligeia the comb of a mermaid; the spirit in " Comus " is adjuring the nymph Sabrina : —

"By Thetis' tinsel-slipper'd feet,
And the songs of Sirens sweet;
By dead Parthenope's dear tomb,
And fair Ligeia's golden comb,
Wherewith she sits on diamond rocks
Sleeking her soft alluring locks."

We do not quarrel with him, however, for turning Ligeia

Sirens from the annihilation into which they had escaped, and degenerated them into one of the lowest reptile forms of America," — the Perennibranchiate Batrachian. If you wish to know what a Perennibranchiate Batrachian is, reader, we refer you to Mr. Broderip's pleasant "Leaves from the Note-Book of a Naturalist."— ED.

* "Country gentlemen," however, must not think that these names have been translated in the order of the Greek; for it is " Parthenope "which is "maiden-faced," and not Ligeia. But it would have had a horrible gaping sound, and most *unsiren-like*, to let the terminating vowel of either of the two other names come before an *and*— Leucosia, *Ligeia, and* Parthenope.

into a mermaid. A great poet, being one of the creating gods of his art, has a right to mould his creatures as he pleases, provided he does it with verisimilitude ; but we shall speak more of this in a minute, when we come to see what Spenser has done. "*Sleeking* her soft *alluring* locks" is a very beautiful line ; you see, and, indeed hear, the passage of the comb through those moist tresses.

Allegorically, the Sirens are sensual pleasures, who, though deriving their charms from one of the Muses, are conquered by a combination of all. *Topographically* (for they have been accounted for, also in that manner), they are said to have alluded to "a certaine bay, contracted within winding straights and broken cliffes ; which, by the singing of the windes, and beating of the billowes, report" (says Archimachus, as quoted by Sandys), "a delightful harmony, alluring those who saile by to approach ; when forthwith they are throwne against the rocks by the waves, and swallowed in the violent eddyes."* *Humanly*, they are thought to have been a set of enticing women, living on the coast of Naples (where divers of the like sort, as Sandys would have said, may to this day be found), and alluring strangers to stop among them, by the pleasures and accomplishments with which they were surrounded. But we are told of them, also, *zoologically;* for some have taken them for certain Indian birds, who set mariners to sleep with their singing and then devour them ; while "some, as Gaza and Trapezuntius" (quoth our old friend), "affirme that they have seene such creatures in the sea ; either the divells assuming such shape, to countenance the fable, or framed in the fantasie by remote resemblances, as we give imaginary formes unto clouds,

---

* See the Notes to the Fifth Book of his "Ovid," fol. edit. p. 101.

and call those monsters of the deepe by the names of land-creatures, which imperfectly carry their similitude."

It is easy to see how Sirens, living near the sea, came to be considered mermaids. A modern Latin poet, quoted by Sandys (Pontanus), adopted this notion, and has a fable of his own upon it. He says that the Sirens were certain Neapolitan young ladies, who, not content with being handsome and accomplished, took to wearing paint and false hair, and went with their necks bare to the waist, — for which Minerva one day, as they were coming out of her temple, suddenly turned their pretty ankles into fish-tails, and sent them rolling into the sea. The poet writes this history in an epistle to his wife, as a warning to all pretty church-goers how they paint and expose themselves.

The writer of the piscatory Italian drama, entitled "Alceo" (Act IV. sc. I.), gives the same figure to the Sirens, but differs from most in his account of their cruelty. He says, that after stopping mariners in their course, they went to the vessel, instead of drawing it ashore, and threw the wretches into the sea.

The moderns, in general, have certainly regarded the Siren as a mermaid. Milton chose to be of that opinion, as we may gather from the passage above quoted. Chaucer, in his translation of the "Romance of the Rose," has inserted some lines, expressly to inform us that what was called a mermaid in England, the French called a Siren.

> " These birdes that I you devise,
> They sung their song as fair and well
> As angels don espirituell;
> And trusteth me, when I them herd
> Full lustily and well I ferd;
> For never yet such melody
> Was heard of men that mighte die.
> Such sweet song was them among,

> That me thought it no birdes song,
> But it was wonder like to be
> Song of meremaidens of the sea,
> That for their singing is so clear;
> Though we meremaidens clepe them here
> In English, as is our usàunce,
> Men clepe them sereins in Fraunce."

But if a poet required express authority in this matter, it is furnished him by the great modern mythologist, Spenser, who, though he had all the learning of the ancient world, vindicated his right to look at the world of poetry with his own eyes, and to recreate its forms, like a Demiurgos, whenever it suited his purposes to do so. He knew that no man better understood the soul of fiction, and therefore, that it was not only allowable, but sometimes proper, for him to embody it as he found convenient. There is something, we confess, to our apprehensions more ghastly and subtle in the ancient notion of a bird with a woman's head; but Spenser, in the passage where he introduces his Sirens, precedes and follows it with an account of things dreadful, and is for placing nothing but a calm voluptuousness in the middle. After all, we are not sure that there would not have been a subtler link with his birds "unfortunate," had he made his charmers partake of their nature; but, however, mermaids he has painted them, and mermaids they are for all poets to come, unless a greater shall arise to say otherwise : —

> "And now they nigh approached to the sted
> Whereat those mermayds dwelt. It was a still
> And calmy bay, on th' one side sheltered
> With the brode shadow of an hoarie hill;
> On th' other side an high rocke toured still,
> That 'twixt them both a pleasaunt port they made,
> And did like an halfe theatre fulfill.
> There those five sisters had continuall trade,
> And used to bath themselves in that deceiptfull shade.

"They were faire ladies, till they fondly striv'd
With th' Heliconian maides for maystery;
Of whom they overcomen were depriv'd
Of their proud beautie, and th' one moyity
Transform'd to fish for their bold surquedry;
But th' upper halfe their hue retayned still,
And their sweet skill in wonted melody;
Which ever after they abus'd to ill,
To allure weeke traveillers, whom gotten they did kill.

"So now to Guyon, as he passed by,
Their pleasaunt tunes they sweetly thus applyde;
'O thou faire sonne of gentle Faëry,
That art in mightie armes most magnifyde
Above all knights that ever batteill tryde,
O turne thy rudder hetherward awhile:
Here may thy storm-beat vessell safely ryde;
This is the port of rest from troublous toyle,
The world's sweet inn, from payne and wearisome turmoyle'

"With that the rolling sea, resounding soft,
In his big base them fitly answered;
And on the rocke, the waves, breaking aloft,
A solemn meane into them measured;
The whiles sweet Zephyrus lowd whisteled
His treble, a straunge kinde of harmony;
Which Guyon's senses softly tickeled,
That he the boteman bade row easily,
And let him heare some part of their rare melody."

BOOK II. c. 12.

"It is plain," says Jortin, in a note on this passage, "that Spenser designed here to describe the mermaids as sirens. He has done it contrary to mythology; for the sirens were not part women and part fishes, as Spenser and other moderns have imagined, but part women and part birds." Upon which Upton remarks, "By the sirens are imagined sensual pleasures; hence Spenser makes their number five. But should you ask, why did not Spenser follow rather the ancient poets and mythologists, than the moderns, in making them mermaids? my answer is, Spenser has a mythology of his own; nor would belie his brethren the romance writers, where merely authority is to be put against authority."

We have thus three out of our four great poets, who are for taking sirens as mermaids; and the fourth is not wanting. Shakespeare's "Mermaid on a dolphin's back," is part of an allegory on England and Queen Elizabeth, and is the most poetical bit of politics on record; but it shows that he entertained the same mixed notion of the mermaid and siren.

> "Once I sat upon a promontory,
> And heard a mermaid on a dolphin's back
> Uttering such dulcet and harmonious breath,
> That the rude sea grew civil at her song,
> And certain stars shot madly from their spheres,
> To hear the sea-maid's music."
> MIDSUMMER NIGHT'S DREAM.

A siren then, in the modern sense of the word, may be regarded as a mermaid who sings. Metaphorically, a siren is any female who charms by singing; and this is the most ancient acceptation of the term, as Plato has shown, by calling the presiders over the spheres of heaven sirens.

> "'Then listen I,'"

says the Genius in Milton's "Arcades,"

> "To the celestial Syrens' harmony,
> That sit upon the nine infolded spheres."

The word, by the way, should be spelled with an *i*, the Greek word not being syren but *seiren;* which, according to Bochart, comes from the Phœnician *seir*, a singer. In this etymology, we are carried back to the probable origin of these and a great many other marvels, which may have commenced with the primeval navigators, who had the world fresh before them, and fanciful eyes to see with. If the fair inhabitants of the south of Italy resembled in those days what they are now (and climate and other local circumstances render it probable), a crew of Phœnician adventurers had only to touch at the coast of Naples to bring away the story at once. In the south, where there is more luxury than fishing, the songs of their mistresses might suggest that of birds, and the sirens be gifted with plumage. Had they gone to the northern seas, where there was more fishing than luxury, the siren would have been the mermaid; and it is possible, that from the romances of the north, the modern idea descended into the poetry of Italy and of Spenser.

"The havfrue (half-woman) or mermaid," says Mr. Keightley, whom we meet in all the pleasant places of fiction, "is represented in the popular tradition (of Scandinavia) sometimes as a good, at other times as an evil and treacherous, being. She is beautiful in her appearance. Fishermen sometimes see her in the bright summer's sun, *when a thin mist hangs over the sea*, sitting on the surface of the water, and combing her long golden hair with a golden comb, or driving up her snow-white cattle to feed on the strands and small islands. At other times she comes as *a beautiful maid, chilled and shivering with the cold of the night*, to the fires the fishers have kindled, hoping by this means to entice them to her love. Her appearance prognosticates both storm and ill-success in their fishing. People that are drowned, and whose bodies are not found, are believed to have been taken into the dwellings of the mermaids. These beings are also supposed to have the power of foretelling future events. A mermaid, we are told, prophesied the birth of Christian IV. of Denmark; and

> 'En Havfrue op af Vandet steg,
> Og spaade Herr Sinklar ilde.'
> SINCLAIR'S " VISA."
>
> 'A mermaid from the water rose,
> And spaed Sir Sinclar ill.' *

These visions have naturally taken a still more palpable shape with some dwellers near the sea, and craft has endeavored to profit by them in the exhibition of their actual bodies. The author of an agreeable abstract of zoology, published some years back, tells us of a King of Portugal, and a Grand Master of the Order of St. James, who "had a suit at law to determine which class of animals these monsters belong to, either man or fish. This," he adds, "is a sort of inductive proof that such animals had been then seen and closely examined; unless we suppose that, as in the case of the child said to have been born with a golden tooth, the discussion took place before the fact was ascertained." †

We ought to know, on these occasions, whether the mermaid is caught fresh, or only shown after death like a mummy. An exhibition of the latter kind took place some years since in London, and was soon detected; but so many deceptions of the sort have been practised, that naturalists seem to think it no longer worth their while to talk about them. A piece of one animal is joined to another, and the two are dried together. Linnæus exposed an imposition of this kind during his travels on the Continent, and is said to have been obliged to leave the town for it.

The writer just quoted proceeds to inform us, that "in

---

* "Fairy Mythology," vol. i. p. 241.
† "A description of more than Three Hundred Animals, &c., with an Appendix on Allegorical and Fabulous Animals," 1826; p. 363.

the year 1560, on the western coasts of the Island of Ceylon, some fishermen are said to have brought up, at one draught of a net, seven mermen and maids, of which *several Jesuits*, and among them F. H. Henriquez, and Dinas Bosquey, physician to the Viceroy of Goa, are *reported* to have been witnesses ; and it is added," he says, "that the physician who examined them, and made dissections of them with a great deal of care, asserted that all the parts, both internal and external, were found perfectly conformable to those of men."

"Several Jesuits," we fear, will be regarded as no better authority than the "five justices" of Autolycus: —

Aut. Here's another ballad, of a fish, that appeared upon the coast on Wednesday, the *fourscore* of April, forty thousand fathom *above* water, and sung this ballad against the hard hearts of maids. It was thought she was a woman, and was turned into a cold fish, for she would not exchange flesh with one that loved her. The ballad is very pitiful, and as true.

Dorcas. Is it true too, think you?

Aut. Five justices' hands at it ! and witnesses more than my pack will hold." — WINTER'S TALE, Act iv. sc. 3.

A later edition (if I mistake not, for I had but a glance of it) of the same work, goes almost so far as to intimate its belief in a mermaid's having been seen by a lady, off the coast of Scotland, in company with three other spectators. The names are mentioned, and letters and deta"s given. That the persons in question thought they beheld such a creature, is to be conceded, supposing the documents to be genuine ; nor would it become any reasonable sceptic, especially in a time like the present, to say what is or is not probable on the part of creation.* But it is to be feared that in this, as in the demands of a less

---

* Sir Walter Scott, in " The Minstrelsy of the Scottish Border," mentions this phenomenon, and says that the evidence serves to show " either that imag-

intellectual appetite, your fish must be "caught" before it is swallowed. Extraordinary particulars were given, in this instance, of the human aspect of the vision, of its tossing its hair back from its brow, and its being much annoyed by a bird which was hovering over it, and which it warned off repeatedly with its hands. The most ingenious conjecture I ever heard advanced respecting the ordinary mistakes about mermaids was, that somebody may have actually seen a mermaid, comb and all, dancing in the water, but that it was a figure of wood, struck off from some shipwrecked vessel.

I am travelling out of the world, however, when I get into these realms of prose and matter-of-fact. I will conclude this paper with the two most striking descriptions of the mermaid I ever met with; — one, indeed, purporting to be that of a true one, but evidently of the wildest oriental manufacture; the other, in the pages of a young living poet, worthy of the name in its most poetical sense.

D'Herbelot, in his article on the "Yagiouge and Magiouge" (Gog and Magog), tells us of a certain Salam, who was sent by Vathek, ninth Caliph of the race of the Abassides, to explore the famous Caspian Gates, and who being in-

---

ination played strange tricks with the witnesses, or that the existence of mermaids is no longer a matter of question."

Simon Wilkin, in one of the notes to his edition of Sir Thomas Browne, makes a learned and ingenious argument on the probable existence of the mermaid; and De Quincey says that Southey once remarked to him, that if the mermaid had been differently named (as, suppose, a mer-ape) nobody would have questioned its existence any more than that of sea-cows, sea-lions, &c. "The mermaid has been discredited by her human name and her legendary human habits. If she would not coquette so much with melancholy sailors, and brush her hair so assiduously upon solitary rocks, she would be carried on our books for as honest a reality, as decent a female, as many that are assessed to the poor-rates." — ED.

vited by the lord of the country to go and fish with him, saw an enormous fish taken, in the inside of which was another still alive, and of a very remarkable description. It had the figure of a naked girl as far as the waist, and wore, down to its *knees*, a sort of *drawers* (*caleçon*) made of a skin like a man's. *It kept its hands over its face*, tore its hair, heaved great sighs, and remained alive but a short time.*

This circumstance of the creature's keeping its hands over its face, is really a fine instance of the ghastly and the pathetic. She seems to have had something too human in her countenance to wish to be looked at by a similar face. How she contrived to tear her hair, without letting her face be seen, we are not told. As knees are mentioned, we are to suppose that the fish commenced just below them, possibly with a double tail. There is no predicating how such extraordinary young ladies will terminate.

Mr. Tennyson's mermaid is in better keeping; as strange and fantastic as need be, but all with the proper fantastic *truth;* just as such a creature might "live, move, and have its being," if such creatures existed. His verse is as strong, buoyant, and wilful as the mermaid herself and the billows around her; and nothing can be happier, or in better or more mysterious sea-taste, than the conglomeration of the wet and the dry, the "forked, and horned, and soft" phenomena at the conclusion. Mark, too, the luxurious and wilful repetition of the words, "for the love of me," and of the rhyme on that word.

---

* "Bibliothèque Orientale." 1783. Tom. iii. p. 271.

SIRENS AND MERMAIDS.

THE MERMAID.

Who would be
A mermaid fair,
Singing alone,
Combing her hair
Under the sea,
In a golden curl,
With a comb of pearl,
On a throne?
I would be a mermaid fair;
I would sing to myself the whole of the day;
With a comb of pearl I would comb my hair;
And still as I combed I would sing and say,
" Who is it loves me? who loves *not* me?"
I would comb my hair till my ringlets would fall,
  Low adown, low adown,
From under my starry sea-bud crown,
  Low adown and around:
And I should look like a fountain of gold
  Springing alone
  With a shrill inner sound,
  Over the throne
  In the midst of the hall;
Till that great sea-snake under the sea,
From his coiled sleeps, in the central deeps,
Would slowly trail himself sevenfold
Round the hall where I sate, and look in at the gate
  With his large calm eyes for the love of me;
  And all the mermen under the sea
  Would feel their immortality
  Die in their hearts *for the love of me.*
But at night I would wander away, away;
 I would fling on each side my low-flowing locks,
And lightly vault from the throne, and play
 With the mermen in and out of the rocks;
We would run to and fro, and hide and seek,
 On the broad seawolds, in the crimson shells,
 Whose silvery spikes are nighest the sea.
But if any came near I would call, and shriek,
And adown the steep like a wave I would leap,
 From the diamond ledges that jut from the dells;
For I would not be kist by all who would list,

Of the bold merry mermen under the sea;
They would sue me, and woo me, and flatter me,
In the purple twilights under the sea;
But the king of them all would carry me,
Woo me, and win me, and marry me,
In the branching jaspers under the sea;
Then all the dry pied things that be
In the hueless mosses under the sea
Would curl round my silver feet silently,
All looking up for the love of me.
And if I should carol aloud, from aloft
All things that are forked, and horned, and soft,
Would lean out from the hollow sphere of the sea,
All looking down for the love of me.

———◆———

TRITONS AND MEN OF THE SEA.

HAVING treated of Sirens, mermaids, and other female phenomena connected with the ocean, we here devote an article to its male gentry — personages for whom, though we may speak of them with a certain familiarity on the strength of old acquaintance, we entertain all the respect due to their ancient renown, and to those sacred places of poetry in which they are still to be found.

And first of the most ancient. The Triton is one of a numerous race begotten by Triton the son of Neptune, whose conch allayed the deluge of Deucalion. Like his ancestors, he is half a man and half a fish, with a great muscular body, and a tail ending in a crescent. There is a variety which has the forefeet of a horse. And sometimes he has two thighs like a man, or great, round, divided limbs resembling thighs, and tending to the orbicular, which end in fish-tails instead of legs. He serves Neptune and the sea-nymphs; is employed in calming billows and helping ships out of danger; and blows a conch-shell before the car he waits on, the sound of which is heard on the remotest shores, and causes the waves there to ripple. You may see him in all his jollity in the pictures of the Italians, waiting upon Galatea and sporting about the chariot with her nymphs; for with the strength he has the good humor of the most gambolling of the great fish; and when not employed in his duties, is for ever making love, and tumbling about the weltering waters.

In one of the divine drawings of Raphael, lately exhibited in St. Martin's-lane (and to be detained, we trust, among us for ever, lest our country be dishonored for want of taste), is a Triton with a nymph on his back, whom he is carrying through the water in a style of exquisite grace and affectionateness; for the higher you go in art, the more lovely does love become, and the more raised above the animal passion, even when it most takes it along with it.

Imagine yourself on a promontory in a lone sea, during an autumnal morning, when the heavens retain the gladness of summer-time, and yet there is a note in the wind prophetical of winter, and you shall see Neptune come by with Amphitrite, strenuously drawn through the billows, in which they are half washed, and Triton blowing his conch before them.

> " First came great Neptune with his three-forkt mace,
> That ,ules the seas and makes them rise or fall;
> *His dewy lockes did drop with brine apace*
> *Under his diademe imperiall;*
> And by his side his queene with coronall,
> Faire Amphitrite, most divinely faire,
> Whose yvorie shoulders weren covered all
> *As with a robe with her owne silver haire,*
> And deckt with pearles which th' Indian seas for her *prepaire.*

And all the way before them, as they went,
Triton his trompet shrill before them blew,
For goodly triumph and great jollyment,
THAT MADE THE ROCKES TO ROARE AS THEY WERE RENT."
FAERIE QUEENE, Book iv. Canto xi.

These pearls which Amphitrite wears, were probably got for her by the Tritons, who are great divers. In one of the pictures of Rubens, there are some of them thrusting up their great hands out of the sea (the rest of them invisible), and offering pearls to a queen.

Some writers have undertaken to describe these sea-deities more minutely, and as partaking a great deal more of the brute-fish than the man. According to them, the Triton has hair like water-parsley; gills a little under the ears; the nostrils of a man; a wide mouth with panther's teeth; blue eyes; fins under the breast like a dolphin; hands and fingers, as well as nails of a shelly substance; and a body covered with small scales as hard as a file. Be this as it may, he was in great favor with the sea-goddesses, and has to boast even of the condescension of Venus. Hear what a triumphant note he strikes up in the pages of Marino.

> Per lo Carpazio mar l'orrida faccia
> Del feroce Triton che la seguia,
> La ritrosa Cimotoe un di fuggia
> Sicome fera sbigottita in caccia.
> Seguiala il rozzo; e con spumose braccia
> L'acque battendo e ribattendo gía,
> E con lubrico piè l'umida via
> Scorreva intento a l'amorosa traccia:
>
> "Qual pro," dicendo, "ov" ha più folta e piena
> L'alga, fuggir quel Dio ch' ogni procella
> Con la torta sua tromba acqueta e frena?

> Tra queste squamme, a la scagliosa ombrella
> Di questa coda, in questa curva schiena
> Vien sovente a seder la Dea più bella.'

> A dreadful face in the Carpathian sea
> After a sweet one like a deer in flight,
> Came ploughing up a trough of thunderous might —
> Triton's — in chase of coy Cymothoe.
> Rugged and fierce, and all afroth, came he,
> Dashing the billowy buffets left and right;
> And on his slippery orbs, with eyes alight
> For thirst, stoop'd headlong tow'rds the lovely she;

> Crying, " What boots it to look out for aid
> In weedy thicks, and run a race with him
> To whom the mastery of the seas is given?
> On this rude back, under the scaly shade
> Of this huge tail, midst all this fishy trim,
> Oft comes to sit the loveliest shape in heaven."

According to Hesiod, Triton is a highly " respectable " god, in the modern sense of the word, for he lives " in a golden house." To be sure, he does that, as residing with his father and mother; but, moreover, he is a god redoubtable on his own account—*deinos*—a god of " awful might," as Mr. Elton excellently renders it; not " eximius " merely, or egregious, as feeble Natalis Comes interpreteth it; nor simply " vehemens," as the common Latin version saith better, but implying the combination of force and terror.

> " From the god of sounding waves,
> Shaker of earth, and Amphitrite, sprang
> *Sea-potent Triton huge;*

(excellently rendered, that)

> Beneath the deep
> He dwells in golden edifice,

(but with his father and mother, quoth Hesiod),

> A god
> Of awful might.*

Mr. Elton appends a curious note to this passage, from the learned and ingenious, but most gratuitous, "Mythology" of Bryant; who, out of a mistaken zeal for identifying every thing with Scripture, undoes half the poetry of old fable "at a jerk," and makes stocks and stones of the gods with a vengeance. We are sorry to find that so poetical a translator has allowed himself, out of a like respectable error, to contract his larger instincts into those of a dogmatist so prosaical. According to Mr. Bryant, Triton is no better than an old brick building; and Amphitrite herself "another."

"The Hetrurians," says he, "erected on their shores towers and beacons for the sake of their navigation, which they called Tor-ain; whence they had a still farther denomination of Tor-aini (Tyrrheni). Another name for buildings of this nature was Tirit, or Turit; which signified a tower or turret. The name of Triton is a contraction of Tirit-on, and signifies the tower of the sun; but a deity was framed from it, who was supposed to have had the appearance of a man upwards, but downwards to have been like a fish. The Hetrurians are thought to have been the inventors of trumpets; and in their towers on the sea-coast there were people appointed to be continually on the watch, both by day and by night, and to give a proper signal if any thing happened extraordinary. This was done by a blast from the trumpet. In early times, however, these brazen instruments were but little known; and people were obliged to use what were near at hand, the

---

* Elton's "Hesiod," p. 194.

conchs of the sea : by sounding these they gave signals from the tops of the towers when any ship appeared; and this is the implement with which Triton is more commonly furnished. Amphi-tirit is merely an oracular tower, which, by the poets, has been changed into Amphitrite, and made the wife of Neptune."

Don't believe a word of it ; or, if you do, admit the possibility of just enough to enable you to admire how the noble imagination of the Greeks restored their rights to the largeness and loudness of Nature, and forced this watchman's tower back again into the ocean which it pretended to compete with. What ! was the sea itself nothing ? its roaring nothing ? its magnitude, and mystery, and eternal motion nothing, that out of all this a Triton and a Neptune could not be framed, without the help of these restorers of Babel?

Bochart, speaking of the river Triton (and, by the way, he was an Eastern scholar, which Bryant was not), derives the name from the Phœnician word *tarit*. Mr. Bryant brings his Triton from *tirit*. In fact you may bring any thing from any thing by the help of etymology; as Goldsmith has shown in his famous derivation of Fohi from Noah ; and Horne Tooke, in his no less learned deduction of " pickled cucumber " from " King Jeremiah." To pretend to come to any certain conclusion in etymology, is to defy time, place, and vicissitude.

Allegorically, Triton is the *noise*, and tumbling, and savageness of the sea ; and therefore may well be represented as looking more brutal than human ; but the savageness of the sea, taking it in the gross, and not the particular, is a thing genial and good-natured, serving the healthiest purposes of the world ; and therefore the same Triton may be represented as abounding in humanity, and appearing in a nobler shape. Be his shape what it may, Venus (universal love) understands his nature; and with the eye of a goddess sees fair-play between him and what is beauteous, difference being only a form, and the elements and essences of things being the same throughout the globe, and secretly harmonizing with one another.

(There is a fine blowing wind, while we are writing this, with a deep tone in its cadences, as if Triton were assenting to what we wrote.) Boccaccio, in identifying him with the noise of the sea, finally says, that he signifies that especial sound of it which announces a more than ordinary swell of the waters, and the approach of his lord and master in his vehemence, "as trumpeters blow their song before the coming of an emperor." *

But allegories are secondary affairs. Triton is a good fellow on his own account, and puts a merriment and visible humanity in the sea, linking us also with things invisible. On this latter account, a living poet, in a fit of tedium with the commonplaces of the "work-a-day world," and their habitual disbelief in any thing beyond themselves, has expressed a wish to see him. But surely, being the great poet he is, he *has* seen him, often; and need not have desponded for a moment over the commonplaces of the world, more than over any other parcel of atoms playing their parts in the vicissitudes and progress of all things. "Great God!" he exclaims (and beautiful is the effusion):

> "I'd rather be
> A pagan, suckled in a creed outworn,
> So might I, standing on this pleasant lea

---

* "Genealogia Deorum," 1511, p. 55. "Voluere ex illo sono comprehendi futurum maris majorem solito æstum; ut sono illo adventante majori cum impetu dominum suum ostendat Triton; uti et tibicines imperatorem de proximo advenire designant tibiarum cantu."

Have glimpses that would make me less forlorn;
Have sight of Proteus coming from the sea,
Or hear old Triton blow his wreathed horn."
                              WORDSWORTH'S SONNETS.

But what is there more marvellous in Triton than in the sea itself? and what glimpses need we desire to reassure us, greater than the stars above our heads, and the wonders in a man's own brain and bosom? To see these, if we look for them, in a healthy spirit, (for the gods, after all, or rather before all, love health and energy, and insist upon them), is to see "the shapes of gods, ascending and descending," and to know them for what they are — no delusions, nor unbeneficent. All that they require is, that we should help the intellectual and moral world to make progress; and as our poet was not doing this at the moment, we suppose the gods suspended his gift, and would not allow him to see them. And yet, behold! he did so, in the midst of his very disbelief! so unable to get rid of his divinity is a true poet.

"In playful reverence, not presumptuous scorn
I speak, nor with my own rebuke, but Jove's,
His teacher mid the stars."

Our old friend Sandys, in the delightful notes to his "Ovid," quotes an Italian author to show that a Triton was once seen and felt, as you might handle a lobster. "Pliny," says he, "writes how an ambassador was sent on purpose from the Olissiponensi (the Lisbon people), unto Tiberius Cæsar, to tell him of a Triton, seene and heard in a certaine cave, winding a shell, and in such a form as they are commonly painted. But I cannot omit what is written by Alexander ab Alexandro, who lived in the last century, how he heard one Draconet Boniface of Naples, a souldier of much experience, report in an honourable assembly, that in the wars of Spaine he saw a sea-monster with the face and body like a man, but below the belly like a fish, brought thither from the farthest shores of Mauritania. It had an old countenance; the hairs and beard rough and shaggy; blew of colour; and high of stature; with finnes between the arms and the body. These were held for gods of the sea, and propitious to sailors! ignorance producing admiration, and admiration superstition. However, perhaps they erre not, who conceived them to be *onely Divells*, assuming that form, to nourish a false devotion." *

Mr. Wordsworth's wish, in certain "moods of the mind," is natural and touching; but we believers of the Muses' "train" are startled, when a great poet, even for a moment, seems to lose sight of those final wonders, which it is poetry's high philosophic privilege to be forever aware of. The deities of past ages are alive still, as much as they ought to be; the divinity that inspires their conception is always alive, and he evinces himself in a thousand shapes of hope, love, and imagination; ay, and of the most commonplace materiality too, which, to beings who beheld us from afar, would be quite as good proof of the existence of things beautiful and supernatural, as Galatea, with all her nymphs, would be to one of us. Let the reader fancy a world, which had but one-half the lovely things in it which ours possesses, or but imagination enough to conceive them, and then let him fancy what it would think of *us*, and of our right to hope for other things supernatural, and to be full of a noble security against all nullification.

---

* Sandys' "Ovid," fol., p. 19.

But to return from these speculations, fit as they are for the remoteness and universality of the seas. We have nothing to do here with Nereus, Proteus, and other watery deities, whose form, though they could change it, was entirely human; neither have we any concern with deities in general, however mixed up with animal natures, unless, like the Triton, they have survived to modern fable, and thus remain tangible. Tritons have been seen in plenty in latter times. Ariosto found them on the shores of romance: they figure in the piscatory dialogues of his countrymen; and our own later poets have beheld them by dozens, whenever they went to the sea-coast, just as other men see fishermen and boats. In the pretty drama entitled "Alceo," written by a promising young poet of the name of Ongaro, who died early, and which the Italians call the *Aminta bagnato* (Amyntas in the water), a Triton performs the part of the Satyr in Tasso.

Our great poet of romance makes express mention of a Sea-Satyr. It is in that "perilous passage" of the last canto of Book the Second, in the perusal of which our imagination becomes as earnest and childlike as the poet's own look of belief. We should lay the whole of it before our readers, had we quoted it twenty times; in the first place, because it contains a list of sea-monsters, and therefore falls in with our subject; and secondly, because we cannot help it. Sir Guyon, with his friend the Palmer, has just passed a dreadful whirlpool: —

> "The heedful boteman strongly forth did stretch
> His brawnie armes, and all his bodie straine,
> That th' utmost sandy breach they shortly fetch,
> Whiles the dredd daunger does behind remaine.
> Suddeine they see, from midst of all the maine,
> The surging waters like a mountaine rise,

And the great sea, puft up with proud disdaine,
  To swell above the measure of his guise,
As threatning to devoure all that his powre despise.

"The waves came rolling, and the billows rore
  Outragiously, as they enraged were,
  Or wrathfull Neptune did them drive before
  His whirling charet *for exceeding feare ;
  For not one puffe of winde there did appeare ;*
  That all the three thereat were much afrayd,
  Unweeting what such horrour straunge did reare.
  Eftsoones they saw an hideous hoast arrayd
Of huge sea-monsters, such as living sence dismayed:

"Most ugly shapes and horrible aspécts,
  Such as dame Nature's self mote feare to see,
  Or shame, that ever should so fowle defects
  From her most cunning hand escaped bee:
  All dreadfull pourtraicts of deformitee ;
  Spring-headed hydres, and SEA-SHOULDERING WHALES,
  Great whirlpooles, which all fishes make to flee,
  Bright scolopendraes, arm'd with silver scales,
Mighty monoceros with *immeasured* tayles:

"The dreadful fish, that hath *deserv'd* the name
  Of Death, and like him lookes in dreadfull hew ;
  The *griesly wasserman*, that makes his game
  The flying ships with swiftness to pursew ;
  *The horrible Sea-Satyre, that doth shew
  His fearefull face in time of greatest storme ;*
  Huge ziffius, whom mariners eschew
  No lesse than rockes, as travellers informe ;
And greedy rosmarines, with visages deforme:

"All these, and thousand thousands many more,
  And more deformed monsters, thousand fold,
  With dreadfull noise, and hollow rombling rore,
  Came rushing, in the fomy waves enroll'd,
  Which seem'd to fly, for feare them to behold ;
  Ne wonder, if these did the knight appall ;
  *For all that here on earth we dreedfull hold,
  Be but as bugs to fearen babes withall,
Compared to the creetures in the seas entrall.*"

There is little doubt that Spenser got some of these monsters out of the natural history of Gesner, the Buffon of his time, and that in a plate of one of his old folio volumes (now before us) is to be seen the identical "fearful face" shown by the poet's "horrible sea-satyr" in "time of greatest storme," the one consequently which the poet himself saw. It is a pity we cannot give it here. The commentators should add it to their notes in the next edition.* With most of Spenser's sea-monsters we have nothing further to do in this article; but the "sea-satyr" is directly to our purpose; and so is the "griesly wasserman," *i. e.* waterman, or man of the sea; a very different personage from your "waterman above bridge."

Gesner's "sea-satyr," or "pan," is taken from an account given by Battista Fulgoso, who says that, in the time of Pope Eugenius the Fourth, it was taken on the coast of Illyria, while endeavoring to drag a boy away with it to its native element. It had a humanish kind of head and body, with a skin like an eel's, two horns on its forehead, a finger and thumb only on each hand, a couple of webbed feet, a great fish's tail, and *wings like a bat!* Such, at least, is the figure to be collected from the description and plate together.

Gesner has two whole chapters upon *Wassermen;* that is, Tritons and Men of the Sea; for, "the Germans call all such creatures *wassermen*, or *seemen*." Of these *watermen* and *seamen*, one of whom an accommodating figure is given, agreeable to his designation (with a caution

---

* "Conradi Gesneri Historia Animalium," p. 1197. Gesner was evidently Milton's as well as Spenser's authority for his animals. In one of his plates (p. 138) is the whale mistaken for an island, which the former speaks of,

' With fixed anchor in his scaly rind."

on the part of the writer against having too much faith in him), is called the *Monk*. The account of it is taken from the work on fishes by Rondelet; who says that the picture was sent him by Margaret, Queen of Navarre. The head is quite human, and has the clerical tonsure! The rest is a compromise between fish-scales and church vestments. This reverend fish was taken in a drag of herrings, and lived only three days, during which it said nothing, "with the exception of uttering certain sighs, indicative of great sorrow and distress."*

Another writer, quoted in the same place, says that the sea-monk is sometimes visible in the British Channel. "He has a white skin on his cranium, with a black circle round it, like a monk newly shaven. He fawns upon people at sea, and entices them into the water, where he satiates himself with their flesh." This species, we suppose, became extinct at the abolition of the monasteries.

But the monk has also a *Bishop*, of whom a figure is likewise given, very episcopal, and as if in the act of giving a charge to his clergy. He has a scaly mitre, a cloak, and an aquiline nose. If the metempsychosis were believed in, it would be difficult not to suppose him an actual bishop, who had been turned into a fish for eating too much turbot. It was caught in 1531, and sent to the King of Poland, to whom it made signs, "apparently indicative of a vehement desire of being returned to the ocean, into which, without further delay, it was accordingly thrown." "I omit other particulars," says Rondelet, "because I hold them to be feigned, for such is the vanity of mankind that, not content with truths sufficiently marvellous in themselves, they are for adding wonders to them of

---

* Gesner, p. 521.

their own invention. As to the likeness of the monster, I give it as I received it, neither affirming nor denying the truth thereof."

In Bochart's "Hierozoicon" is a very curious and learned chapter on fabulous animals, in which he gives us a variety of those of the sea from Arabian authors. They remind us of Eastern tales, and of Sindbad. Not that Sindbad's Old Man of the Sea (that admirable fiction, full of verisimilitude) has any thing of the sea in him but his name, and his living on the sea-shore; but the wonders are of the same wild and remote cast, linking the extremity of the marvellous with a look of nature and an appeal to our sympathies.

The first is named *Abu-Muzaina*, that is, says Bochart, "*Paterdecoræ* (the Father of the seemly)." Gentlemen of this species have the form of the sons of Eve, with glutinous skins, and are very well made. They weep and wail when they fall into human hands. They come out of the sea to walk about, and are then taken by hunters, who are so touched by their weeping as to dismiss them unhurt.*

The next is the *Old Jew*, who has a face like a man, a gray beard, a body like a frog's, hair like an ox, and is of the size of a calf. He comes out of the sea on Sabbath nights, and walks about till next evening, when he leaps frog-like into the sea.

Then comes a proper "Wasserman" by name, the *Homo Aquaticus*, or *Man of the Water;* called likewise *Old Man of the Sea*, from his gray beard. He is just like a man, only he has a tail. His appearance presages great lowness in the price of crops. A king of Damascus married one of them to a female of the country, in order

---

* Bochart, "Opera Omnia," fol., vol. ii., part 2, p. 858.

that he might learn what language he spoke from their offspring! The result was a son, and one remark on the part of the old gentleman, expressing an unaccountable amazement.

Lastly cometh one *Duhlak* (the name is not interpreted), who haunts islands, riding upon an ostrich, and eating people that are shipwrecked. Some say that he will board ships, have a fight with the crew, and cry aloud "with a voice of boasting." Bochart is of opinion that this "voice of boasting" should rather be translated "glad and agreeable voice;" for, says he, the sirens are the creatures intended, who had maidens' faces, were birds in the lower parts of their bodies, and eat human flesh. But for a reason to be noticed presently, this decision appears to be a mistake.

"In these Arabian stories," says our good old author, "there may be some truth; for it has been proved that there are creatures in the sea possessing, or nearly possessing, the human form. You may read of some that have endeavored to get into ships by the cables, of others who come upon land to walk about, and who strike fire in the night-time with flints, and of others who behave very ill to women, unless you are quick to prevent them. Some have been taken and lived a long time in human society; among others a female one in Pomerania, of the name of Eda, very lively and amorous. And Gassendi, in his life of Peiresc, describes one that had been seen not long before, on the coast of Brittany. Ancient as well as modern history bears witness that such creatures have been found on the surface as well as in the depth of the ocean. Hence the origin of Tritons and Nereids. *I regard, however, as plainly fabulous* what is said of their being gifted with speech, and the Arabian stories of *a species which keep the Sabbath;* though a writer of a former age, Lodovicus Vives, who was not at all given to trifling, confidently asserts that they have spoken, and thence concludes that the sea contains a generation of real men. 'There are men,' says he, 'in the sea as there are on the land — Pliny tells us so; entire men — and I have no doubt of it. One was taken twelve years ago in Holland, and seen by many. He was kept above two years, and was just *beginning to speak*, when being seized a second time with the plague, he was restored to his native element, into which he went *leaping and rejoicing*.' But we are to conclude that this marine species of man originated with the land species."*

In the "Persian Tales," a genuine oriental production, is a story of a manifest species of Duhlak, or ship-invading and boasting man of the sea, which corroborates what appeared to Bochart a misinterpretation of the "voice" above mentioned. It is drawn in apparent emulation of Sindbad's old man, to which it is very inferior, especially in the conclusion; yet the dramatic surprise of his behavior after he gets on board the vessel is startling; and though his boasting is overdone and made of too "knowing" and human a cast, yet when we see that this attribute of bullying was part of the popular faith in such beings, the narrative acquires additional interest, and has a diminished look of impossibility. His impatient stamping, the impenetrability of his skin, and his sticking his claws into the vessel when they tried to throw him overboard, are also striking circumstances. His face is described a good deal after the fashion of the ancient Triton. We shall commence the narrative with a few of those introductory details, *à la* Defoe, which give such a look of nature to

---

* Bochart, "Opera Omnia," fol., vol. ii., part 2, p. 860.

these "monstrous lies." The person speaking is "Aboulfauris, the Great Voyager," whose name one repeats with involuntary respect for his great beard and truly prodigious experience.

"Having sailed," says this illustrious personage, "almost round the Isle of Serendib, we entered the Gulf of Bengal, which is the greatest gulf in Asia, at the lower end of which are the kingdoms of Bengal and Golconda. Just as we entered it there rose a violent storm of wind, the like of which had never been seen in those seas. We wanted a south wind, and this was a north-west, quite contrary to our course for Golconda. We lowered our sails, and the seamen did all they could to save the ship, which they were at last forced to let drive at the mercy of the wind and waves. The storm lasted fifteen days, and blew so furiously that we were in that time driven six hundred leagues out of our way. We left the long isles of Sumatra and Java to our larboard, and the ship drove to the strait of the Moluccas, south of the Philippines, into a sea unknown to our mariners. The wind changed at last and turned to an easterly wind; it blew pretty gently, and great was the joy of the ship's company. But their joy did not last long; 'twas disturbed by an adventure which you will hardly believe, it being so very extraordinary. We were beginning merrily to resume our course, and were got to the east point of the island of Java, when, not far off, we spied a man quite naked, struggling with the waves, and in danger of being swallowed up; he held fast by a plank that kept him up, and made a signal to us to come to his assistance. We sent our boat to him out of compassion, and found, by experience, that if pity be a laudable passion it must be owned that it is also sometimes very dangerous. The seamen took up the man and brought him aboard; he looked to be about forty years old, was of a monstrous shape, had a great head, and short, thick, bristly hair. His mouth was excessively wide, his teeth long and sharp, his arms nervous, his hands large, with a long crooked nail on each finger. His eyes, which are not to be forgotten, were like those of a tiger; his nose was flat, and his nostrils wide. We did not at all like his physiognomy, and his mien was such that it soon changed our pity into terror.

"When this man, such as I have described him, appeared before Dehaousch, our master, he thus addressed him: 'My Lord, I owe my life to you, I was at the point of destruction when you came to my assistance.'—'Indeed,' replied Dehaousch, 'it would not have been long ere you had gone to the bottom, had you not had the good fortune to have met with us.'—'I am not afraid of the sea,' replied the man, smiling; 'I could have lived whole years in the water without any inconvenience; what tormented me much more is hunger, which has devoured me these twelve hours, for so long it is since I ate any thing, and that is a very long while for a man who has so good a stomach as I have. Therefore, pray let me have something as soon as possible to repair my spirits almost spent with such a fasting as I have been forced to keep. You need not look for niceties; I am not squeamish; I can eat any thing.'

"We looked at one another very much surprised at his discourse, and doubted not that the peril he had been in had cracked his brain. Our master was of the same mind, and imagining he might want something to eat, he ordered meat enough for six hungry stomachs to be set before him, and clothes to be brought him for his covering. 'As for the clothes,' says the stranger, 'I shall not meddle with them; I always go naked.'—'But,' replied Dehaousch, 'decency will not permit that you should stay with us in that condition.' The man took him up short— 'Oh!' says he, 'you will have time enough to accustom yourself to it.' This brutal answer confirmed us in the opinion that he had lost his senses. Being sharp-set, he was very impatient that he was not served to his mind. He stamped with his foot upon the deck, ground his teeth, and rolled his eyes so ghastly that he looked both furious and menacing. At last what he wanted appeared; he fell upon it with a greediness that surprised us, and though there was certainly sufficient for any other six men, he despatched it in a moment.

"When we had cleared the table which had been spread for him, he, with an air of authority, bade us bring him some more victuals. Dehaousch, being resolved to try how much this devouring monster could really swallow, ordered he should be obeyed. The table was spread as before, and as much victuals again set before him; but this second service lasted him no longer than the first— it was gone in a moment. We thought, however, he would stop there, but we were mistaken, he demanded more meat still; upon which one of the slaves aboard the ship, going up to this brute, was about to chastise him for his insolence, which the other observing prevented, laying his two paws upon his shoulders, fixing his nails in his flesh and tearing him to pieces. In an instant fifty sabres were drawn to revenge this dreadful murder; every one pressed forward to strike him and chastise his insolence, but they very soon found to their terror that the skin of their enemy was as impenetrable as adamant; their sabres broke, and their edges turned without so much as raising the skin. Though he received no hurt by their blows, they did not strike him with impunity; he took one of the most forward of his assailants, and with amazing strength tore him to pieces before our eyes.

"When we found our sabres were useless, and that we could not wound him, we threw ourselves upon him to endeavor to fling him into the sea, but we could not stir him. Besides his huge limbs and prodigious nerve, he stuck his crooked nails in the timber of the deck, and stood as immovable as a rock in the midst of the waves. He was so far from being afraid of us that he said with a sullen smile, 'You have taken the wrong course, friends, you will fare much better by obeying me; I have tamed more indocile people than you. I declare if you continue to oppose my will, I will serve you all as your two companions have been served.'

"These words made our blood freeze in our veins. We a third time set a large quantity of provisions before him, he fell aboard it, and one would have thought by his eating that his stomach rather increased than diminished. When he saw we were determined to submit he grew good-humored. He said he was sorry we had forced him to do what he did, and kindly assured us he loved us on account of the service we had done him in taking him out of the sea, where he should have been starved if he had stayed there a few hours longer without succor; that he wished, for our sakes, he could meet with some other vessel laden with good provisions, because he would throw himself aboard it and leave us in quiet. He talked thus while he was eating, and laughed and bantered like other men, and we should have thought him diverting enough had we been in a disposition to relish his pleasantry. At the fourth service he gave over, and was two hours without eating any thing at all. During this excess of sobriety he was very familiar in his discourse; he asked us one after another what country we were of, what were our customs, and what had been our adventures. We were in hopes that the fumes of his victuals he had eaten would have got up in his head and made him drowsy; we impatiently expected that sleep would seize him, and were resolved to take him napping, and fling him into the sea before he had time to look about him. This hope of ours was our only resource, for though we had great store of provisions aboard, yet, after his rate of eating, he would have devoured them all in a very little while. But, alas! in vain did we flatter ourselves with these false hopes. The cruel wretch, guessing our design, told us he never slept; that the great quantity of victuals he ate repaired the wearisomeness of nature, and supplied the want of sleep.

"To our grief we found what he said was true; we told him long and tedious stories on purpose to lull him asleep, but the monster never shut his eyes. He then deplored our misfortune, and our master despaired of ever seeing Golconda again; when on a sudden a cloud gathered over our heads. We thought at first it was a storm which was gathering, and we rejoiced at it; for there was more hope of our safety in a tempest than in the state we were in. Our ship might be driven ashore on some island; we might save ourselves by swimming; and by this means be delivered from this monster, who doubtless intended to devour us when he had eaten up all our provisions. We wished, therefore, that a violent storm would overtake us; and, what perhaps never happened before, we prayed to heaven to be drowned. However, we were deceived; what we took for a cloud was the greatest rokh that was ever seen in those seas. The monstrous bird darted himself on our enemy, who was in the middle of our ship's company; and mistrusting nothing, had no time to guard himself against such an attack: the rokh seized him by his claws, and flew up into the air with his prey, before we were aware of it.

"We then were witnesses of a very extraordinary combat. The man recollecting himself, and finding he was hoisted up in the air between the talons of a winged monster, whose strength he made trial of, resolved to defend himself. He struck his crooked nails into the body of the rokh, and setting his teeth to his stomach, began to devour him, flesh, feathers, and all. The bird made the air resound with his cries, so piercing was his pain; and to be revenged tore out his enemy's eyes with his claws. The man, blind as he was, did not give over. He ate the heart of the rokh, who, re-collecting all his force at the last gasp, struck his beak so forcibly into his enemy's head, that they both fell dead into the sea, not many paces from our ship's side." *

In the "Arabian Nights" is an account of a nation who live under the sea, but they differ in nothing from men, except in their power of so doing, and coming to and fro with dry clothes, "as if nothing had happened;" all of which is not in the usual fine taste of that work.†

Of men of the sea, in their connection with the more shadowy nation of the Fairies, we have treated elsewhere, in a separate article on that people, and therefore say nothing of them here; and what we might have had to say on Mermen has been anticipated, as far as the genus is

---

* "Persian Tales; or, the Thousand and One Days." Ed. 1800, vol. ii., p. 133.
† See the story of Prince Beder and the Princess Giauhara.

concerned, in the paper on "Sirens and Mermaids;" but as we extracted into that paper Mr. Tennyson's poem on the female of this genus, we cannot but indulge ourselves here with giving his companion-piece.

THE MERMAN.

  Who would be
  A merman bold,
  Sitting alone,
  Singing alone,
  Under the sea,
  With a crown of gold,
  On a throne?
I would be a merman bold.
I would sit and sing the whole of the day:
 I would fill the sea-halls with a voice of power;
But at night I would roam abroad and play
With the mermaids in and out of the rocks,
 Dressing their hair with the white sea-flower;
And, holding them back by their flowing locks,
 I would kiss them often under the sea,
 And kiss them again, till they kiss'd me,
  Laughingly, laughingly.
And then we would wander away, away,
To the pale-green sea-groves, straight and high,
 Chasing each other merrily.

There would be neither moon nor star;
But the wave would make music above us afar —
Low thunder and light in the magic night —
 Neither moon nor star.
We would call aloud in the dreamy dells, —
Call to each other, and whoop and cry
 All night merrily, merrily.
They would pelt me with starry spangles and shells,
Laughing and clapping their hands between,
 All night merrily, merrily.
But I would throw to them back in mine
Turkis, and agate, and almondine;
Then leaping out upon them unseen,

I would kiss them often under the sea,
And kiss them again, till they kiss'd me,
   Laughingly, laughingly.
Oh! what a happy life were mine,
Under the hollow-hung ocean green!
Soft are the moss-beds under the sea:
We would live merrily, merrily.

The most charming story connected with beings of the sea is that of Acis and Galatea; the most wildly touching, that of the *Neck*, or Scandinavian Water-spirit, who wept when he was told he would not be "saved" (related in the fairy article above mentioned); the sublimest is the famous one of the voice which announced the death of the "Great Pan." Plutarch relates it, in his essay on the "Cessation of Oracles," upon the authority of one Philippus, who said he had it from the hearer's own son, and who was corroborated in his report by several persons present. The original narrator alluded to gave the account as follows.* He said, "that, during a voyage to Italy, the wind fell in the night-time, as they were nearing the Echinades; and that, while almost all the people on board were on the watch, a great voice was heard from the Island of Paxos, calling upon one of them of the name of Thamnus; which voice, for the novelty of the thing, excited them all to great astonishment." This Thamnus was an Egyptian, and master of the vessel. He was twice called and gave no answer. He was called a third time, and then he acknowledged the call; upon which the voice, with much greater loudness than before, cried out, "When you come to the Marsh, announce that the Great Pan is dead," a command which struck all the listeners with terror.

---

* We quote from Gesner, as above, p. 1198.

Accordingly, when they arrived off the Marsh, Thamnus, looking out from his rudder towards the land, cried, with a loud voice, " The Great Pan is dead ; " upon which there was suddenly heard a mighty groaning, as of many voices — " yea, of voices innumerable, all wonderfully mixed up together." And because there were many people in that ship, as soon as they came to Rome the rumor was spread through the whole city, and the Emperor Tiberius sent for Thamnus, and was so struck with his relation, that he applied to the philosophers to know what Pan it could be ; and the conjecture was that it must be the Pan who was the son of Mercury and Penelope.

The announcement of the death of Pan was awkward ; for Pan signifies *all*, and was the most universal of the gods ; but luckily, by the help of the Platonists and others, every god was surrounded with minor intelligences of the same name, after the fashion of a Scottish clan ; so that the philosophers found a god convenient for the occasion in this particular Pan, the offspring of Mercury and Penelope. It has been supposed that the story was a trick to frighten the vicious and superstitious emperor, which is not very likely. There is no authority, beyond Plutarch's report, who lived long after, and was very credulous, for the story itself ; and if a voice was actually heard, it does not follow that it said those exact words, or that the subsequent delivery of the message produced any thing more than a fancied acknowledgment. A sceptic at court might have resolved it into some common message, perhaps a watchword : perhaps some smugglers meant to tell their correspondent that "*all* was up with them !" Joking and scepticism apart, however, the story is a fine one ; so much so, that it is surprising Milton did not make a more particular allusion to it in his noble juvenile ode on the "Nativity," where he speaks of the voices heard at the cessation of the oracles: —

> "The lonely mountains o'er,
> And the resounding shore,
> A voice of weeping heard, and loud lament."

ON GIANTS, OGRES, AND CYCLOPS.

IT would be difficult to find an early national history without a giant in it. Any thing great in its effects, and supposed not to be very tender-hearted, was a giant. A violent set of neighbors were giants. An opposer of the gods was a giant, and threw mountains at them instead of sceptical essays. Evil genii were gigantic. The same Persian word came to signify a giant, a devil, and a magician. An older word, in the Persian language, meaning a giant, gave its name to the ancient dynasty of the Caianides. Kings, in ancient times, when physical more than moral dignity was in request, were sometimes chosen on account of their stature. Agamemnon is represented as taller, by the head and shoulders, than any man in his army; and probably it was as much on account of his height as his other supremacy that he was called *Anax Andron*, King of Men. An etymologist would even see in the word *Anax* a resemblance to the *Anakites* of Scripture. It is remarkable that Virgil, in his "Elysium," has given the old poet Musæus a similar superiority over his brethren; as if every kind of power in the early ages was associated with that of body. Moral enormity was naturally typified by physical. "It may be observed," says

Mr. Hole, "that a giant, in Arabic or Persian fables, is commonly a negro or infidel Indian, as he is in our old romances a Saracen Paynim, a votary of Mahound and Termagaunt."—"Were the negroes authors," he pleasantly adds, "they would probably characterize their giants by whiskers and turbans; or by hats, wigs, and a pale complexion." *

In like manner, if the English wrote allegorical story-books nowadays, the oppressive lord or magistrate would be a giant. Fierce upholders of the old game-laws would be monsters of the woods, that devoured a man if he dared to touch one of their rabbits. "In books of chivalry," says Bishop Hurd, "the giants were oppressive feudal lords; and every lord was to be met with, like the giant, in his stronghold or castle. Their dependants of the lower form, who imitated the violence of their superiors, and had not their castles, but their lurking places, were the savages of romance. The greater lord was called a giant, for his power; the less, a savage for his brutality. All this is shadowed out of the Gothic tales, and sometimes expressed in plain words. The objects of the knight's vengeance go indeed by the various names of giants, paynims, Saracens, and savages. But of what family they all are, is clearly seen from the poet's description:—

> ' What, mister wight, quoth he, and how far hence
> Is he, that doth to travellers such harmes?
> He is, said he, a man of great defence,
> Expert in battell and in deedes of armes:
> And more emboldened by the wicked charmes
> With which his daughter doth him still support:
> Having great lordships got and goodly farmes

---

* " Remarks on the Arabian Nights' Entertainments," p. 80.

GIANTS, OGRES, AND CYCLOPS. 233

> Through strong oppression of his powre extort;
> By which he still them holds, and keeps with strong effort.
> And dayly he his wrongs encreaseth more,
> For never wight he lets to pass that waye
> Over his bridge, albee he rich or poore,
> But he him makes his passage-penny paye;
> Else he doth hold him backe or beate awaye.
> Thereto he hath a groom of evil guise,
> Whose scalp is bare, that bondage doth bewraye,
> Which pols and pils the poore in piteous wise,
> But he himself upon the rich doth tyrannise.'

"Here," says the Bishop, "we have the great oppressive baron very graphically set forth. And the *groom of evil guise* is as plainly the baron's vassal. The romancers, we see, took no great liberty with these respectable personages, when they called the one a giant, and the other a savage." *

That men of gigantic stature have existed here and there, we have had testimony in our own days. Some of them, probably not the tallest, have been strong. The others are weak and ill-formed, like children that have outgrown their strength. Whether giants ever existed as a body is still a question. The Patagonians of Commodore Byron have come down to a reasonable stature; and the bones that used to be exhibited as proofs undeniable of enormous men, turn out to be those of the mammoth and the elephant. But this is the prose of gigantology. In poetry they are still alive and stalking.

The earliest giants were monstrous as well as huge. Those that warred with the gods, and heaped Ossa upon Pelion, had a multitude of heads and arms, with serpents instead of legs. Typhon, the evil principle, the dreadful wind (still known in the East under the same name, the

---

* Todd's "Spenser," vol. vi. p. 7.

Tifoon), had dragons, instead of human heads, and out of each of them threw the shriek of a different animal. Enceladus was thrust under Mount Etna, from which he still vomits fire and smoke, and when he turns his side there is an earthquake. Otus and Ephialtes grew nine inches a month, and at nine years old made their campaign against the gods. Now and then a giant undertook to be more courtly and pious. When Juno, Neptune, and Minerva conspired to dethrone Jupiter, Briareus went up into heaven, and seating himself on his right hand, looked so very shocking that the deities were fain to desist.

There is a confusion of the giants with the Titans, but their wars were different. Those of the Titans were against Cœlus and Saturn; the giants warred against Jupiter. They were also of a different nature, the Titans being of proper celestial origin, whereas the birth of the giants was as monstrous as their shapes. As to the great stature of the Titans, all the gods were gigantic. It was only in their visits to earth that they accommodated themselves to human size, and then not in their wars. One of the noblest uses ever made of this association of bodily size with divine power is in "Paradise Lost," where Milton, in one of those passages in which his theology is as weak and perplexed as his verse is powerful, makes Abdiel say to the leader of the infernal armies, —

> "Fool! not to think how vain
> Against the Omnipotent to rise in arms;
> Who out of smallest things could without end
> Have raised incessant armies to defeat
> Thy folly; or with *solitary hand*
> *Reaching beyond all limit*, at one blow,
> Unaided, could have *finished* thee, and whelm'd
> Thy legions under darkness."

"Solitary hand," says Bishop Newton, "means his

single hand." Oh no! it is much finer than that. It means his hand, visibly alone, — with nothing round about it, — solitary in the great space of existence. It stretches out into the ether, dashing, at one blow, a great host into nothing; then draws back into heaven, and there is a silence as if existence itself were annihilated.

The Cyclops is a variety of the giant monstrous. He has one eye, and is a man-eater. Mr. Bryant, who, in his "Elements of Ancient Mythology," amidst a heap of wild and gratuitous assumptions, has some ingenious conjectures, is of opinion that a Cyclops was a watch-tower, with a round window in it showing a light, and that by the natural progress of fable the tower became a man. If the light however was for good purposes, the charge of man-eating is against the opinion. The Cyclopes, a real people, who left the old massy specimens of architecture, called after their name, are said to have been in the habit of carrying shields with an eye painted on them, or wore visors with a hole to see through. But these conjectures are not necessary to our treatise. The proper, huge, cannibal giant, the Fee-faw-fum of antiquity, is our monster. Homer, who wandered about the world, and took marvels as they came, has painted him in all his cruelty. Theocritus, writing pastorals at the court of Ptolemy, and more of a "sweet Signior," found out a refinement for him, which, to say the truth, is superior to jesting, and has touched a chord which the inventor of the character of Hector would have admired. He made Polyphemus in love; and we are sorry for the monster, and wish Galatea to treat him with as much tenderness as is compatible with her terrors.* His discovery of his forlorn condition,

---

* Those who wish to know how music can express a giant's misery con-

his fear that his senses are forsaking him, and his eagerness to suppose that he is not altogether alien to humanity, because the village girls, when he speaks to them from his mountain at night-time, *laughed at him*, render him no longer a monstrosity odious, but a difference pitiable.*

There is a Polyphemus in the story of " Sindbad " so like Homer's, that the ingenious author of the " Remarks on the Arabian Nights' Entertainments " pronounces it to be copied from him. Homer, however, might have copied it from the Orientals. He might have heard it from Eastern traders, granting it was unknown to the Greeks before. The wanderings of Ulysses imply a compilation of wonders from all parts of the world. The Greeks, except in this instance, appear to have had no idea of a nation of giants. Even Polyphemus they mixed up with their mythology, making him a son of Neptune. On the other hand, the grandiosity of the Orientals supplied them with giants in abundance, and Sir John Mandeville had no need, as Mr. Hole imagines, to go to Virgil and Ovid for his descriptions of huge monsters, eating men as they go, "all raw and all quicke."

Ariosto, in the seventeenth book of his great poem, has a Polyphemus with two projecting bones, instead of eyes, of the color of fungus. This is very ghastly. He calls

---

trasted with the happiness of two innocent lovers, should hear the serenata of " Acis and Galatea," by Handel, the giant of the orchestra.

(" Where giant Handel stands,
    Arm'd, like Briareus, with his hundred hands."— POPE.)

The terrible intonations of Polyphemus in his despair, with those lovely unweeting strains of the happy pair immediately issuing out upon them, " Ere I forsake my love," &c., offer perhaps the finest direct piece of contrast in the whole circle of music.

* Theocritus, " Idyll." xi. v. 72.

him an *orco*, that is to say, an *ogre*. Ogre, whether derived from the Latin *orcus*, or from Oigour (a tribe of Tartars), or Hongrois, or Hungarian,* is a man-eater; and *orco* appears to be the same, though not confined to the man-monster. The same poet, in his rifacimento of the story of Andromeda (canto 10), calls the fish an *orc;* and the word is used in a like sense in our elder poetry. Ariosto's Polyphemus (for he gives him a cavern, sheep, &c., exactly like those of the old Cyclops) has no sight at all with those horrible goggles of his. An exquisite sense of smelling supplies the want of it; and he comes running upon his prey, dipping his nose towards the ground.

> "Mentre aspettiamo, in gran piacer sedendo,
> Che da caccia ritorni il signor nostro,
> Vedemmo l'orco a noi venir correndo
> Lungo il lito del mar, terribil mostro.
> Dio vi guardi, signor, che 'l viso orrendo
> De l'orco a gli occhi mai vi sia dimostro.
> Meglio e per fama aver notiza d'esso,
> Ch' andargli, si che lo veggiate, appresso.

> "Non si puo compartir quanto sia lungo,
> Si smisuratamente è tutto grosso.
> In luogo d' occhi, di color di fungo
> Sotto la fronte ha due coccole d'osso.
> Verso noi vien, come vi dico, lungo
> Il lito: e par ch'un monticel sia mosso.
> Mostra le zanne fuor, come fa il porco:
> Ha lungo il naso, e'l sen bavoso e sporco.

> "Correndo viene, e'l muso a guisa porta
> Che'l braccio suol, quando entra in su la traccia.
> Tutti che lo veggiam, con faccia smorta
> In fugo andiamo ove il timor ne caccia.

---

* See "Fairy Mythology," vol. ii.

> Poco il veder lui cieco ne conforta ;
> Quando fiutando sol par che piu faccia,
> Ch 'altri non fa ch 'abbia odorato e lume:
> E bisogno al fuggire eran le piume."

> While thus we sat, prepared for mirth and glee,
> Waiting the king's appearance from the chase,
> Suddenly, to our horror, by the sea,
> We saw the ogre coming towards the place.
> God keep you, Sir, in his benignity,
> From setting eyes on such a dreadful face !
> Better, by far, of such things to be told,
> Than see a sight to make a man turn old.

> I cannot tell you his immeasured size,
> So huge he was, and of a bulk throughout.
> Upon his horrid front, instead of eyes,
> Two bony roundels, fungus-hued, stuck out.
> Thus, like the only thing 'twixt earth and skies,
> He came along; and under his brute snout
> Tusks he put forth, bared like the boar's in wrath ;
> And his huge breast was filthy with a froth.

> Running he comes, projecting towards the ground
> His loathly muzzle, dog-like, on the scent.
> With ashy faces we arise, and bound,
> Fast as we can, before the dire intent.
> Small comfort to us was his blindness found ;
> Since with his smelling only as he bent,
> More sure he seem'd than creatures that have sight ;
> And wings alone could match him for a flight.

The poverty-stricken propriety of Mr. Hoole regarded these circumstances as "puerilities." He ventured to turn Ariosto's wine into water, and then judged him in his unhappy sobriety. Mr. Hoole was not man enough to play the child with a great southern genius. Ariosto's poem is a microcosm, which sees fair-play to all the circles of imagination, at least to all such as are common to men in their ordinary state ; and he did not omit those that include childhood, and that, in some measure, are never forgotten by us. This literally construed, is in high epic taste, as much so as the homely similes of the Iliad and the Odyssey. We should be thankful, for our parts, to an epic poet who could manage to introduce the big-headed and bushy-haired ogres of our own story-books, with the little ogres, their children, all with crowns on their heads. We sympathize with the hand of the diminutive "giganticide," who felt them as they lay in their grim slumber, all in a row. Was this, by the way, a satire on royalty? It is an involuntary one. The giant Gargantua, in " Rabelais," who ate three men in a salad was a king.

Several of Spenser's allegorical personages are giants. The allegory is incidental, and helps to vary the individual character; but otherwise the bodily pictures are complete specimens of the giants of chivalry. One of them is Disdain —

> "Who did disdain
> To be so called, and whoso did him call."

Of another giant, of the same name, he tells us that

> "His lookes were dreadfull, and his fiery eies,
> Like two great beacons, glared bright and wyde,
> Glauncing askew, as if his enemies
> He scorned in his overweening pryde;
> And stalking stately, like a crane, did stryde
> At every step upon the tiptoes hie;
> And all the way he went, on every syde
> He gaz'd about, and stared horriblie,
> As if he with his looks would all men terrifie.
>
> "He wore no armour, ne for none did care,
> As no whit dreading any living wight;
> But in a jacket, quilted richly rare
> Upon checklaton,* he was straungely dight,

---

* Checklatoun (Fr. *ciclatoun*) is supposed to be intended by Spenser for cloth of gold.

> And on his head a roll of linnen plight,
> Like to the Moors of Malaber, he wore,
> With which his lockes, as black as pitchy night,
> Were bound about and voyded from before;
> And in his hand a mighty yron club he bore."
> FAERIE QUEENE, Book vi., Canto vii.

A third great giant is Orgoglio (or Pride), a good swallowing name. A knight is enjoying himself with his mistress, when suddenly he hears

> "A dreadful sownd,
> Which through the wood loud bellowing did rebownd,
> That all the earth for terror seemed to shake,
> And trees did tremble. Th' Elfe, therewith astownd,
> Upstarted lightly from his looser make,
> And his unready weapons gan in hand to take.
>
> "But ere he could his armour on him dight,
> Or get his shield, his monstrous enimy
> With sturdie steps came stalking in his sight,
> An hideous giant, horrible and hye;
> The grownd all groned under him for dread."

Orgoglio has a

> "Dreadful club
> All arm'd with ragged snubbes and knottie grain."

With this, in a battle with Prince Arthur, he aims a terrible blow, which, missing him —

> "Did fall to ground, and with his heavy sway,
> So deeply dented in the driven clay,
> That three yardes deep a furrow up did throw.
> The sad earth, wounded with so sore essay,
> Did groan full grievous underneath the blow,
> And trembling with strange feare, did like an earthquake show."

Then follows one of the noblest similes ever produced. Upton says that Longinus would have written a whole chapter upon it: —

> "As when Almightie Jove, in wrathful mood,
>   To wreake the guilt of mortal sins is bent,
>   Hurls forth his thund'ring dart with deadly food,
>   Enroll'd in flames and smouldering dreriment,
>   Through riven clouds and molten firmament:
>   The fierce three-forked engine, making way,
>   Both loftie towres and highest trees hath rent,
>   And all that might his angry passage stay;
>   And, shooting in the earth, castes up a mount of clay."
>   Book i. Canto viii.

Spenser writes the word variously — giant, gyaunt, and geaunt; for no man had a stronger sense of words as the expressions of things, nor delighted more to call in every aid to the emphasis and conscious enjoyment of what he was writing. His very rhymes are often spelled in an arbitrary manner, to enforce the sound; and he tells a dreadful story with all the shuddering epithets, and lingering, fearful fondness of a child.

Take another of his giants — one Corflambo, whose eyes are very new and terrible: —

> "At length they spied where towards them with speed
> A squire came galloping, as he would flie,
> Bearing a little dwarfe before his steed,
> That all the way full loud for aide did crie,
> That seem'd his shrikes would rend the brasen skie:
> Whom after did a mightie man pursew,
> Riding upon a dromedare on hie,
> Of stature huge, and horrible of hew,
> That would have mazed a man his dreadfull face to view:
>
> For from his fearfulle eyes *two fierie beames*,
> *More sharpe than points of needles*, did proceede,
> Shooting forth farre awaye two flaming streames,
> Full of *sad powre*, that poysnous bale did breede
> To all that on him lookt without good heed,
> And secretly his enemies did slay:
> Like as the basiliske, of serpent's seede,
> From powrefull eyes *close* venim doth convay
> Into the looker's hart, and *killeth farre away*."
>   Book iv. Canto viii.

This Corflambo is another good name. The names of
the giants in the beautiful romance of "Amadis of Gaul"—
(superior, undoubtedly, to "Palmerin of England," though
the latter also is delightful for its bits of color, and its
green and flowery places)—are very bulky, and "talk big."
There is Gandalac and Albadanger; and Madanfabul,
of the Vermilion Tower; and Gromadaga, the Giantess
of the Boiling Lake; and Ardan Canileo, the Dreadful;
and above all, the mighty and most mouthing *Famongom-
adan*, who seems to inform his enemies that he means to
flame and gobble 'em. Gandalac makes the least oral
pretensions; and "he was not so wicked as other giants,
but of a good and gentle demeanor, except when he was
enraged, and then would he do great cruelties." * But he
was very terrible. He was "so large and mismade, that

---

* See the excellent version of Mr. Southey, vol. i., p. 37.

[" Amadis of Gaul " and " Palmerin of England " were among Don Quixote's
favorite romances of chivalry. He and the curate used to dispute long and
learnedly as to who was the better knight, Palmerin of England or Amadis of
Gaul.

Bernardo Tasso, father of the poet, translated "Amadis de Gaul" into
Italian; and Tasso himself, as quoted by Ticknor, says that the "Amadis"
"is the most beautiful, and perhaps the most profitable, story of its kind that
can be read, because in its sentiments and tone it leaves all others behind
it, and in the variety of its incidents yields to none written before or since."
Sir Philip Sidney says he had known men "made better and braver by its
perusal." According to Burton, the work was a favorite among the English
gentry of the seventeenth century. Southey's version of "Amadis of Gaul"
was published by Longman in 1803, and was the subject of Sir Walter Scott's
first contribution to the "Edinburgh Review." "Amadis is an extraordinary
book," wrote Southey, in a letter to Miss Barker (the Bhow Begum of
"The Doctor"); "and now the job is done, I am glad I undertook it. . . .
I have a sort of family love for Vasco Loberia, more than for Ariosto or Milton, approaching to what I feel for Spenser; and certainly, when I get to
heaven, he will be one of the very first persons to whom I shall desire to be
introduced." — ED.]

never man saw him without affright;" and when he makes his appearance in Chapter IV., "the women ran, some among the trees and others fell down, and shut their eyes, that they might not see him."

By degrees, as men found out that a gigantic stature did not always imply strength, or even courage, they began to change their fear into contempt, and to laugh, like children, at the great bugbear that had amazed them. At length, they discovered that a giant could even be good-natured; and then the more philosophical romancers thought it necessary to do them justice. Hence the pleasant, mock-heroical giant of Pulci, and the amiable one (Dramuziando) of "Palmerin of England." Being no longer formidable, however, they were for the most part found to be dull and awkward, probably not without some ground in nature. It is observed, says Fuller (or in some such language), that, for the most part, those who exceed their fellows in a reasonable measure of height "are but indifferently furnished in the cockloft."* The little knights have as much advantage over them in battle, as the light brigantines had against the overgrown Spanish Armada. Our nursery acquaintance, Jack the Giant Killer (if he be not a burlesque on Thor himself), is an incarnation of the superior strength of wit over bulkiness. He has a cousin a monstrous giant, having three heads, and who would beat five hundred men in armor. On one occasion, Jack comes to a large house in a lonesome place, and knocking at the gate, there issues forth a giant with two heads, who nevertheless "did not seem so fiery as the former giant; for," says the Saxon author, "he was a Welsh giant."

---

* Fuller's exact words are: "Ofttimes such who are built four stories high, are observed to have little in their cockloft." — ED.

In the opening book of the "Morgante Maggiore" of Pulci, the father of modern banter and burlesque (though a genius at the same time, capable of great seriousness and pathos), there is a remarkable scene, in which Orlando comes upon a set of monks in a desert, who are pestered by three giants, their neighbors. The giants, who are of course infidels or Mahometans, are in the habit of throwing great stones at the abbey, so that the monks cannot go out for provisions. Orlando, in his errantry, comes to the abbey door, and knocks for some time in vain. At length he is let in, and the abbot apologizes, by stating the blockade in which they are kept. The holy father then proceeds to make some very singular comments, in a stanza that seems to contain the first germs of the style of Voltaire.

"Gli antichi padri nostri nel deserto,
Se le lor opre sante erano e giuste,
Del ben servir da Dio n'avean buon merto;
Ne creder sol viversin *di locuste*:
Piovea dal ciel la manna, *questo e certo*:
Ma qui convien, che spesso *assagi e guste
Sassi*, che piovon di sopra quel monte,
Che gettano Alabastro e Passamonte.

" E'l terzo ch'e Morgante piò fiero,
Isveglie e pini, e faggi, e cerri, e gli oppi,
E gettagli infin qui: questo e pur vero:
Non posso far che d'ira non iscoppi.
Mentre che parlan cosi in cimitero,
Un sasso par che Rondel quasi sgroppi ;
Che da giganti giù venne da alto
Tanto, ch'e prese sotto il tetto un salto.

" Tirati dentro, cavalier, per Dio,
Disse l'abate, *che la manna casca*.
Rispose Orlando: caro abate mio,
Costui non vuol che 'l mio caval piu pasca :
Veggo che lo guarebbe del restio:
Quel sasso par che di buon braccio nasca.

Rispose il santo padre; io non t'inganno,
Credo che 'l monte un giorno gitteranno."

"The Eremites of old, if just and true,
  And righteous in their works, had blessed cheer;
God's servants in those days no hunger knew,
  Nor lived *on those same locusts* all the year.
Doubt not, they had the rain of manna too:
  But as for us, *our pretty dishes here
Are stones;* which Passamont and Alabaster
  Rain down upon our heads, by way of taster.

"And yet those two are nothing to the third.
  He tears me up whole trees, whole horrid oaken
Trunks by the root; he does upon my word;
  Our heads infallibly will all be broken."
While thus, as if he could be overheard,
  The monk stood talking low, there came a token
So close upon the house, it seem'd all over
  With the poor devil, who leap'd under cover.

"For God's sake, come in doors, Sir!" cried the priest;
  "The manna's falling." "'Tis indeed," said t'other:
"They seem to grudge his feed to the poor beast;
  They'd cure his restiveness. Well, such another
Stunner as this proves no weak arm at least,
  No son, dear abbot, of a feeble mother."
"The Lord," exclaimed the monk, "look down upon us!
Some day, I think, they'll cast the mountain on us."

Orlando proposes to go and settle the giant; which the monk, after in vain endeavoring to dissuade him, permits.

"Disse l'abate col segnarlo in fronte, —
Va, che da Dio e me sia benedetto.
Orlando, poi che salito ebbe il monte
Si dirizzò, come l'abate detto
Gli avea, dove sta quel Passamonte;
Il quale Orlando veggendo soletto
Molto lo squadra di drieto e davante;
Poi domandò, se star volea per fante.

"E' promettava di farlo godere.
Orlando disse; pazzo Saracino,

> Io vengo a te, com' è di Dio volere,
> Per dar ti morte, e non per ragazzino.
> A'monaci suoi fatto ha dispiacere:
> Non puo piu comportarti, can mastino.
> Questo gigante armar si corse a furia,
> Quando sentì ch' e'gli diceva ingiuria."

> He cross'd the forehead of the knight, and said,
> "Go then, of God, and of our prayers befriended."
> Orlando went, and keeping in his head
> The monk's directions, hastily ascended
> The height, and struck for Passamonte's shed,
> Who seeing him thus coming unattended,
> Perused him well, then cried, "I like his plan!
> What, my new footboy? eh, my little man?"

> And then he promised him his board and pallet.
> "You stupid Saracen!" Orlando cried,
> "I come to be your death, and not your valet;
> Think of these saints here, whom you keep inside
> Their abbey: 'tisn't to be borne, nor shall it,
> You hound, you; so prepare your stupid hide."
> The giant, hearing him pour forth such evil,
> Ran in to arm him, like a very devil.

The hero kills Alabaster and Passamonte, and converts Morgante, who was prepared for him by a dream. The giant becomes a faithful servant, both of the knight and the church, and after many enormous achievements, dies of the bite of a crab; — an edifying moral. His conversation, in the course of his studies in divinity, is no less instructive; but we are at a loss how to quote it, from the reverential feelings we have for certain names, whose misuse he helps to expose. We would fain see them kept sacred against better days. There is another giant, Margutte, who speaks still more plainly, and is the prototype of a worldly philosophy, the natural offspring of a profaner superstition. "Margutte," says Ugo Foscolo, "is a very infidel giant, ready to confess his failings, and full of drollery. He sets all a-laughing, readers, giants, devils, and heroes, and he finishes his career by laughing till he bursts." *

We do not choose, however, to leave off speaking of our old friends with a burlesque; and, therefore, we shall conclude the present chapter with a few right earnest giants out of the "History of Prince Arthur." A jest cracked by that hero upon one of them is no joke infidel. It is only, as the poet says, "the ornament of his gravity." Arthur, in a battle with the Emperor of Rome, smites off by the knees the legs of a giant of the name of Galapar. "Now," quoth he, "art thou better of a size to deal with, than thou wert." The Emperor of Rome had got together fifty giants, who were "born of fiends," to break the front of the warriors' battle. But a chapter in that once popular compilation will present the reader with the complete giant of the old story-books. The style of the work is incorrect. The compiler pieces out the fine things of the old romances with a poverty of language that is a poor substitute for their simplicity; but the present extract is "a favorable specimen;" and the repetitions, and other gossiping fervors, have the proper childlike effect. We ascend the giant's mountain by due degrees. The picture of him, "baking his broad limbs by the fire," is in sturdy epic taste; and "the weltering and wallowing" of the fighters does not mince the matter. There is a Cornish hug in the battle.†

---

* See a masterly criticism in the "Quarterly Review," said to be translated from a contribution of this gentleman, and entitled "Narrative and Romantic Poems of the Italians."

† Fuller, in the "Worthies," gives this definition of a Cornish hug: "The Cornish are masters of the art of wrestling; so that if the Olympian games were now in fashion, they would come away with victory. Their hug is a

"HOW A MAN OF THE COUNTRY TOLD HIM OF A MAR-
VELLOUS GIANT, AND HOW HE FOUGHT AND CON-
QUERED HIM.

"Then came to him a husbandman of the country, and told him how there was, in the country of Constantine, beside Britain, a great giant, which had slain, murthered, and devoured much people of the country, and had been sustained seven years with the children of the commons of that land, insomuch that all the children be all slain and destroyed. And now late he hath taken the Duchess of Brittany, as she rode with her men, and had led her to his lodging, which is in a mountain: and many people followed her, more than five hundred; but all they might not rescue her, but they left her shrieking and crying lamentably; wherefore I suppose that he hath slain her in fulfilling his foul lust; she was wife unto your cousin, Sir Howel, the which was full nigh of your blood. Now, as ye are a rightful king, have pity on this lady, and revenge us all as ye are a valiant conqueror.

"'Alas!' said King Arthur, 'this is a great mischief; I had rather than the best realm that I have that I had been a furlong before him, for to have rescued that lady. Now, fellow,' said King Arthur, 'canst thou bring me there whereas this giant haunteth?'

"'Yea, Sir,' said the good man; 'lo, yonder whereas ye see the two great fires, there shall ye not fail to find him, and more treasure, as I suppose, than is in all the realm of France.'

"When King Arthur had understood this piteous case,

---

cunning close with their fellow-combatant; the fruit whereof is his fair fall, or foil at the least. It is figuratively applicable to the deceitful dealing of such, who secretly design their overthrow whom they openly embrace."—ED.

he returned into his tent, and called unto him Sir Kaye and Sir Bedivere, and commanded them secretly to make ready horse and harness for himself, and for them twain; for after evensong he would ride on pilgrimage, with them two only, unto Saint Mighel's Mount. And then anon they made them ready, and armed them at all points, and took their horses and their shields; and so they three departed thence, and rode forth as fast as they might, till they came unto the furlong of that mount, and there they alighted, and the king commanded them to tarry there, and said he would himself go up to that mount.

" And so he ascended up the mount till he came to a great fire, and there found he a careful widow wringing her hands and making great sorrow, sitting by a grave new made. And then King Arthur saluted her, and demanded her wherefore she made such lamentation. Unto whom she answered and said, 'Sir Knight, speak soft, for yonder is a devil; if he hear thee speak he will come and destroy thee. I hold thee unhappy: what dost thou here in this mountain? for if ye were such fifty as ye be, ye were not able to make resistance against this devil: here lieth a duchess dead, which was the fairest lady of the world, wife unto Sir Howel of Britain.'

"'Dame,' said the King, 'I come from the great conqueror, King Arthur, for to treat with that tyrant for his liege people.'

"'Fie upon such treaties,' said the widow; 'he setteth nought by the King, nor by no man else; but and if thou hath brought King Arthur's wife, Dame Guenever, he shall be gladder than if thou hadst given him half France. Beware; approach him not too nigh; for he hath overcome and vanquished fifteen kings, and hath made him a coat full of precious stones, embroidered with their beards, which they sent him to have his love for salvation of their people this last Christmas, and if thou wilt speak with him at yonder great fire, he is at supper.'

"'Well,' said King Arthur, 'I will accomplish my message for all your fearful words,' and went forth by the crest of that hill, and saw where he sat at supper gnawing on a limb of a man, baking his broad limbs by the fire, and breechless, and three damsels turning three broaches, whereon was broached twelve young children, late born, like young birds.

"When King Arthur beheld that piteous sight, he had great compassion on them, so that his heart bled for sorrow, and hailed him, saying in this wise: 'He that all the world wieldeth give thee short life and shameful death, and the devil have thy soul! Why hast thou murthered these young innocent children, and this duchess? Therefore arise and dress thee, thou glutton, for this day shalt thou die of my hands.'

"Then anon the giant start up, and took a great club in his hand, and smote at the King that his coronal fell to the earth. And King Arthur hit him again, that he carved his belly, and that his entrails fell down to the ground. Then the giant with great anguish threw away his club of iron and caught the King in his arms, that he crushed his ribs. Then the three damsels kneeled down, and called unto our Lord Jesus Christ, for help and comfort of the noble King Arthur. And then King Arthur weltered and wrung, that he was one while under, and another while above; and so weltering and wallowing, they rolled down the hill, till they came to the sea-mark; and as they so tumbled and weltered, King Arthur smote him with his dagger, and it fortuned they came unto the place whereas the two knights were that kept King Arthur's horse. Then when they saw the King fast in the giant's arms, they came and loosed him; and then King Arthur commanded Sir Kaye to smite off the giant's head, and to set it upon a truncheon of a spear, and bear it to Sir Howel, and tell him 'that his enemy is slain; and after let his head be bound to a barbican, that all the people may see and behold it; and go ye two to the mountain, and fetch me my shield, and my sword, and also the great club of iron; and as for the treasure, take it to you, for ye shall find there goods without number; so that I have his kirtle and the club, I desire no more. This was the fiercest giant that ever I met with, save one in the mount of Araby, which I overcame; but this was greater and fiercer.'" *

---

* "Of the two proposed books, respecting which you ask me the particulars," writes Leigh Hunt to John Forster, "one is 'The Fabulous World,' the chief portion of which, though not under that title, or, indeed, under any general one, appeared many years ago in the 'New Monthly Magazine,' as articles on Satyrs, Nymphs, Giants, Mermaids, &c. They were written with my customary painstaking, interspersed with quotations from poets of divers languages (translated when necessary), and very much approved. Everybody, to whom their incorporation into a volume was talked of, seemed to hail the notion; and, in truth, there is no such book in the language, nor, I believe, in any other. I propose to complete what was wanting to it in the 'New Monthly,' and to add the miraculous goods and chattels belonging to my fabulous people, such as Enchanted Spears, Flying Sophas, Illimitable Tents that pack up in nutshells, &c." "The Fabulous World" was never published, and the articles that were to have formed the greater part of the volume are here first collected together. — ED.

GOG AND MAGOG, AND THE WALL OF DHOULKARNEIN.

SHADOW seems to fall upon our paper at the very mention of the words, "Gog and Magog," — fine, mouth-filling, mysterious names; and of whom? Nobody knows. The names, we doubt not, have helped to keep up the interest; but the mystery is a mighty one of itself, and is found in reverend places. The grand prophet Ezekiel has a long mention of Gog and Magog, and describes them as a terrible people; but nobody has yet discovered who they are. They have been thought to be Goths, Celts, Germans, Tartars, &c.; but the most received opinion is, that they are Scythians; and there is a curious chapter in Bochart, which would corroborate a notion that is said to have prevailed among the Turks, and to which late events have given additional color: to wit, that the Russians are a part of their family.* At all events, dear reader, Gog and Magog are *not* the giants of Guildhall; albeit the latter, like the former, are unappropriated phenomena — supposed, we believe, to represent an ancient Briton and a Roman, and to be the relics of some quondam city pageant.

It seems agreed, however, that although nobody knows who Gog and Magog are, they are mixed up somehow

---

* "Geographia Sacra," cap. 13. [The reader will find a pleasant passage concerning Bochart in the article on " Bricklayers and an Old Book," in " The Seer." Hallam, too, in the " Literature of Europe," has a good word for the fine old scholar. — ED.]

THE WALL OF DHOULKARNEIN.

with the region about Caucasus; and the Orientals, who call them Yàjouje and Màjouje,* think they are to come out of the mountains on the Caspian, and overrun the world. Some hold them to be giants; others say they are an innumerable race of pigmies. Bruce was asked about them during his travels, and informed that they were horribly little. "By God's help," said the traveller, "I shall not be afraid of them, though they be a hundred times less."

An old tradition, at strange variance with prophecy, says that Gog and Magog are Jews, and that they are to appear at the time of anti-Christ, and do great harm to believers. Hear Mandeville on the subject, whose old language adds to the look of seriousness and mystery: "Among thes hillis that be there," quoth the knight, "be the Jews of the ix. kyndes enclosed, that men call Gog and Magog, and they may not come out on no syde. Here were enclosed xxii. kynges, with her folke that dwellyd ther before, and between the hilles of Sichy (Scythæ? Scythians) and the kingdom of Alisaunder. He droffe hem theder among thes hillis, for he trowed for to have enclosyd hem there thourgh strength and worckyng of mannys hond, but he myght not. And than he prayed God that he wold fullfill that he had begon, and God hard his prayer, and enclosyd thes hillis togedyr, so that the Jews dwell there as they were lokyd and speryd inne (sparred, i.e. shut up); and there be hillis all abought hem but on one syde. Why ne

---

* It is a whim of the Eastern nations, when names are familiarly coupled in history, to make them rhyme. Thus, Cain and Abel, are Cabil and Habil; and there are several other instances, but we have not time to look for them. If Beaumont and Fletcher had written among them, they would have tried hard to call them Beaumont and Fleaumont.

go they not out? seist thou. But therto I answer, thou yt be soo that yt be called a cee, yt ys a stanke (standing water) stonding among hillis. And yt ys the greatest stanke of all the world, and yf they went over the cee, they wot not where to aryve, for they wot not to speke but her owne langage; and ye shall (knowe) that the Jues have no lond of her owne in all the worlde, but they that dwellen in the hillis, and yet they bere tribute to the quene of Ermony. And sometyme yt ys soo that some Jewes gon on the hill, but they mey not passe, for thes hillis be so heigh; neverthelesse men seye of that cuntre ther bye, that in the tyme of Antecriste they shall comen out, and do moch yll herme to Cristen men. And therefore all the Jewes that dwellen in dyvers partise of the world lern to speke Ebrewe, for they trowe that dwell amonge thes hillis schall com out, and (if) they speke Ebrewe and not ellis. And in tyme of Antecriste shall thyse Jewes comen out and speke Ebrewe, and leden other Jewes into Cristendom for to destroy Cristenmen; for they wotte be her prophecies that they shall com out of Cristenmen, shall be in her subieccion, as they be now under Cristenmen. An yf ye will wit howe they shall com and fynd passage out as I have hard saye, I schall tell you. At the comynge of Antecrist, a fox schall com and make his den in the sam place where that kyng Alisaunder ded make the gattes, and schall travaille so on the erth and perce yt thorowe till that he com among the Jewes; and whan they see thys fox, they schall have great marwell of hym, for they seye never such maner of bestes, for other bestes they have amonge hem many, but non such; and they schall chese the fox, and pursue him till he be fled agen to the hole ther he cam out of; and than schall they grave after hym tyll the time they com to the gates that kyng Alisaunder dyde make of gret stonys will dight with symend (cement); and they schall brek thes gates, and so schall they fynd issue." *

The story of the fox is idle enough; but in the Pecorone of Sir Giovanni Fiorentino, quoted by the same authority, is a version of this story, in which a very romantic manœuvre of Alexander is mentioned. In order to keep his captives in subjection, "he fixed a number of trumpets on the top of the mountains, so cunningly framed *that they resounded in every breeze*. In the course of time certain birds built their nests in the mouths of the trumpets, and stopped them up, *so that the clangour gradually lessened. And when the trumpets were quite silent, the Jews ventured to climb over the mountains, and sallied forth.*"

It is curious to fancy the imprisoned nation listening year after year, and finding the sound of Alexander's dreadful trumpets grow less and less, till at length they are "silent." What has happened? Is the king dead? Have his army grown less and less, or feebler and feebler, so as to be unable to blow them? Are they all dead? Let us go and see. And forth they go, but cautiously — climbing the mountains with due care, and many listening delays. At length they arrive at the top, and see nobody — only those mighty scarecrows of trumpets, their throats stuffed up with the nests of birds! †

In these traditions there is a confusion common in the East of Alexander of Macedon, called by the Orientals

---

* Quoted by Mr. Weber in the notes to his "Metrical Romances," vol. iii. p. 323. It has long been supposed that the Jews had a national settlement somewhere about this quarter. See D'Herbelot, "Bibliothèque Orientale," art. *Jahoud;* and the late English travellers, particularly Elphinstone in his "Account of Caubul."

† Leigh Hunt tells this story more minutely in his fine poem entitled *The Trumpets of Doolkarnein.* — ED.

Dhoulkarnein, or Zulkarnein (that is to say, the Two-horned, or Lord of the East and West), with another Dhoulkarnein, who lived before the time of Abraham, and is styled Dhoulkarnein the Greater. Powerful as they think the former, the latter was still more so; and was, besides, a prophet. He was a Mussulman by anticipation; and lived sixteen hundred years. It is supposed, however, that the Greek Alexander is both Dhoulkarneins inclusive; and that in consequence of the figure he made in the East, he threw that mightier shadow of his greatness upon the mists of antiquity.

The essay towards the history of Old Arabia, by Major Price, contains a summary of this Dhoulkarnein's adventures with Gog and Magog, taken out of an Eastern historian, and containing the best account hitherto given of this awful people. The following is the amount of it: Among the children of Japhet was one of the name of Mensheje, or Meshech, who was the father of two sons called Yàjouje and Màjouje. From these descended a progeny so numerous, that, according to Abdullah, the son of Omar, if the inhabitants of the whole earth were divided into ten equal parts, nine out of the ten would be found to consist of the Yàjouje-Màjouje. They were so long-lived, that no one died till he had seen a thousand descendants of his body; and as to their stature, the race might be divided into three classes, — the Kelim-goush, or *cloth-eared*, only four cubits big; the class a hundred and twenty cubits in height; and the class who were a hundred and twenty cubits both in height and breadth. Had there been any more, we suppose that they would have been measured by the square mile. They were of enormous strength; and, though their ordinary food was the wild mulberry, were eaters of men. Agreeably to these bodily symptoms, they lived without a god, government, or good manners; and made horrible visitations in the countries about them, who lived in constant dread of their enormities.

Dhoulkarnein, in the course of an expedition which he took to survey all the countries of the earth, arrived at a territory bordering on these people, and was met with great reverence by the king of it, who, after becoming a convert to the hero's faith, begged his assistance against his dreadful neighbors. The two-horned gave his consent, but it appears that even he had no expectation of being able to conquer them, for he did not attempt it. He contented himself with building a mighty wall, called by the Eastern historian *sedde-Zulkarnein*, or bulwark of Zulkarnein; the remains of which are supposed to exist in certain ruins still visible, near the city of Derbent, on the Caspian. This wall fills the imagination almost as much as the race whom it was built to keep out; and the details of its construction are worth repeating. The monarch commenced by causing an immense ditch to be excavated between the two mountains through which the Yàjouje-Màjouje were accustomed to pass. He then filled up the ditch with enormous masses of granite, by way of foundation; and upon these (though we are not told how he contrived it) he heaped huge blocks of iron, copper, and other metals, in alternate layers like brick; the whole of which being put in a state of fusion by great fires, became, when cooled, one solid bulwark of metal, stretching from side to side, and on a level with the mountains. "On the top of all," says our author, —

[*Hiatus valde deflendus!* — We had made a memorandum of this passage some time ago, and cannot on the sudden again meet with the book, not even in the British Museum.]

The length of the wall was "one hundred and fifty parasangs, or five hundred and twenty-five miles; its breadth fifty miles; and its height two thousand eight hundred cubits, or about the height of Ben Nevis."

There is no doubt that an important barrier of some kind existed in the defiles of Caucasus, on the Caspian; there are considerable remains of one. According to some, Nouschirvan, King of Persia, a prince of the dynasty of the Sassanides, had the honor of completing what Alexander began. Others have suspected, that by the account of its magnitude the wall of China must have been meant. But these questions, into which our hankering after the truth is continually leading us, are not necessary to that other truth of fable. The wall may or may not be a truth historical; Gog and Magog are a fine towering piece of old history fabulous.

In D'Herbelot, * is an account of a Journey of Discovery made by order of a caliph of the house of the Abbasides, to inquire into this structure. With the exception of a story of a mermaid, which we have transferred to its proper place, Warton gives a better account in his "History of English Poetry."† We have taken the best circumstances from both, and proceed to lay the result before the reader.

About the year 808, the caliph Al Amin, having heard wonderful reports concerning this wall or barrier, sent his interpreter Salam, with an escort of fifty men, to view it. Salam took the route of Nouschirvan, or Northern Media, in which Filan-Schah reigned at that time. From Nous-

---

* Art. "Jagiouge et Magiouge," tom. iii. p. 270.

† Vol. i. "Dissertation I." (Quoted by Weber in the notes to his "Metrical Romances," vol. iii. p. 325.)

chirvan he passed into the territory of the Alani, and thence into the district of the lord of the marches, who dwelt in the city of Derbent, and whose title was *Lord of the Golden Throne.* For the extraordinary fish which he caught in company with their ruler, see the article upon "Sirens and Mermaids."

The Lord of the Golden Throne furnished our travellers with guides to conduct them farther north, into which quarter, having marched twenty-six days, they arrived at a land which emitted a fearful odor. They beheld, as they went, many cities destroyed by the Yàjouje-Màjouje, and in six days arrived at that part of the mountains of Caucasus, in which was the stronghold, enclosing those *captives* of Dhoulkarnein. They saw the tops of the fortress long before they reached it. On coming up, it was found to consist partly of iron and partly of a huge mountain, in an opening in which stood the gate, of enormous magnitude. This gate was supported by vast buttresses, and had an iron bulwark, with turrets of the same metal, reaching to the top of the mountain itself, which was too high to be seen. The valves, lintels, threshold, lock and key, were all of proportionate magnitude. The governor of certain places in the neighborhood comes to this castle once every week, with an escort of ten men all mounted on horseback, and striking it three times with a great hammer, *lays his ear to the door and listens.* A murmuring noise comes from within, *which is the noise of the Yàjouje-Màjouje.* Salam was told, that they often appeared on the battlements of the bulwark.

Do you not fancy, reader, that you take a journey to that awful place, and that after waiting there a long time you behold some of them looking over — huge, blackheaded giants, looking down upon you with a shadow, and making you hold your breath?

AERONAUTICS, REAL AND FABULOUS.

HE balloon, by the help of fashionable encouragement and the intrepid frequency of the ascents of Messrs. and Mesdames Green and Graham, appears to be again hovering on the borders of a little improvement. There is a talk of its being made use of for the purpose of surveying land. The only practical account it was ever turned to, was of this sort — a survey of the field of battle at Fleurus; where the French prevented a surprise by means of it. Ascents have been made, indeed, for scientific experiments, but not with any particular result.

Should you like, dear reader, to go up in a balloon?
Some readers. Very much indeed.
Others. Can't exactly say. Must reflect a little.

If these latter wish to have a friend to stand by them in their hesitation, I, for one, must own myself of the same mind. It would take much to make me undergo so practical a lift to the imagination. I can imagine it, "methinks," well enough as I am, — on terra firma.

> " Suave Vauxhall Gardens, turbantibus æthera throatis,
> E terra magnum alterius spectare balloonem."

> "'Tis sweet, when at Vauxhall throats tear the skies,
> To see in his balloon *another* rise."

I cannot withhold my admiration from those who go up; otherwise, perhaps, to spite them for my sense of the advantage they have over me, I would; nor can I say how immense my own valor might become, and how independent of the necessity for some prodigious cause or principle, if, instead of these sedentary turnings of paragraphs, I could grow young again, and go through a course of horseback, felicity, and the Fives' Court. But meantime, as a king of Naples once, climbing up a tree, told the courtiers who assisted him that he "found he had an antipathy to the buffalo;" so I find my antipathy is to height. I could shudder now, this moment, to recollect, that when I was a youth I once walked to the edge of Shakespeare's Cliff (higher then than at present), and looked over; though even then I was fain to stretch myself along the ground, while the friend who was with me nobly kept his legs. I should have more respect for this infirmity, if I could persuade myself that it was unavoidable by the imaginative; but Rousseau was famous for his love of these altitudes; nor is the reverse courage to be attributed to a destitution of thought for others: for the late admirable writer and most kind human being, Charles Lamb, one of the most considerate of kinsmen, and highly imaginative also in his way, could run (as he once actually did) along the top of a high parapet wall in the Temple,— so much to the terror of Hazlitt, that the latter cried out, in a sort of rage and cruel transport of sympathy, "Lamb, if you don't come down, I shall push you over." On the other hand, that I may not be supposed to be indulging myself in the lowest of all egotisms, that of parading a weakness, or the want of some common quality, I beg leave to say, that I trust I could do any sort of duty, if required of me, as well as most men, even to the walking on the edge of a precipice; though I should beg leave to be permitted to do it with a pale face. I should want that sort of courage, which removes peril by feeling none; and which, when it does not arise from having no thought at all (though the last instance forms a perplexing exception), seems to originate in some exquisite, healthy balancing of the faculties, bodily and mental ;—a thing admirable, and which I envy to the last degree. I sometimes fancy I have it, when I have been taking vigorous exercise ; but the emotion of a single morning's work over my writing-table puts it to flight. I attribute the change in myself (with regard to the power of enduring height), to a long illness I had, during which, happening to read of a similar infirmity, the impression it made upon me, when I again looked down from a high place, was tremendous ; and I have never since been able to avoid thinking of it, on the like occasions. When I was in Italy, I tried to get rid of it by pedestrian experiments on mountainous places, upon Alps and Apennines ; but it would not do. I only mortified myself to no purpose. (I find I am getting egotistical, after all ; and must beg the reader to excuse me. I would gladly hear as much about himself, or from any man.)

Hail then, gallant Greens and Grahams! and gallant Captain Currie ! and thou, Marquis of Clanricarde, worthy of thine ancestry ! It is not easy to know how far mind and matter are duly mixed up in any given aeronaut ; but the gallant Marquis, issuing from his house of legislation, where he has speech as well as a voice, taketh me mightily; and though captains are bound by office to be both gàllant and gallànt, it is not every one of them that would have the poetical enthusiasm to exclaim, when up in the clouds, " Oh, Mrs. Graham ! let us *never return to earth !*" We, envious fixtures to the ground, may smile at the exclamation ; but the critic who thought he was bantering it the other day in the newspapers, felt himself in his candor obliged to give up the laugh, and allow that the occasion justified the outbreak. I confess, I think the

Captain could not have said a better thing. On all occasions there is some one thing to be said which is better than all others; and this appears to me to have been the very one for the present. It combines the smile of pleasantry with the seriousness of a deep feeling. The clouds were looking gorgeous; the scene was new and heavenly; the world, with all its cares, was under their feet; the thought naturally arose, " Why cannot we quit all care, and live in some new and heavenly place, such as this seems to lead to? Let us do it: — let us " never return to earth."

On turning to the narrative, I find the words to be still better put, — with more of will in them, justified by the excess of beauty: " The range of clouds," Mrs. Graham tells us, were at this minute " forming an indescribable extensive circle around, in one part resembling the immense ocean, the darker clouds having the appearance of snow-clad mountains, the tops of which looked like frosted silver, from the effects of the glorious beams of the great luminary of the day." Captain Currie was so delighted with the grandeur of the scene, that in the moment of ecstasy, he suddenly exclaimed, " Oh! how awfully beautiful — how enchanting! — Oh, Mrs. Graham! *we will never return to the earth again!*" He had made up his mind.

They had at this time " obtained an altitude of above three miles and a half, having surmounted the highest strata of clouds." What a place for two human beings to find themselves in, looking upon sights never beheld but by the sun and moon, and by eyes spiritual! Who is to wonder at any enthusiasm excited by them? It seems to me that if I had been there I should have felt as if I had no business in such a region till disembodied; life and death would have seemed to meet together, and their united wonders oppressed me beyond endurance. But there is no knowing. Imagination itself familiarizes us to spectacles of things which are too much for the mechanical. It is the body which is in fault when the mind is overborne in its own business. Again, I like Mrs. Graham's committal of herself about Pope. The scene, she says, was one which, she is "convinced, would have given an energetic impetus to the ideas of the *immortal Pope himself*, to have given an adequate description." She betrays, to be sure, the extent of her reading; and though Pope is an immortal, one is accustomed to confine the epithet to immortals greater than he; but what could she do better than resort to the utmost limits of her book-knowledge, to show the height of her sensations? Poetry itself may be glad of any compliment paid it, at an elevation of three miles and a half above terra firma!

It is not improbable that they who feel apprehensive at the idea of ascending in a balloon, would feel less so when fairly up in the air, especially at a great height. There is something in the air itself at those altitudes, which supports and delights. I remember I used to have less of the feeling I have been speaking of, when standing on the greatest mountainous precipices, than on the top of a house. I have looked from a platform of the maritime Apennines, down upon the Gulf of Genoa, where the towns on the opposite coast appeared like toys in a shop-window, at a less distance from the edge of the mountain than I could have borne at a far less elevation. Extremes meet. It seemed so idle to contest a point, or to have a will not in unison with so many thousand feet, that the counter idea itself mitigated the fascination of its terror. Besides, there is a tendency in the pure air to put the bodily feelings into a state of tranquillity. It seemed as if the great, good-natured elements themselves would have supported me.

> "Ye gentle gales, upon my body blow,
> And softly lay me on the waves below."

Perhaps they might really do so if one had a good cloak on, or some such expanding piece of drapery! There was a marvellous paragraph the other day in the newspapers, stating that a young lady at Odessa had ascended in a balloon made of *paper*, which burst at a great height, and dismissed her to the earth, where she landed, nevertheless, in safety! The winds must have been conveniently opposed to her, and her garments have formed an extempore parachute, after the fashion of the hoop-petticoat described in the "Spectator." But does it not seem a shame for men to have a thought of danger, while ladies can go up in paper balloons, or in any balloons at all? One is forced, in self-defence, to conclude that these fair aërial voyagers cannot, at all events, superabound in imagination. They would hardly irritate a perverse husband with an excess of the gentle. Not that they may not be very good-humored either, nor are they bound to be masculine in an ill sense. The truth is, they stand a chance of being either very pleasant or very unpleasant people — pleasant, if their courage arises from good health, or confidence in science, and a willingness to go where their husbands go, and the reverse, in all conscience, if it be sheer want of fancy and abundance of will. I confess, if I were seeking a wife, that, on the face of the matter, I should not be desirous to fetch —

> "E'en from the golden chariot of balloon,
> A fearless dame, who touch'd a golden fee;"

and yet circumstances might render even that circumstance a touching proof of her womanhood; and I might fare worse, on the score of the truly feminine, with a screamer at a frog.

Poets go up in the air without balloons, and arrive at sensations which others must ascend in actual cars to experience. The Psalmist takes "the wings of the morning," (how beautiful!) and remains "in the uttermost parts of the sea." Goethe heard the sun rolling in thunder round the throne of God, and young Milton anticipated the grandeurs of his epic poem, and saw the thunders themselves lying in cloudy piles and mountains of sullen snow. Milton, in his nineteenth year, seems to have meditated a poem on some aërial subject, like the "Extasy," subsequently published by his contemporary Cowley, whom he is known to have highly admired in spite of his conceits. There is even a dash of Cowley's mixture of great and little things (the taste of the day) in the following lines, which, however, are a true announcement of the future Milton: —

> "I have some naked thoughts that rove about,
> And loudly knock to have their passage out;
> And, weary of their place, do only stay
> Till thou hast deck'd them in thy best array;
> That so they may, without suspect of fears,
> Fly swiftly to this fair assembly's ears.
> Yet I had rather, if I were to choose,
> Thy service in some graver subject use;
> Such as may make thee search thy coffers round,
> Before thou clothe my fancy in fit sound;
> Such where the deep transported mind may soar
> *Above the wheeling poles, and at heaven's door
> Look in,*"

(How well pitched is the pause here!)

> "and see each blissful deity,
> How he *before the thund'rous throne* does lie,

*Listening to what unshorn Apollo sings
To the touch of golden wires*, while Hebe brings
Immortal nectar to her kingly sire ;
Then passing through the spheres of watchful fire,
And misty regions of wide air next under,
And hills of snow, *and lofts of piled thunder,*
May tell at length how green-eyed Neptune raves,
In heaven's defiance mustering all his waves."

Cowley's "Extasy" is a very curious poem, provoking for its excessive mixture of mean and grand ideas. Had Cowley and Milton, instead of being kept apart by difference of political opinion, had the luck to become friends, they might have done one another great service. Milton might have saved Cowley's taste from the homely drawbacks to which good nature rendered it liable, and the highly rational amiableness of Cowley's heart might have softened the sternness of Milton, and saved it from degenerating into puritanical sourness. The opening of this poem might serve for an aëronaut when quitting the ground ; but how ludicrous is the misplaced waiving of ceremony in the second line, especially after the mighty universality of the first ! —

" I leave mortality and things below ;
I have no time in compliments to waste ;
Farewell to ye all in haste,
For I am call'd to go.
A whirlwind bears up my dull feet,
Th' officious clouds beneath them meet ;
And lo ! I mount, and lo !
How small the biggest parts of earth's proud title show !

." Where shall I find the noble British land ?
Lo ! I at last a northern speckespy,
Which in the sea does lie,
And seems a grain o' the sand !
For this will any sin or bleed ?
Of civil wars is this the meed ?
And is it this, alas ! which we — "

(Here comes a fine line),

"Oh, irony of words!—do call Great Britannie?"

He then seems to be imitating the lines of his contemporary, but in a very inferior strain. The third and fourth lines are in laughably bad taste:—

"I pass by th' arched magazines which hold
Th' eternal stores of frost, and rain, and snow;
Dry and secure I go,
Nor shake with fear or cold.
Without affright or wonder,
I meet clouds charg'd with thunder;
And lightnings on my way,
Like harmless lambent fires, about my temples play."

I pass two stanzas to come to a most noble line—

"*Where am I now?* ANGELS AND GOD IS HERE."

I know nothing finer than the use of this word *is* instead of *are*, making the idea of the presence of God swallow up that of the angels, and yet leaving a sense of them too. It is a feeling of this sort, which appears to me as if it would be overwhelming, up in that unaccustomed region of silence and vastness. This transport, in spite of some quaintness of expression, is not unworthily followed up in the succeeding lines, though in the concluding one the poet falls plump down into familiar inanity—

"Where am I now? Angels and God is here;
An unexhausted ocean of delight
Swallows my senses quite,
And drowns all what, or how, or where.
Not Paul, who first did thither pass,
And this great world's Columbus was,
The *tyrannous pleasure* can express."

That's fine; but look at the next!

"*O! 'tis too much for man! but let it ne'er be less!!*"

The next stanza is worth repeating, if only for the excessive comedy of the concluding verse: —

> " The mighty Elijah mounted so on high,
> That second man who leap'd the ditch where all
> The rest of mankind fall,
> And went not downwards to the sky.
> With much of pomp and show
> (As conqu'ring kings in triumph go)
> Did he to heaven approach;
> *And wond'rous was his way, and wond'rous was his* COACH!!"

The word "coach," it must be confessed, was not in quite such undignified repute then, as now; but still the poet had no business with it. He proceeds, however, to make good his words, by a refinement on Ovid's description of Phaeton's : —

> "'Twas gaudy all, and rich in every part:
> Of essences, and gems, and spirit of gold," &c.

There is something not so bad in "spirit of gold;" but he goes on to tell us how it was not only with "moonbeams silver'd bright," but

> " *Double-gilt* with the sun's light!"

Enough, however, of the vagaries of dear, noble-hearted, genial Cowley, who was among the Tories what Thomson was among the Whigs — one of the best specimens of hearty British nature, and only liable to want of selectness in his taste, because he had a love for every thing. My volume of Shelley happens to be lent at this moment, otherwise I could quote some fine things out of his ethereal pages; nor am I lucky enough to have by me that of Mr. Southey, in which he gives us his beautiful fiction of the Glendoveer with his heavenly boat.

Poetry and matter-of-fact meet oftener than is supposed. The first hints of aërostation may be truly said to be lost in the clouds of antiquity; but real and fabulous things of all kinds are naturally so confounded in those obscure periods of time, that it is not improbable there was some foundation in fact for the stories of Abaris, Dædalus, and others, beyond even the supposed solution of the difficulty by means of a ship. Sciences have been lost and recovered. The Chinese had been in possession, for many centuries, of inventions supposed to be original to Europe. Should there have been no art of printing, the fact of the Channel's having been crossed by men in balloons, and of the fate of poor Pilâtre de Rozier, might, in the course of time, become stories of no greater credibility than that of Dædalus and his son. Immortal poetry, at all events, keeps the tradition alive in some shape or other, not omitting those verisimilitudes which enable all stories, real or fabulous, to be true to the human heart. With what pretty pathos does Ovid describe little Icarus enjoying his father's manufacture of the wings, unconscious of the death they were to give him!

> " Puer Icarus una
> Stabat; et ignarus sua se tractare pericla,
> Ore renidenti, modo quas vaga moverat aura
> Captabat plumas; flavam modo pollice ceram
> Mollibat; lusuque suo mirabile patris
> Impediebat ópus." METAM. lib. viii.

> " Young Icarus stood by, who little thought
> That with his death he play'd; and, smiling, caught
> The feathers, tossed by the wandering air;
> Now chafes the yellow wax with busy care,
> And interrupts his sire." SANDYS.

"But for men to flye is impossible" (says this fine old translator in his notes, where he thinks to make up for his natural credulity by an occasional peremptory standing out for some matter of fact); "although," continues he,

"I am not ignorant that the like is reported of Simon Magus; which others, by the breaking of their necks, have as miserably, as foolishly, attempted. Nero exhibited this spectacle to the Romanes in their amphitheater; the poor youth fell not far from his throne, whose blood, to upbraid his cruell pastime, besprinkled his garments." Contemporary with Sandys, however, arose a learned divine, Bishop Wilkins, who was of opinion that men might not only fly, but fly to the moon. After contending for points which are now admitted (such as that the moon is a separate planet, has probably sea and land, &c.), and the supposed absurdity of which at former periods helps to give his remaining propositions a less air of the ridiculous, he gives the three following answers to the objection as to ascending above the sphere of the earth's attraction: —

"1. It is not perhaps impossible, that a man may be able to flye by the application of wings to his owne body; as angels are pictured, and as Mercury and Dædalus are fained, and as hath been attempted by divers, particularly by a Turk in Constantinople, as Busbequius relates. 2. If there be such a great *Rock* in *Madagascar*, as Marcus Polus the Venetian mentions, the feathers in whose wings are twelve foot long, which can swoope up a horse and his rider, or an elephant, as our kites doe a mouse; why, then, it is but teaching one of these to carry a man, and he may ride up thither, as Ganymed does upon an eagle. 3. Or if neither of these ways will serve, yet I doe seriously, and upon good grounds, affirm it possible to make a flying chariot; in which a man may sit, and give such a motion into it, as shall convey him through the aire. And this perhaps might be made large enough to carry divers men at the same time, together with food for their viaticum, and commodities for traffique. It is not the bignesse of any thing in this kind, that can hinder its motion, if the motive faculty be answerable thereunto. We see a great ship swim as well as a small cork, and an eagle flies in the aire as well as a little gnat. This engine may be contrived from the same principles by which Archytas made a wooden dove, and Regiomontanus a wooden eagle. I conceive it were no difficult matter if a man had leisure, to show more particularly the meanes of composing it. The perfecting of such an invention would be of such excellent use, that it were enough, not only to make a man, but the age also wherein he lives. For besides the strange discoveries that it might occasion in this other world, it would be also of inconceivable advantage for travelling, above any other conveiance that is now in use. So that, notwithstanding all these seeming impossibilities, 'tis likely enough, that there may be a meanes invented of journeying to the moone. And how happy shall they be, that are first successful in this attempt?

'' Fœlicesque animæ, quas nubila supra
Et turpes fumos, plenumque vaporibus orbem
Inserit Cœlo sancti scintilla Promethei!'

"Having thus finished this discourse, I chanced upon a late fancy to this purpose, under the feigned name of Domingo Gonzales, written by a late reverend and learned Bishop (Godwin); in which (besides sundry particulars, wherein this latter chapter did unwittingly agree with it) there is delivered a very pleasant and well-contrived fancy concerning a voyage to this other world." *

---

* " Biographical Dictionary," art. Wilkins.
[Addison, in the following letter from a projector, quietly satirizes Wilkins and his brother philosophers in the art of flying: —

The bishop, however, has here overlooked the still more formidable objection as to the power of breathing at so great an altitude. He seems to have forgotten that a man above a certain limit of the atmosphere is like a fish out of water. I have not his book at hand to see whether he notices this dilemma; though, doubtless, he would get

---

"Knowing that you are a great encourager of ingenuity, I think fit to acquaint you that I have made considerable progress in the art of flying. I flutter about my room two or three hours in a morning: and when my wings are on, can go above a hundred yards at a hop, step, and jump. I can fly already as well as a Turkey-cock, and improve every day. If I proceed as I have begun, I intend to give the world a proof of my proficiency in this art. Upon the next public thanksgiving day, it is my design to sit astride the dragon upon Bow steeple, from whence, after the first discharge of the Tower guns, I intend to mount into the air, fly over Fleet-street, and pitch upon the Maypole in the Strand. From thence, by a gradual descent, I shall make the best of my way for St. James's Park, and light upon the ground near Rosamond's pond. This, I doubt not, will convince the world that I am no pretender; but before I set out, I shall desire to have a patent for making of wings, and that none shall presume to fly, under pain of death, with wings of any other man's making. I intend to work for the court myself, and will have journeymen under me to furnish the rest of the nation. I likewise desire that I may have the sole teaching of persons of quality, in which I shall spare neither time nor pains, till I have made them as expert as myself. I will fly with the women on my back for the first fortnight. I shall appear at the masquerade, dressed up in my feathers and plumage like an Indian prince, that the quality may see how pretty they will look in their travelling habits. You know, Sir, there is an unaccountable prejudice against projectors of all kinds; for which reason, when I talk of practising to fly, silly people think me an owl for my pains; but, Sir, you know better things. I need not enumerate to you the benefits which will accrue to the public from this invention; as how much the roads of England will be saved when we travel through these new *highways*, and how all family accounts will be lessened in the article of coaches and horses. I need not mention posts and packet-boats, with many other conveniences of life, which will be supplied this way. In short, Sir, when mankind are in possession of this art, they will be able to do more business in three-score and ten years, than they could do in a thousand by the methods now in use. I therefore recommend myself and art to your patronage, and am

"Your most humble servant." — ED.]

over it with his usual vivacity. It is not a little that can stop a man who has taken his first step towards the moon. And yet the banter of the most confident of us may be balked by observing that, two years after the publication of this book, he sent forth another, "tending to prove that it is *probable* our earth is one of the planets." The man is laughed at now who ventures to think such an established tenet improbable. The "flying chariot" has been realized since Wilkins's time, in the car of the balloon; but the only persons that have succeeded in getting to the moon are Cyrano de Bergerac, Domingo Gonzales, and Ariosto's hero, Astolfo.

The first undoubted succeeders in raising a man into the air, and enabling him to continue there, were the brothers Stephen and Joseph de Montgolfier, papermakers at Lyons: the first person who so rose, but in a balloon secured to the earth by ropes, was M. Pilâtre de Rozier; and the first persons who quitted the earth entirely were the same De Rozier and the Marquis d'Arlandes. They went up together. The following is the interesting *procès verbal*, giving an account of this ascent, and signed, among others, by the illustrious Franklin, who was then commissioner in France, from the new American government:—

"To-day, Nov. 21, 1783, at the Château de la Muette, took place the experiment with the aërostatic machine of M. de Montgolfier. The sky was partly clouded, wind N. W. At eight minutes after noon, a mortar gave notice that the machine was about to be filled. In eight minutes, notwithstanding the wind, it was ready to set off, the Marquis d'Arlandes and M. Pilâtre de Rozier being in the car. It was at first intended to retain the machine awhile with ropes, to judge what weight it would bear, and see that all was right. But the wind prevented it from rising vertically, and directed it towards one of the garden walks : the ropes made several rents in it, one of six feet long. It was brought down again, and in two hours was set right. Having been filled again, it set off at fifty-four minutes past one, carrying the same persons. It rose in the most majestic manner, and when it was about two hundred and seventy feet high, the intrepid voyagers took off their hats and saluted the spectators. No one could help feeling a mingled sentiment of fear and admiration. The voyagers were soon undistinguishable ; but the machine, hovering upon the horizon, and displaying the most beautiful figure, rose at least three thousand feet high, and remained visible all the time. It crossed the Seine below the barrier of La Conférence ; and passing thence between the Ecole Militaire and the Hôtel des Invalides, was in view of all Paris. The voyagers, satisfied with their experiment, and not wishing to travel farther, agreed to descend ; but seeing that the wind was carrying them upon the houses of the Rue de Sève, Faubourg St. Germain, they preserved their presence of mind, increased the fire, and continued their course through the air till they had crossed Paris. They then descended quietly on the plain, beyond the new boulevard, opposite the mill of Croulebarbe, without having felt the slightest inconvenience, and having in the car two-thirds of their fuel. They could then, if they had wished, have gone three times as far as they did go, which was 5000 toises, done in from twenty to twenty-five minutes. The machine was seventy feet high ; forty-six feet in diameter ; it contained 60,000 cubic feet, and carried a weight of from 1600 to 1700 pounds. Given at the Château of La Muette, at five in the afternoon. Signed, Duc de Polignac, Duc de Guisnes, Comte de Polastron,

Comte de Vaudreuil, D'Hunaud, Benjamin Franklin, Faujas de St. Fond, de Lisle, le Roy, of the Academy of Sciences."

This *procès verbal* is taken from an excellent summary on the balloon, in the "Penny Cyclopædia," where it is followed by the ensuing extract from a letter of the Marquis d'Arlandes, who, after stating that he had obtained permission from M. Montgolfier to ascend alone, but that, by the advice of the latter, M. de Rozier was associated with him the evening before the ascent, proceeds thus: "We set off at 54 minutes past one. The balloon was so placed that M. de Rozier was on the West, and I on the East. The machine, says the public, rose with majesty. I think few of them saw that, at the moment when it passed the hedge, it made a half turn, and we changed our positions, which, thus altered, we retained to the end. I was astonished at the smallness of the noise or motion occasioned by our departure among the spectators. I thought they might be astonished and frightened, and might stand in need of encouragement" (a beautiful trait of coolness from the man in the balloon to those on *terra firma*). "I waved my arm with little success; I then drew out and shook my handkerchief, and immediately perceived a great movement in the garden. It seemed as if the spectators all formed one mass, which rushed by an involuntary motion towards the wall, which it seemed to consider as the only obstacle between us. At this moment M. de Rozier called out, 'You are doing nothing, and we do not rise.' I begged his pardon, took some straw, moved the fire, and turned again quickly; but I could not find La Muette. In astonishment, I followed the river with my eye, and at last found where the Oise joined it. Here then, was Conflans; nearest to them, I repeated, Poissy,

St. Germain, St. Denis, Sève, then I am still at Poissy, or at Chaillot. Accordingly, looking down through the car, I saw the Visitation de Chaillot. M. Pilâtre said to me at this moment, 'Here is the river, and we are descending.' 'Well, my friend,' said I, 'more fire;' and we set to work. But, instead of crossing the river, as our course towards the Invalides seemed to indicate, we went along the Ile des Cygnes, entered the principal bed again, and went up the stream till we were above the Barrière la Conférence. I said to my brave associate, 'Here is a river, which is very difficult to cross.' 'I think so,' said he; 'you are doing nothing.' 'I am not so strong as you,' I answered; 'and we are well as we are.' I stirred the fire, and seized a bundle of straw, which, being too much pressed, did not light well. I shook it over the flame, and the instant after I felt as if I had been seized under the arms, and I said to my friend, 'We are rising now, however.' 'Yes, we are rising,' he answered, coming from the interior, where he had been seeing all was right. At this moment I heard a noise high up in the balloon, which made me fear it had burst. I looked up, and saw nothing; but, as I had my eyes fixed on the machine, I felt a shock, the first I had experienced. The shock was upwards, and I cried out, 'What are you doing, — are you dancing?' 'I am not stirring.' 'So much the better,' I said; 'this must be a new current, which will, I hope, take us off the river.' Accordingly, I turned to see where we were, and found myself between the Ecole Militaire and the Invalides, which we had passed by about 400 toises. M. Pilâtre said, 'We are in the plain.' 'Yes,' I said, 'we are getting on.' 'Let us set to work,' he replied. I heard a noise in the machine, which I thought came from the breaking of a cord. I looked in and saw that the southern part was full of round holes, several of them large. I said, 'We must get down.' 'Why?' 'Look,' said I. At the same time, I took my sponge (pyrotechnical term), and easily extinguished the fire, which was enlarging such of the holes as I could reach.; but on trying if the balloon was fast to the lower circle, I found it easily came off. I repeated to my companion, 'We must descend.' He looked round him, and said, 'We are over Paris.' Having looked to the safety of the cords, I said, 'We can cross Paris.' We were now coming near the roofs: we raised the fire, and rose again with great ease. I looked under me and saw the Missions Etrangerès, and it seemed as if we were going towards the towers of St. Sulpice, which I could see. Raising ourselves, a current turned us south. I saw on my left a wood, which I thought was the Luxembourg. We passed the Boulevard; and I called out, 'Pied à terre.' We stopped the fire, but the brave Pilâtre, who did not lose his self-possession, thought we were coming upon mills and warned me. . . . We alighted at the Butte aux Cailles, between the mill Des Merveilles and the Moulin Vieux. The moment we touched land, I held by the car with my two hands: I felt the balloon press my head lightly. I pushed it off, and leaped out. Turning towards the balloon, which I expected to find full, to my great astonishment, it was perfectly empty and flattened."

The second balloon voyage was that of Messrs. Charles and Robert, at sunset, from the Tuileries, Dec. 1, 1783. M. Charles reascended immediately afterwards, alone, to the height of nearly two miles, and *saw the sun rise again.* "I was the only illuminated object," he says; "all the rest of nature being plunged in shadow."

M. de Rozier ascended for the third time, in the third voyage, in company with Joseph Montgolfier, and six other persons. The balloon was "intended for six only, and these were found too many, but no one could be induced to give up his place. The instant after the ropes had been cut, a seventh person jumped in. A rent in the balloon caused it to descend with great velocity, but no one was hurt."

February 22, 1784, a small balloon, launched by itself, from Sandwich, crossed the channel.

March 2, 1784, M. Blanchard made his first ascent from Paris, carrying a parachute in case of need.

April 25, 1784, Messrs. de Morveau and Bertrand ascended 13,000 English feet, at Dijon, and thought they found some effect produced by the use of oars.

May 20, 1784, ladies first went up, four of them with two gentlemen, but in a balloon secured by ropes. Madame Thible, however, ascended on the 4th of June, with one other person in a free balloon.

September 15, 1784, the first voyage in England was made by Vincenzo Lunardi, who took with him a dog, a cat, and a pigeon. He rose from the artillery-ground, and landed at Standon, near Ware, in Hertfordshire.

January 7, 1785, M. Blanchard and Dr. Jeffries crossed the channel. June 15, 1785, M. Pilâtre de Rozier, and M. Romain ascended from Boulogne, with the intention of crossing the channel, when the balloon took fire, and the gallant De Rozier, the *first aëronaut*, together with his unfortunate companion, fell from a height of a thousand yards, and was killed on the spot.

July 22, General Money ascended at Norwich, and the balloon dropped in the water, where the voyager remained six hours before he was rescued.

In 1807, M. Garnerin ascended from Paris, and landed at, or rather "was dashed against Mount Tonnerre, 300 miles from that place, after running very great risks."

September 21, 1802, M. Garnerin descended from a balloon by means of a parachute, near the Small-pox Hospital, at St. Pancras. I remember seeing him, frightfully swung about at first, but afterwards coming down steadily, to the great relief of an enormous multitude, whose sudden gathering together in the fields almost astonished me as much as the parachute.

Several ascents have been made for the purpose of scientific experiments; among others, one by M. Gay Lussac, at Paris, to the height of 23,000 feet.

"In 1806, Carlo Brioschi, astronomer-royal at Naples, ascended with Signor Andreani, who had been the first Italian aëronaut. Trying to rise higher than M. Gay Lussac, they got into an atmosphere so rarefied as to burst the balloon. Its remnants checked the velocity of their descent; and this, with their falling on an open space, saved their lives; but Brioschi contracted a complaint, which brought him to his grave."

Since this period many ascents have been made both in France and England, by a variety of aëronauts, one of whom, in the latter country, generally keeps possession of the public curiosity for a certain time, and makes the balloon a sort of profession. It is said in the publication above quoted, that the balloon is now a "toy in which ascents are sometimes made to amuse a crowd," and that what "was honorable risk, so long as any thing could be gained to science, is now mere foolhardiness, and will continue to be so until some definite object be proposed, and some probable means suggested of attaining it." But this is surely too harsh a judgment. Amusement is worth something for its own sake, and courage too; and by familiarity with the machine, gradual improvements in its construction must be acquired, and its safety made greater, for greater purposes. It is a long time since any catastrophe has happened to a balloon made of the ordinary materials.

The greatest fault to be found with aërial voyagers is the dulness of the narratives which they put forth. One would expect from their strange experiences more lively and copious accounts; but whether it is that they are not gifted with too much observation themselves, or have less to observe than might be supposed, — whether they are not imaginative or well informed enough, or the air is for the most part as barren of sights as the ocean, nothing can be more barren or brief than their narratives in general. All which the traveller tells us is, that he rose to a certain height, and went to a certain distance; that the spectacle around him was very imposing, or grand, or magnificent; that he saw Kensington Gardens distinctly, or the old London docks; that the trees looked like hedges; and that he alighted safely at such and such a place, where he was treated with great hospitality by Mr. Jenkins; after which, he and his balloon returned to town the same evening by a post-chaise. Truth is certainly not "more wondrous than fiction" here. Ariosto's hippogriff and Mr. Southey's aërial boat are abundantly more entertaining.

In the first navigations of this kind, allowance is to be made for the fluttered feelings of the voyagers, which, indeed, are a zest of themselves. And perhaps the same allowance is to be made now, especially as there is still a tendency in the parties to compliment one another upon their courage. The thing to be desired, however (besides going up in more picturesque and varied countries — mountainous, in particular), is, that they would tell us *all* they feel or see, giving us the minutest details, scenery, sensation, experiment, disappointment, every thing. It is hard if the results would not be more interesting than at present. Why does not Lord Clanricarde favor us with an account? Or Captain Currie? It would be curious to see the characters of the different minds, and of the impressions made upon them. By and by, people would be going up to record their experiences; and being on the watch for observation, new appearances would be noticed. How should *you* feel, reader, up in the sky? What should you say or do? Do you think you should be inclined to be merry or grave? or timid or bold?—or neither? Should you think most of the third heaven, or of Piccadilly?

Horace is of opinion that the man who first went to sea must have had a heart triple-hooped with brass. What would he have said to the first aëronaut? He has anticipated without knowing it, in the same ode: —

> Cœlum ipsum petimus stultitiâ.
> Our folly strives to reach the heav'ns themselves.

It is thought a fearful thing at sea to have only a plank between you and death; but you have a comparatively kindly element to fall into, something more substantial, and which gives you a chance. You can struggle with it, swim, cry out, get upon a piece of wood or a hen-coop. Being a swimmer myself, I never feel as if I should be lost in water, as long as I had only myself to attend to. But think of a plank's being between you and a distance of three miles and a half, — all' sheer emptiness! Down you go, precipitate, chucked out; a dreg at once tragical and ridiculous; a fluttering bit of humanity, no securer than a lump of lead, no stronger than a feather. To be sure, there are instances of being saved; but who could think of them at the moment of ejaculation?

Should a time, however, arrive when balloons shall be equally safe and guidable, steerable against the wind, &c., (and who, in this age of science and steam-engines, shall say there will not?) it is very pleasant to fancy one's self *keeping one's balloon*, like a carriage, ordering it hither and thither, visiting one's friends over the house-tops, and "looking in," not at the street door, but at the drawing-room window, &c. The poet wishes that he could fly; so that when pleasure flagged in the East, he might

"Order his wings, and be off to the West."

This undoubtedly would be pleasanter; more convenient, and not so expensive. But he might have both; and wings, compared with a balloon, would be like horse-keeping, compared with a carriage. Beaux, instead of cantering beside barouches, would then flutter three miles high by the side of a car; and a hero in a novel would gloriously catch his mistress in his arms, if her balloon burst, and convey her safely to earth, as Mercury did Psyche. People would then be accused, not of running, but of flying after the girls; and we should see an air-lounger fifty feet above Regent Street, pursuing some maid-servant, or pretty milliner, in and out the chimneys.*

---

* "I have fully considered the project of these our modern Dædalists," says Addison, in the "Guardian," "and am resolved so far to discourage it, as to prevent any person from flying in my time. It would fill the world with innumerable immoralities, and give such occasions for intrigues, as people cannot meet with who have nothing but legs to carry them. You should have a couple of lovers making a midnight assignation upon the top of the monument, and see the cupola of St. Paul's covered with both sexes, like the outside of a pigeon-house. Nothing would be more frequent than to see a beau flying in at a garret window, or a gallant giving chase to his mistress, like a hawk after a lark. There would be no walking in a shady wood without springing a covey of toasts. The poor husband could not dream what was doing over his head: if he were jealous, indeed, he might clip his wife's wings; . . . what con-

But war! What a horrible thing to be shot in a balloon! To "fall gloriously" *that* way, in battle!

"'There was *mounting* 'mong Graemes of the Netherby clan;
Forsters, Fenwicks, and Musgraves, they '*rose*,' and they ran."

Think of two armies, or navies rather, meeting over Salisbury Plain, and commencing their broadsides! What a tumbling forth of bodies and cocked hats; of mid-balloon-men, and admirals of the sky-blue! " Sky-scraper " would then indeed be a proper term for the top of a vessel; and " Pegasus," and " Bellerophon," names to some purpose. But war must go out, as nations advance, whether they arrive at these altitudes or not. Peaceful railroads will supersede hostile inroads (as old Fuller would have said): nations will no more go to war, when they become such close neighbors and their interests are so bound up together, than Middlesex will fight with Surrey, or tradesmen with their employers.

ON THE TALKING OF NONSENSE.

HERE is no greater mistake in the world than the looking upon every sort of nonsense as want of sense. Nonsense, in the bad sense of the word, like certain suspicious ladies, is very fond of bestowing its own appellation,—particularly upon what renders other persons agreeable.

---

cern would the father of a family be in all the time his daughter was upon the wing? Every heiress must have an old woman flying at her heels. In short, the whole air would be full of this kind of *gibier*, as the French call it."
— ED.

But nonsense, in the good sense of the word, is a very sensible thing in its season; and is only confounded with the other by people of a shallow gravity, who cannot afford to joke.

These gentlemen live upon credit, and would not have it inquired into. They are perpetual beggars of the question. They are grave, not because they think, or feel the contrast of mirth, for then they would feel the mirth itself; but because gravity is their safest mode of behavior. They must keep their minds sitting still, because they are incapable of a motion that is not awkward. They are waxen images among the living, — the deception is undone, if the others stir, — or hollow vessels covered up, which may be taken for full ones, — the collision of wit jars against them, and strikes out their hollowness.

In fact, the difference between nonsense not worth talking, and nonsense worth it, is simply this: the former is the result of a want of ideas, the latter of a superabundance of them. This is remarkably exemplified by Swift's "Polite Conversation," in which the dialogue, though intended to be a tissue of the greatest nonsense in request with shallow merriment, is in reality full of ideas, and many of them very humorous; but then they are all commonplace, and have been said so often, that the thing uppermost in your mind is the inability of the speakers to utter a sentence of their own; — they have no ideas at all. Many of the jokes and similes in that treatise are still the current coin of the shallow; though they are now pretty much confined to gossips of an inferior order, and the upper part of the lower classes.

On the other hand, the wildest rattling, as it is called, in which men of sense find entertainment, consists of nothing but a quick and original succession of ideas, — a finding, as it were, of something in nothing,—a rapid turning of the hearer's mind to some new face of thought and sparkling imagery. The man of shallow gravity, besides an uneasy half-consciousness that he has nothing of the sort about him, is too dull of perception to see the delicate links between one thought and another; and he takes that for a mere chaos of laughing jargon, in which finer apprehensions perceive as much delightful association, as men of musical taste do in the most tricksome harmonies and accompaniments of Mozart or Beethoven. Between such gravity and such mirth, there is as much difference as between the driest and dreariest psalmody, and that exquisite laughing trio, — E voi ridete, — which is sung in Cosi Fan Tutte. A quaker's coat and a garden are not more dissimilar;— nor a death-bell, and the birds after a sunny shower.

It is on such occasions indeed that we enjoy the perfection of what is agreeable in humanity,— the harmony of mind and body,— intellect and animal spirits. Accordingly the greatest geniuses appear to have been proficients in this kind of nonsense, and to have delighted in dwelling upon it, and attributing it to their favorites. Virgil is no joker, but Homer is: and there is the same difference between their heroes, Æneas and Achilles, the latter of whom is also a player on the harp. Venus, the most delightful of the goddesses, is philomeides, the laughter-loving;— an epithet, by the bye, which might give a good hint to a number of very respectable ladies, "who love their lords," but who are too apt to let ladies less respectable run away with them. Horace represents Pleasantry as fluttering about Venus in company with Cupid, —

   Quem *Jocus* circumvolat, et Cupido ;

and these are followed by Youth, the enjoyer of animal

spirits, and by Mercury, the god of persuasion. There is the same difference between Tasso and Ariosto as between Virgil and Homer; that is to say, the latter proves his greater genius by a completer and more various hold on the feelings, and has not only a fresher spirit of Nature about him, but a truer, because a happier; for the want of this enjoyment is at once a defect and a deterioration. It is more or less a disease of the blood; — a falling off from the pure and uncontradicted blithesomeness of childhood; a hampering of the mind with the altered nerves; — dust gathered in the watch, and perplexing our passing hours.

It may be thought a begging of the question to mention Anacreon, since he made an absolute business of mirth and enjoyment, and sat down systematically to laugh as well as to drink. But on that very account, perhaps, his case is still more in point; and Plato, one of the gravest, but not the shallowest, of philosophers, gave him the title of the Wise. The disciple of Socrates appears also to have been a great enjoyer of Aristophanes; and the divine Socrates himself was a wit and a joker.

But the divine Shakespeare; — the man to whom we go for every thing, and are sure to find it, grave, melancholy, or merry, — what said he to this exquisite kind of nonsense? Perhaps next to his passion for detecting nature, and over-informing it with poetry, he took delight in pursuing a joke; and the lowest scenes of his in this way say more to men whose faculties are fresh about them, and who prefer enjoyment to criticism, than the most doting of commentators can find out. They are instances of his animal spirits, — of his sociality, — of his passion for giving and receiving pleasure, — of his enjoyment of something wiser than wisdom.

The greatest favorites of Shakespeare are made to resemble himself in this particular: Hamlet, Mercutio, Touchstone, Jaques, Richard the Third, and Falstaff, "inimitable Falstaff," are all men of wit and humor, modified according to their different temperaments or circumstances, — some from health and spirits, others from sociality, others from a contrast with their very melancholy. Indeed melancholy itself with the profoundest intellects, will rarely be found to be any thing else than a sickly temperament, induced or otherwise, preying in its turn upon the disappointed expectation of pleasure, — upon the contradiction of hopes, which this world is not made to realize, though (let us never forget) it is made, as they themselves prove, to suggest. Some of Shakespeare's characters, as Mercutio and Benedick, are almost entirely made up of wit and animal spirits; and delightful fellows they are; and ready, from their very taste, to perform the most serious and manly offices. Most of his women, too, have an abundance of natural vivacity. Desdemona herself is so pleasant of intercourse in every way, that upon the principle of the respectable mistakes above mentioned, the Moor, when he grows jealous, is tempted to think it a proof of her want of honesty. But we must make Shakespeare speak for himself, or we shall not know how to be silent on this subject. What a description is that which he gives of a man of mirth, — of a mirth too, which he has expressly stated to be within the limit of what is becoming! It is in Love's Labor Lost.

> "A merrier man,
> Within the limit of becoming mirth,
> I never spent an hour's talk withal.
> His eye begets occasion for his wit:
> For every object that the one doth catch,
> The other turns to a mirth-moving jest;

ON THE TALKING OF NONSENSE.   289

> Which his fair tongue, conceit's expositor,
> Delivers in such apt and gracious words,
> That aged ears play truant at his tales,
> And younger hearings are quite ravished;
> So sweet and voluble is his discourse."

We have been led into these reflections, partly to introduce the conclusion of this article, — partly from being very fond of a joke ourselves, and so making our self-love as proud as possible, — and partly from having spent some most agreeable hours the other evening with a company, the members of which had all the right to be grave and disagreeable that rank and talent are supposed to confer, and yet from the very best sense or forgetfulness of both, were as lively and entertaining to each other as boys. Not one of them perhaps but had his cares, — one or two, of no ordinary description; but what then? These are the moments, if we can take advantage of them, when sorrows are shared, even unconsciously; — moments, when melancholy intermits her fever, and hope takes a leap into enjoyment; — when the pilgrim of life, if he cannot lay aside his burden, forgets it in meeting his fellows about a fountain; and soothes his weariness and his resolution with the sparkling sight, and the noise of the freshness.

To come to our anticlimax, for such we are afraid it must be called after all this grave sentiment and mention of authorities. The following dialogue is the substance of a joke (never meant for its present place) that was started the other day upon a late publication. The name of the book it is not necessary to mention, especially as it was pronounced to be one of the driest that had appeared for years. We cannot answer for the sentences being put to their proper speakers. The friends, whom we value most, happen to be great hunters in this way; and the reader may look upon the thing as a specimen of a joke run down, or of the sort of nonsense above mentioned; so that he will take due care how he professes not to relish it. We must also advertise him, that a proper quantity of giggling and laughter must be supposed to be interspersed, till towards the end it gradually becomes too great to go on with.

A. Did you ever see such a book?

B. Never, in all my life. It's as dry as a chip.

A. As a chip? A chip's a slice of orange to it.

B. Ay, or a wet sponge.

A. Or a cup in a currant tart.

B. Ah, ha; so it is. You feel as if you were fingering a brick-bat.

A. It makes you feel dust in the eyes.

B. It is impossible to shed a tear over it. The lachrymal organs are dried up.

A. If you shut it hastily, it is like clapping together a pair of fresh-cleaned gloves.

B. Before you have got far in it, you get up to look at your tongue in a glass.

A. It absolutely makes you thirsty.

B. Yes:— If you take it up at breakfast, you drink four cups instead of two.

A. At page 30 you call for beer.

B. They say it made a Reviewer take to drinking.

A. They have it lying on the table at inns to make you drink double. The landlord says "A new book, Sir," and goes out to order two neguses.

B. It dries up every thing so, it has ruined the draining business.

A. There is an Act of Parliament to forbid people's passing a vintner's with it in their pockets.

B. The Dutch subscribed for it to serve them instead of dykes.*

---

* A witty correspondent of Leigh Hunt—probably Charles Lamb—thus "pampers" into pleasant "exaggeration" the joke about the "dry book:"—

What? and do you really mean to say that this is "a specimen of a joke run down?" For "run down," read "wound up." There are limits to human wisdom, but none to folly. Hercules might come to a stand-still, but our merry friend with the bauble was never heard to exclaim *ne plus ultra*. After reading your pleasant article in our coterie the other evening, we took down "the book" you allude to (it gets into most libraries of any size), and it quickly inspired us with the following dry jokes:—

A. Et certamen erat, Corydon cum Thyrside, magnum,—Posthabui——seria ludo. Allons. I know an infant who, on merely seeing it, was cured of water in the head.

B. A dropsical gentleman, given over by his physicians, was never tapped again after he had read it.

A. Carry a copy under your arm, and you need no umbrella.

B. A number were sent over to Ireland, just at the time they had almost abandoned the idea of reclaiming bogs.

C. A friend of mine on the coast has recovered ninety acres of land from the sea, by possessing a copy. He calls it his Copyhold land.

A. Southey tells me, that Kehama had one in his pocket when he walked into the ocean, and it divided.

B. When I travel, I always take it to read in bed; and though I never use a warming pan, I never had the rheumatism in my life.

A. It must be a very ancient work, for we owe to it the origin of the terms "dry study," "dry reading," &c.

C. It is not generally known, but the conjurer rubs himself with it, before he dips his arm in boiling water.

B. Some one swearing, kissed it in jest, which brought on the complaint of parched lips. Feeling this, he threw it down, and trampling on it, was laid up with chilblains.

C. It is an excellent substitute in bathing for an oil-skin cap.

A. It is said to be very superior in efficacy to a deviled biscuit.

D. It is found in most libraries, which occasions such an accumulation of dust in those places.

B. A nurse, who took it up by accident, was obliged to wean the child directly.

D. A widow that I know, after burying her husband, retired to her closet,

A RAINY DAY.

HE day that we speak of is a complete one of its kind, beginning with a dark wet morning, and ending in a drenching night. When you come down stairs from your chamber, you find the breakfast-room looking dark, the rain-spout pouring away, and unless you live in a street of traffic, no sound out of doors but a clack of pattens and an occasional clang of milk-pails. (Do you see the rogue of a milkman? He is leaving them open to catch the rain.)

We never see a person going to the window on such a morning, to take a melancholy look out at the washed houses and pavement, but we think of a reanimation which we once beheld of old Tate Wilkinson. But observe how sour things may run into pleasant tastes at last. We are by no means certain that the said mimetic antique, Tate Wilkinson, was not Patentee of the York Theatre, wore a melancholy hat tied the wrong way, and cast looks of

---

and having read a page, never shed another tear. This may be considered its greatest miracle!

C. Its author, who is said to have run mad during the dog-days, wrote it on the sands of Africa, from whence it was brought to this quarter of the globe by means of the Sirocco. "Nil dictum, quod non dictum prius," is, as you now see, a mighty foolish maxim; and, as a foolish bit of Latin makes a very appropriate conclusion to the English that precedes it,

> "*Vivas in amore jocisque* —
> Vive vale."

> [Live and preserve your health for other folks,
> And don't forget to love, and crack your jokes] — ED.

unutterable dissatisfaction at a rainy morning, purely to let his worthy successor and surpasser in mimicry, Mr. Charles Mathews, hand down his aspect and countenance for the benefit of posterity. We once fell into company with that ingenious person at a bachelor's house, where he woke us in the morning with the suspicious sound of a child crying in another room. It was having its face washed; and had we been of a scandalizing turn, or envied our host for his hospitality, we should certainly have gone and said that there was a child in his house who inherited a sorrowful disposition from somebody, and who might be heard (for all the nurse's efforts of a morning) whining and blubbering in the intervals of the wash-towel; — now bursting into open-mouthed complaint, as it left him to dip in the water; and anon, as it came over his face again, screwing up its snubbed features and eyes, and making half-stifled obstinate moan with his tight mouth. The mystery was explained at breakfast; and as it happened to be a rainy morning, we were entertained with the reanimation of that "living dead man," poor Tate aforesaid, — who had been a merry fellow, too, in his day. Imagine a tall, thin, withered, desponding-looking old gentleman, entering his breakfast-room with an old hat on, tied under his chin the wrong way of the flap, — a beaver somewhat of the epicene order, so that you do not know whether it is his wife's or his own. He hobbles and shrinks up to the window, grunting gently with a sort of preparatory despair; and having cast up his eyes at the air, and seen the weathercock due east and the rain set in besides, drops the corners of his mouth and eyes into an expression of double despondency, not unmixed (if we may speak unprofanely) with a sort of scornful resentment; and turns off with one solitary, brief, comprehensive, and groaning ejaculation of "Eh — Christ!" — We never see anybody go to the window of a rainy morning, but we think of this poor old barometer of a Patentee, whose face, we trust, will be handed down in successive fac-similes to posterity, for their edification as well as amusement; for Tate had cultivated much hypochondriacal knowledge in his time, and been a sad fellow, in a merry sense, before he took to it in its melancholy one.

The preparation for a rainy day in town is certainly not the pleasantest thing in the world, especially for those who have neither health nor imagination to make their own sunshine. The comparative silence in the streets, which is made dull by our knowing the cause of it, — the window-panes drenched and ever-streaming, like so many helpless cheeks, — the darkened rooms, — and at this season of the year, the having left off fires; — all fall like a chill shade upon the spirits. But we know not how much pleasantry can be made out of unpleasantness, till we bestir ourselves. The exercise of our bodies will make us bear the weather better, even mentally; and the exercise of our minds will enable us to bear it with patient bodies in-doors, if we cannot go out. Above all, some people seem to think that they cannot have a fire made in a chill day, because it is summer-time, — a notion which, under the guise of being seasonable, is quite the reverse, and one against which we protest. A fire is a thing to warm us when we are cold; not to go out because the name of the month begins with J. Besides, the sound of it helps to dissipate that of the rain. It is justly called a companion. It looks glad in our faces; it talks to us; it is vivified at our touch; it vivifies in return; it puts life and warmth and comfort in the room. A good fellow is bound to see that he leaves this substitute for his company when he goes out, especially to a lady; whose solitary work-table in a chill room on such a day, is a very melancholy refuge. We exhort her, if she can afford it, to take a book and a footstool, and plant herself before a good fire. We know of few baulks more complete, than coming down of a chill morning to breakfast, turning one's chair as usual to the fireside, planting one's feet on the fender and one's eyes on a book, and suddenly discovering that there is no fire in the grate. A grate, that ought to have a fire in it, and gapes in one's face with none, is like a cold, grinning, empty rascal.

There is something, we think, not disagreeable in issuing forth during a good, honest summer rain, with a coat well buttoned up, and an umbrella over our heads. The first flash open of the umbrella seems a defiance to the shower, and the sound of it afterwards, over our dry heads, corroborates the triumph. If we are in this humor, it does not matter how drenching the day is. We despise the expensive effeminacy of a coach; have an agreeable malice of self-content at the sight of crowded gate-ways; and see nothing in the furious little rain-spouts, but a lively emblem of critical opposition, — weak, low, washy, and dirty, gabbling away with a perfect impotence of splutter.

Speaking of malice, there are even some kinds of legs which afford us a lively pleasure in beholding them splashed.

Lady. Lord, you cruel man!

Author. Nay, I was not speaking of yours, madam. How could I wish ill to any such very touching stockings? And yet, now I think of it, there are very gentle and sensitive legs (I say nothing of beautiful ones, because all gentle ones are beautiful to me), which it is possible to behold in a very earthy plight; — at least the feet and ankles.

L. And pray, sir, what are the very agreeable circumstances under which we are to be mudded?

Author. Fancy, madam, a walk with some particular friend, between the showers, in a green lane; the sun shining, the hay sweet-smelling, the glossy leaves sparkling like children's cheeks after tears. Suppose this lane not to be got into, but over a bank and a brook, and a good savage assortment of wagon-ruts. Yet the sunny-green so takes you, and you are so resolved to oblige your friend with a walk, that you hazard a descent down the slippery bank, a jump over the brook, a leap (that will certainly be too short) over the ploughed mud. Do you think that a good thick-mudded shoe and a splashed instep would not have a merit in his barbarous eyes, beyond even the neat outline of the Spanish leather, and the symbolical whiteness of the stocking? Ask him.

L. Go to your subject, do.

Author. Well, I will. You may always know whether a person wishes you a pleasant or unpleasant adventure, by the pleasure or pain he has in your company. If he would be with you himself (and I should like to know the pleasant situation, or even the painful one, if a share of it can be made pleasant, in which we would not have a woman with us), you may rest assured that all the mischief he wishes you is very harmless. — At the same time, if there are situations in which one could wish ill even to a lady's leg, there are legs and stockings which it is possible to fancy well-splashed upon a very different principle.

Gentleman. Pray, sir, whose may those be?

Author. Not yours, sir, with that delicate flow of trouser, and that careless yet genteel stretch-out of toe. There is an humanity in the air of it, — a graceful, but at the same time manly, sympathy with the drapery beside it. I allude, sir, to one of those portentous legs, which belong to an over-fed money-getter, or to a bulky methodist parson, who has doating dinners got up for him by his hearers. You know the leg I mean. It is "like unto the sign of the leg," only larger. Observe, I do not mean every kind of large leg. The same thing is not the same thing in every one, — if you understand that profound apophthegm. As a leg, indifferent in itself, may become very charming, if it belongs to a charming owner; so even when it is of the cast we speak of in a man, it becomes more or less unpleasant according to his nature and treatment of it. I am not carping at the leg of an ordinary jolly fellow, which good temper as well as good living helps to plump out, and which he is, after all, not proud of exhibiting; keeping it modestly in a boot or trousers, and despising the starched ostentation of the other: but at a regular, dull, uninformed, hebetudinous, "gross, open, and palpable" leg, whose calf glares upon you like the ground-glass of a post-chaise lamp. In the parson it is somewhat obscured by a black stocking. A white one is requisite to display it in all its glory. It has a large balustrade calf, an ankle that would be monstrous in any other man, but looks small from the contrast, a tight knee, well buttoned, and a seam inexorably in the middle. It is a leg at once gross and symbolical. Its size is made up of plethora and superfluity; its white cotton stockings affect a propriety; its inflexible seam and side announce the man of clock-work. A dozen hard-worked dependants go at least to the making up of that leg. If in black, it is the essence of infinite hams at old ladies' Sunday dinners. Now, we like to see a couple of legs, of this sort, in white, kicking their way through a muddy street, and splashed unavoidably as they go, till their horrid glare is subdued into spottiness. A lamplighter's ladder is of use, to give him a passing spurn: upon which the proprietor, turning round to swear, is run against in front by a wheelbarrow; upon which, turning round again to swear worse, he thrusts his heel upon the beginning of a loose stone in the pavement, and receives his final baptism from a fount of mud.

Our limits compel us to bring this article to a speedier conclusion, than we thought; and, to say the truth, we are not sorry for it; for we happened to break off here in order to write the one following, and it has not left us in a humor to return to our jokes.*

We must therefore say little of a world of things we intended to descant on,— of pattens, — and eaves, — and hackney-coaches, — and waiting in vain to go out on a party of pleasure, while the youngest of us insists every minute that "it is going to hold up," — and umbrellas dripping on one's shoulder, — and the abomination of soaked gloves, — and standing up in gate-ways, when you hear now and then the passing roar of rain on an umbrella, — and glimpses of the green country at the end of streets,— and the footmarked earth of the country-roads,— and clouds eternally following each other from the west,— and the scent of the luckless new-mown hay, — and the rainbow, — and the glorious thunder and lightning, — and a party waiting to go home at night, — and, last of all, the delicious moment of taking off your wet things, and resting in the dry and warm content of your gown and slippers.†

---

* "The Italian Girl," in the "Indicator." — ED.

† Years after the publication of this sprightly effusion, the author wrote another article on "A Rainy Day," which the reader will find (if he cares to look for it) in "The Seer." — ED.

THE TRUE ENJOYMENT OF SPLENDOR.

A CHINESE APOLOGUE.

DOUBTLESS, saith the illustrious Me, he that gaineth much possession hath need of the wrists of Hong and the seriousness of Shan-Fee, since palaces are not built with a teaspoon, nor are to be kept by one who runneth after butterflies. But above all it is necessary that he who carrieth a great burden, whether of gold or silver, should hold his head as lowly as is necessary, lest on lifting it on high he bring his treasure to nought, and lose with the spectators the glory of true gravity, which is meekness.

Quo, who was the son of Quee, who was the son of Quee-Fong, who was the five-hundred and fiftieth in lineal descent from the ever-to-be-remembered Fing, chief minister of the Emperor Yau, one day walked out into the streets of Pekin in all the lustre of his rank. Quo, besides the greatness of his birth and the multitude of his accomplishments, was a courtier of the first order, and his pigtail was proportionate to his merits, for it hung down to the ground and kissed the dust as it went with its bunch of artificial roses. Ten huge and sparkling rings, which incrusted his hands with diamonds, and almost rivalled the sun that struck on them, led the ravished eyes of the beholders to the more precious enormity of his nails, which were each an inch long, and by proper nibbing might have taught the barbarians of the West to look with just scorn on their many writing-machines. But even these were nothing to the precious stones that covered him from head to foot. His bonnet, in which a peacock's feather was stuck in a most engaging manner, was surmounted by a sapphire of at least the size of a pigeon's egg; his shoulders and sides sustained a real burden of treasure; and as he was one of the handsomest men at court, being exceedingly corpulent, and indeed, as his flatterers gave out, hardly able to walk, it may be imagined that he proceeded at no undignified pace. He would have ridden in his sedan, had he been lighter of body, but so much unaffected corpulence was not to be concealed, and he went on foot that nobody might suspect him of pretending to a dignity he did not possess. Behind him, three servants attended, clad in the most gorgeous silks; the middle one held his umbrella over his head; he on the right bore a fan of ivory, whereon were carved the exploits of Whay-Quang; and he on the left sustained a purple bag on each arm, one containing opium and Arecanut, the other the ravishing preparation of Gin-Seng, which possesses the Five Relishes. All the servants looked the same way as their master, that is to say, straight forward, with their eyes majestically half-shut, only they cried every now and then with a loud voice, "Vanish from before the illustrious Quo, favorite of the mighty Brother of the Sun and Moon."

Though the favorite looked neither to the right nor to the left, he could not but perceive the great homage that was paid him as well by the faces as the voices of the multitude. But one person, a Bonze, seemed transported beyond all the rest with an enthusiasm of admiration, and followed at a respectful distance from his side, bowing to the earth at every ten paces and exclaiming, "Thanks to my lord for his jewels!" After repeating this for about six times, he increased the expressions of his gratitude, and said, "Thanks to my illustrious lord from his poor servant for his glorious jewels,"—and then again, "Thanks to my illustrious lord, whose eye knoweth not degradation, from his poor servant, who is not fit to exist before him, for his jewels that make the rays of the sun look like ink." In short, the man's gratitude was so great, and its language delivered in phrases so choice, that Quo could contain his curiosity no longer, and turning aside, demanded to know his meaning: "I have not given you the jewels," said the favorite, "and why should you thank me for them?"

"Refulgent Quo!" answered the Bonze, again bowing to the earth, "what you say is as true as the five maxims of Fo, who was born without a father:—but your slave repeats his thanks, and is indeed infinitely obliged. You must know, O dazzling son of Quee, that of all my sect I have perhaps the greatest taste for enjoying myself. Seeing my lord therefore go by, I could not but be transported at having so great a pleasure, and said to myself, 'The great Quo is very kind to me and my fellow-citizens: he has taken infinite labor to acquire his magnificence; he takes still greater pains to preserve it, and all the while, I, who am lying under a shed, enjoy it for nothing.'"

A hundred years after, when the Emperor Whang heard this story, he diminished the expenditure of his household one half, and ordered the dead Bonze to be raised to the rank of a Colao.

RETROSPECTIVE REVIEW — MEN WEDDED TO BOOKS — THE CONTEST BETWEEN THE NIGHTINGALE AND MUSICIAN.

E have often had occasion to think of the exclamation of that ingenious saint, who, upon reading a fine author, cried out "Pereant male qui ante nos nostra dixerunt!"— "Deuce take those who have said our good things before us!"— Now, without mentioning the extendibility (we are writing in high spirits, early on a fine morning, and cannot stop to find a better word)— without mentioning the extendibility of this judicious imprecation to deeds, as, "Deuce take those who have anticipated our exploits.;" or to possessions, as "Confound those fellows that ride in our coaches and eat our asparagus;"— we cannot help thinking the phrase particularly applicable to those who have read our authors — "Plague take those who anticipate our articles, — who quote our highly interesting passages out of old books."

Here is a Retrospective Review set up, which with an alarming precision of prepositions undertakes to make "Criticisms upon, Analyses of, and Extracts from, curious, useful, and valuable Books in all languages, that have been published from the Revival of Literature to the Commencement of the Present Century;"— And what is very inconsiderate, it performs all this, and more. Its criticisms are of a very uncritical kind; deep and well-tempered. It can afford to let other people have their merits. Proud of the literature of past ages, it is nevertheless not at all contemptuous of the present; and even in reading a lecture to modern critics, as it does admirably in its second number in an article on the once formidable John Dennis, it expostulates in so genial and informing a spirit, that he must be a very far gone critical old woman indeed, who does not feel inclined to leave off the brandy-drinking of abuse, — the pin-sticking of grudging absurdity. It is extremely pleasant to see it travelling in this way over so wide a range of literature, warming as well as penetrating as it goes, with a sunny eye, — now fetching out the remotest fields, and anon driving the shadows before it and falling in kindly lustre upon ourselves. The highest compliment that we can pay it, or indeed any other work, is to say, that the enthusiasm is young, and the knowledge old ; — a rare, a wise, and a delightful combination.*

It is lucky for us that we happened to speak of this work in another publication, the very day before the appearance of the second number ; for the latter contained a very kind mention of the little work now before the reader ; and thus our present notice might have been laid

---

* "The Retrospective Review," says Lowell, in a pleasant passage of his uncollected prose writings, "continues to be good reading, in virtue of the antique aroma (for wine only acquires its *bouquet* by age) which pervades its pages. Its sixteen volumes are so many tickets of admission to the vast and devious vaults of the sixteenth and seventeenth centuries, through which we wander, tasting a thimbleful of rich Canary, honeyed Cyprus, or subacidulous Hock, from what dusty butt or keg our fancy chooses. The years during which this Review was published were altogether the most fruitful in genuine appreciation of old English literature. Books were prized for their imaginative, and not their antiquarian, value, by young writers who sat at the feet of Lamb and Coleridge." One of the best and most agreeable contributors to the "Retrospective Review" was Thomas Noon Talfourd, the biographer of Lamb, and the early friend and literary guide of Dickens. He wrote the article on John Dennis, mentioned above, and those on North's "Life of Lord Guilford," "Rymer on Tragedy," Colley Cibber's "Apology for his Life," and Wallace's "Prospects of Mankind, Nature, and Providence." — ED.

to the account of a vanity, which, however gratified, is not the cause of it. The value of praise as well as rebuke does indeed depend upon the nature of the persons from whom it comes; and it is as difficult not to be delighted with panegyric from some, as it is easy to be indifferent to it, or even pained by it, from others. But when we confess our pleasure in this instance, we can say with equal truth, that all our feelings and hopes being identified with the cause of what we think good and kind, our very self-love becomes identified with it; and we would consent to undergo the horrible moment of annihilation and oblivion the next instant, could we be assured that the world would be as happy as we were unremembered. And yet what a Yes! would that be!

But to get from under the imagination of this crush of our being, and emerge into the lightness and pleasurability of life, — it was very hard of the Retrospective Review, that, while it praised us, it should pick our intentional pockets of an extract we had long thought of making from an old poet. We allude to the poem called "Music's Duel" from Crashaw. Here the feelings expressed at the head of our paper come over us again. It has been said of fond students that they were "wedded to their books." We have even heard of ladies who have been jealous of an over-seductive duodecimo; as perhaps they might, if every literary husband or lover were like the collegian in Chaucer, who would rather have

> At his bed's head,
> A twenty books, clothed in black or red,
> Of Aristotle and his philosophy,
> Than robes rich, or fiddle, or psaltry.

And yet we feel that we could very well like them too at the bed's head, without at all diminishing our regard for what should be at the bed's heart. We could sleep under them as under a bower of imaginations. We are one of those who like to have a book behind one's pillow, even though we know we shall not touch it. It is like having all our treasures at hand.

But if people are to be wedded to their books, it is hard that under our present moral dispensations, they are not to be allowed the usual exclusive privileges of marriage. A friend thinks no more of borrowing a book nowadays, than a Roman did of borrowing a man's wife; and what is worse, we are so far gone in our immoral notions on this subject, that we even lend it as easily as Cato did his spouse. Now what a happy thing ought it not to be to have exclusive possession of a book,—one's Shakespeare, for instance; for the finer the wedded work, the more anxious of course we should be, that it should give nobody happiness but ourselves. Think of the pleasure not only of being with it in general, of having by far the greater part of its company, but of having it entirely to one's self; of always saying internally, " It is my property ; " of seeing it well-dressed in "black or red," purely to please one's own eyes; of wondering how any fellow could be so impudent as to propose borrowing it for an evening; of being at once proud of his admiration, and pretty certain that it was in vain; of the excitement nevertheless of being a little uneasy whenever we saw him approach it too nearly; of wishing that it could give him a cuff of the cheek with one of its beautiful boards, for presuming to like its beauties as well as ourselves ; of liking other people's books, but not at all thinking it proper that they should like ours ; of getting perhaps indifferent to it, and then comforting ourselves with the reflection that others are not so, though to no purpose; in short, of all the mixed transport and anxiety to which the exclusiveness of the book-wedded state would be liable; not to mention the impossibility of other people's having any literary offspring from our fair unique, and consequently of the danger of loving any compilations but our own. Really if we could burn all other copies of our originals, as the Roman Emperor once thought of destroying Homer, this system would be worth thinking of. If we had a good library, we should be in the situation of the Turks with their seraglios, which are a great improvement upon our petty exclusivenesses. Nobody could then touch our Shakespeare, our Spenser, our Chaucer, our Greek and Italian writers. People might say, "Those are the walls of the library!" and "sigh, and look, and sigh again;" but they should never get in. No Retrospective rake should anticipate our privileges of quotation. Our Mary Woolstonecrafts and our Madame de Staëls,—no one should know how finely they were lettered,—what soul there was in their disquisitions. We once had a glimpse of the feelings which people would have on these occasions. It was in the library of Trinity College, Cambridge. The keeper of it was from home; and not being able to get a sight of the Manuscript of Milton's "Comus," we were obliged to content ourselves with looking through a wire work, a kind of safe, towards the shelf on which it reposed. How we winked, and yearned, and imagined we saw a corner of the all-precious sheets, to no purpose! The feelings were not very pleasant, it is true; but then as long as they were confined to others, they would of course only add to our satisfaction.

But to come to our extract; for not being quite recovered yet from our late ill-health, we mean to avail ourselves of it still. It is remarkable, as the Reviewer has observed, for "a wonderful power over the resources of our language." The original is in the "Prolusions of Strada," where it is put into the mouth of the celebrated Castiglione, as an imitation of the style of Claudian. From all that we recollect of that florid poet, the imitation, to say the least of it, is quite as good as any thing in himself. Indeed, as a description of the niceties of a musical performance, we remember nothing in him that can come up to it. But what will astonish the reader, in addition to the exquisite tact with which "Strada" is rendered by the translator, is his having trebled the whole description, and with an equal minuteness in his exuberance. We cannot stop to enter into the detail of the enjoyment, as we would; and indeed we should not know perhaps how to express our sense of it but by repeating his masterly niceties about the "clear unwrinkled song," the "warbling doubt of dallying sweetness," the "ever-bubbling spring," the kindling of the bird's

> " soft voice
> In the close murmur of a sparkling noise,"

the "quavering coyness," with which the musician "tastes the strings," the "surges of swoln rhapsodies," the "full-mouthed diapason swallowing all;" and, in short, the whole "pride, pomp, and circumstance" of masterly playing, from its lordly sweep over the full instrument to the "capering cheerfulness" of a guitar accompaniment. The man of letters will admire the power of language; and to the musician and other lovers of music we are sure we are affording a great treat. Numbers of them will never have found their sensations so well analyzed before. Part of the poetry, it is true, is in a false and overcharged taste; but in general the exuberance is as true as it is surprising, for the subject is exuberant and requires it.

We should observe, before the concert begins, that

Castiglione is represented by Strada as having been present at this extraordinary duel himself; and however fabulous this may seem, there is a letter extant from Bartolomeo Ricci to Giambattista Pigna, contemporaries of Tasso, in which he says, that Antoniano, a celebrated improvisatore of those times, playing on the lute after a rural dinner which the writer had given to his friends, provoked a nightingale to contend with him in the same manner. Dr. Black, in his "Life of Tasso," by way of note upon this letter, quotes a passage from Sir William Jones, strongly corroborating such stories; and indeed, when we know what parrots and other birds can do, especially in imitating and answering each other, and hear the extravagant reports to which the powers of the nightingale have given rise, such as the story of an actual dialogue in Buffon, we can easily imagine that the groundwork of the relation may not be a mere fable. "An intelligent Persian," says Sir William, "declared he had more than once been present, when a celebrated lutanist, surnamed Bulbul (the nightingale), was playing to a large company in a grove near Shiraz, where he distinctly saw the nightingales trying to vie with the musician; sometimes warbling on the trees, sometimes fluttering from branch to branch, as if they wished to approach the instrument, and at length dropping on the ground in a kind of ecstasy, from which they were soon raised, he assured me, by a change in the mode."

MUSIC'S DUEL.

Now westward Sol had spent the richest beams
Of noon's high glory, when hard by the streams
Of Tiber, on the scene of a green plat,
Under protection of an oak, there sat
A sweet lute's-master: in whose gentle airs
He lost the day's heat and his own hot cares.
   Close in the covert of the leaves there stood

A nightingale, come from the neighbouring wood :
(The sweet inhabitant of each glad tree,
Their muse, their syren, harmless syren she)
There stood she list'ning, and did entertain
The music's soft report : and mould the same
In her own murmurs, that whatever mood
His curious fingers lent, her voice made good:
The man perceiv'd his rival and her art,
Dispos'd to give the light-foot lady sport
Awakes his lute, and 'gainst the fight to come
Informs it, in a sweet præludium
Of closer strains ; and ere the war begin,
He lightly skirmishes on every string,
Charg'd with a flying touch : and straightway she
Carves out her dainty voice as readily,
Into a thousand sweet distinguish'd tones,
And reckons up in soft divisions,
Quick volumes of wild notes; to let him know
By that *shrill taste*, she could do something too.

His nimble hands' instinct then taught each string
A cap'ring cheerfulness, and made them sing
To their own dance ; now *negligently rash*
He throws his arm, and *with a long-drawn dash*
Blends all together; then distinctly trips
From this to that ; then quick returning skips
And snatches this again, and pauses there.
She measures every measure, everywhere
Meets art with art ; sometimes, as if in doubt,
Not perfect yet, and fearing to be out,
Trails her plain ditty in one long-spun note,
Through the sleek passage of her open throat,
A clear unwrinkled song; then doth she point it
With tender accents, and severely joint it
By short diminutives, that being rear'd
In controverting warbles evenly shar'd,
With her sweet self she wrangles. He amaz'd
That from so small a channel should be rais'd
The torrent of a voice, whose melody
Could melt into such sweet variety,
Strains higher yet, that tickled with rare art
The tattling strings (each breathing in his part)
Most kindly do fall out ; the grumbling base
In surly groans disdains the treble's grace :

The high-perch'd treble chirps at this, and chides,
Until his finger (moderator) hides
And closes the sweet quarrel, rousing all
Hoarse, shrill, at once; as when the trumpets call
Hot Mars to th' harvest of death's field, and woo
Men's hearts into their hands: this lesson too
She gives him back; *her supple breast thrills out*
Sharp airs, and staggers in a warbling doubt
Of dallying sweetness, hovers o'er her skill,
And folds in wav'd notes, with a trembling bill,
The pliant series of her slippery song;
Then starts she suddenly *into a throng*
Of short thick sobs, whose thund'ring volleys float,
And roll themselves over her lubric throat
In panting murmurs, still'd out of her breast.
That ever-bubbling spring, the sugar'd nest
Of her delicious soul, that there does lie
Bathing in streams of liquid melody;
Music's best seed-plot, where, in ripen'd airs
A golden-headed harvest fairly rears
His honey-dropping tops, plow'd by her breath
Which there reciprocally laboureth.
In that sweet soil, it seems a holy choir,
Founded to th' name of great Apollo's lyre,
Whose silver roof rings with the sprightly notes
Of sweep-lipp'd angel-imps, that swill their throats
In cream of morning Helicon, and then
Prefer soft anthems to the ears of men,
To woo them from their beds, still murmuring
That men can sleep while they their matins sing:
(Most divine service) whose so early lay
Prevents the eye-lids of the blushing day!
There you might hear her kindle her soft voice
In the close murmur of a sparkling noise,
And lay the ground-work of her hopeful song,
Still keeping in the forward stream, so long
Till a sweet whirlwind (striving to get out)
Heaves her soft bosom, wanders round about,
And makes a pretty earthquake in her breast,
Till the fledg'd notes at length forsake their nest,
Fluttering in wanton shoals, and to the sky,
Wing'd with their own wild echoes, prattling fly.
She opes the floodgate, and lets loose a tide

MUSICAL DUEL.

Of streaming sweetness, which in state doth ride
On the wav'd back of every swelling strain,
Rising and falling in a pompous train.
And while she thus discharges *a shrill peal
Of flashing airs, she qualifies their zeal
With the cool epode of a graver note,*
Thus high, thus low, as if her silver throat
Would reach the brazen voice of war's hoarse bird ;
Her little soul is ravish'd: and so pour'd
Into loose ecstasies, that she is plac'd
Above herself, music's enthusiast.

Shame now and anger mix'd a double strain
In the musician's face ; yet once again,
Mistress, I come ; now reach a strain, my lute,
Above her mock, or be forever mute.
But tune a song of victory to me ;
As to thyself, sing thine own obsequy ;
*So said, his hands sprightly as fire he flings,
And with a quavering coyness tastes the strings,*
The sweet-lip'd sisters musically frighted,
Singing their fears, are fearfully delighted.
Trembling as when Apollo's golden hairs
Are fann'd and frizzled in the wanton airs
Of his own breath: which, married to his lyre,
Doth tune the spheres, and make heaven's self look higher.
*From this to that, from that to this he flies,
Feels music's pulse in all her arteries,*
Caught in a net which there Apollo spreads,
His fingers struggle with the vocal threads,
Following those little rills, he sinks into
A sea of Helicon ; his hand does go
Those parts of sweetness which with nectar drop,
Softer than that which pants in Hebe's cup.
The humourous strings expound his learned touch
By various glosses ; now they seem to grutch,
And murmur in a buzzing din, then gingle
In shrill-tongu'd accents, striving to be single.
Every smooth turn, every delicious stroke
Gives life to some new grace ; thus doth invoke
Sweetness by all her names ; thus, bravely thus
(Fraught with a fury so harmonious)
The lute's light genius now does proudly rise,
Heav'd on the surges of swoln rhapsodies,

Whose flourish (meteor-like) doth curl the air
With flash of high-born fancies; here and there
Dancing in lofty measures, and anon
*Creeps on the soft touch of a tender tone:
Whose trembling murmurs melting in wild airs
Run to and fro, complaining his sweet cares;*
Because those precious mysteries that dwell
In music's ravish'd soul he dares not tell,
But whisper to the world: thus do they vary,
Each string his note, as if they meant to carry
Their master's blest soul (snatch'd out at his ears
By a strong ecstasy) through all the spheres
Of music's heaven, and seat it there on high
In th' empyreum of pure harmony.
At length, (after so long, so loud a strife
Of all the strings, still breathing the best life
Of blest variety, attending on
His fingers' fairest revolution,
In many a sweet rise, many as sweet a fall)
A full-mouth'd diapason swallows all.
 This done, he lists what she would say to this,
And she, although her breath's late exercise
Had dealt too roughly with her tender throat,
Yet summons all her sweet powers for a note.
Alas! in vain! for while (sweet soul) she tries
To measure all those wild diversities
Of chatt'ring strings, by the small size of one
Poor simple voice, rais'd in a natural tone;
She fails, and failing grieves, and grieving dies.
She dies: and leaves her life the victor's prize,
Falling upon his lute; O fit to have
(That liv'd so sweetly) dead, so sweet a grave!

This exquisite story has had another relator in Ford, the dramatist, and according to a great authority, a finer one.* The passage is very beautiful, certainly, especially in the outset about Greece; and if the story is to be taken

---

* Charles Lamb; who says, in one of the notes to his "Specimens of English Dramatic Poets," "This story, which is originally to be met with in 'Strada's Prolusions,' has been paraphrased in rhyme by Crashaw, Ambrose

as a sentiment, it must be allowed to surpass the other;
but as an account of the Duel itself, it is assuredly as
different as playing is from no playing. Sentiment, however, completes everything, and we hope our readers will
enjoy with us the concluding from Ford:—

> *Menaphon.* Passing from Italy to Greece, the tales
> Which poets of an elder time have feign'd
> To glorify their Tempe, bred in me
> Desire of visiting that paradise.
> To Thessaly I came, and living private,
> Without acquaintance of more sweet companions
> Than the old inmates to my love, my thoughts,
> I day by day frequented silent groves
> And solitary walks. One morning early
> This accident encounter'd me: I heard
> The sweetest and most ravishing contention
> That art and nature ever were at strife in.
> *Amethus.* I cannot yet conceive what you infer
> By art and nature.
> *Men.* I shall soon resolve ye.
> A sound of music touch'd mine ears, or rather
> Indeed entranc'd my soul; as I stole nearer,
> Invited by the melody, I saw
> This youth, this fair-fac'd youth, upon his lute,
> With strains of strange variety and harmony,
> Proclaiming, as it seem'd, so bold a challenge
> To the clear choristers of the woods, the birds,
> That as they flock'd about him, all stood silent,
> Wond'ring at what they heard. I wonder'd too.
> *Amet.* And so do I; good, on!
> *Men.* A nightingale,
> Nature's best skill'd musician, undertakes
> The challenge, and for ev'ry several strain
> The well-shap'd youth could touch, she sung her down;
> He could not run division with more art
> Upon his quaking instrument, than she,

Phillips, and others; but none of these versions can at all compare for harmony
and grace with this blank verse of Ford's; it is as fine as anything in Beaumont
and Fletcher; and almost equals the strife it celebrates." — ED.

The nightingale, did with her various notes
Reply to. For a voice, and for a sound,
Amethus, 'tis much easier to believe
That such they were, than hope to hear again.
   Amet. How did the rivals part?
   Men.   You term them rightly,
For they were rivals, and their mistress harmony.
Some time thus spent, the young man grew at last
Into a pretty anger, that a bird
Whom art had never taught clefs, moods, or notes,
Should vie with him for mastery, whose study
Had busied many hours to perfect practice:
To end the controversy, in a rapture
Upon his instrument he plays so swiftly,
So many voluntaries, and so quick,
That there was curiosity and cunning,
Concord in discord, lines of diff'ring method
Meeting in one full centre of delight.
   Amet. Now for the bird.
   Men.   The bird, ordain'd to be
Music's first martyr, strove to imitate
These several sounds: which, when her warbling throat
Fail'd in, for grief down dropp'd she on his lute
And brake her heart. It was the quaintest sadness,
To see the conqueror upon her hearse,
To weep a funeral elegy of tears,
That, trust me, my Amethus, I could chide
Mine own unmanly weakness, that made me
A fellow-mourner with him.
   Amet.   I believe thee.
   Men. He look'd upon the trophies of his art,
Then sigh'd, then wip'd his eyes, then sigh'd and cried,
" Alas, poor creature! I will soon revenge
This cruelty upon the author of it;
Henceforth this lute, guilty of innocent blood,
Shall never more betray a harmless peace
To an untimely end:" and in that sorrow,
As he was dashing it against a tree,
I suddenly stept in.

THE MURDERED PUMP.

A STORY OF A WINTER'S NIGHT.

THE hero of the following sketch is a real person, and the main points in it, the pump and the refuge in the cellar, are recorded as facts. The latter took place in the house of Sir John Trevor, the Master of the Rolls, a kinsman of Mr. Lloyd's, who was a proud and irritable Welshman.

TIME. *The Beginning of the Last Century.*

SCENE. *A Fog in Holborn towards Dawn. Enter Two Middle-aged Gentlemen, of the names of* LANE *and* LLOYD, *coming towards an old Pump*

Lane. You're so quarrelsome, when you drink.
Lloyd. (*Hiccuping.*) No, I ain't.
Lane. Always contradicting everybody.
Lloyd. (*Hiccuping.*) No, I ain't.
Lane. So eager to say No, merely because other people say Yes.
Lloyd. (*Hiccuping.*) No, I ain't.
Lane. Why, you do it this very instant.
Lloyd. No, I don't.
Lane. You can't say Yes, if you would.
Lloyd. (*Hiccuping.*) Yes, I can.
Lane. No, you can't. Your very Yes is a No. You merely say it to contradict.
Lloyd. No, I don't.
Lane. Pooh, nonsense! And then you must draw your sword, forsooth, and add fury to folly. You'll get some tremendous lesson some day, and you really need it. I should like to give it you.
Lloyd. (*Violently.*) Take care, George Lane. (LLOYD *stumbles.*)
Lane. Take you care, of the gutter. I shan't pick you up. I shall leave you to cool yourself.
Lloyd. (*Hiccuping.*) No, you won't.
Lane. Oh, what, you remember my carrying you home last Thursday, do you? And this is your gratitude.

Lloyd. Damn gratitude! I'll not be insulted.
Lane. Yes, you will, — by forgiveness. You'll insult others, and be forgiven.
Lloyd. No, I won't. Nobody shall forgive Roderick Lloyd. I should like to see 'em. (*Standing still, putting his hand on his sword, and trying to speak very loudly.*) Who forgives me? Who forgives Lloyd, I say? Come into the court, you rascal.
Lane. (*Laughing.*) Come along. Nonsense.
Lloyd. Who forgives Roderick Lloyd, — Promontory, Pro—thonotary of—
Lane. Of North Wales, Marshal to Baron Price, and so forth. Come along, and don't be an ass.
Lloyd. Fire and fury! A what? (*Drawing his sword, and coming on.*) A prothonotary called — (*He stumbles against the Pump.*) Who the devil are you? Get out of the way.
Lane. (*Aside.*) A good thing, faith. He shall have it out.
Lloyd. (*To the Pump.*) Who are you, I say? Why don't you speak?
Lane. He says you may go to the devil.
Lloyd. The devil he does! Draw, you scoundrel, or you're a dead man.
Lane. He stands as stiff as a post.
Lloyd. (*Furiously.*) Draw, you infernal fool.
Lane. He says he defies your toasting-fork, and your Welsh-rabbit to boot.
Lloyd. Blood and thunder! (*He runs the Pump through the body.*)
Lane. Good Heavens, Lloyd! what have you done? We must be off.
Lloyd. Pink'd an infernal Welsh-rabbit — I mean a toasting, damnation prothonotary. Who's afraid?
Lane. Come along, man. This way, this way. Here, down the lane. The constables are coming, and you've done it at last, by Heavens!

[*Exeunt down Chancery Lane.*

SCENE II. *Daylight in a cellar.* LLOYD *and* LANE *discovered listening.*

Lane. It's nobody, depend on't. It's too early. Nobody is stirring yet. Don't be down-hearted, Rory. You're a brave man, you know; and the worse the luck, the greater the lion.
Lloyd. But I've left my sword in him.
Lane. No, have you though? That's unlucky.
Lloyd. Oh, that punch, that punch! and that cursed fool — poor fool, I should say, — Progers. I shall come to shame, George. Oh, I shall. To shame and to suffering. (*He walks to and fro.*)
Lane. No, no. The sword had no name on it?
Lloyd. Yes, it had.
Lane. But only initials.

Lloyd. No. Full length.
Lane. What, titles and all? Roderick Lloyd, Prothono—-
Lloyd. No, no. But name and address. Oh, wouldn't it be better if you would go out and see how matters are going on?
Lane. What, the crowd, and all that? No, I think best not. We are too well known hereabouts.
Lloyd. Then why didn't you go further?
Lane. You were too far gone already, Rory. I don't mean to jest. You can't suppose me guilty of that. But it's a phrase, you know. You were very drunk, and to say the truth, very wilful.
Lloyd. Oh, I was, I was.
Lane. You wouldn't be guided at all.
Lloyd. Too true, too true.
Lane. I was twenty minutes getting you away from that apple-woman, and half an hour, I'm sure, in persuading you to rise from the door-way. (*Lloyd groans.*) Then you wouldn't let me take your sword (for I was afraid of some mischief), and you must have stood, I think, ten minutes against that shop-window, damning us all round — all the friends you had been disputing with.
Lloyd. Oh, don't tell me all that again. It's cruel of you, George. Listen ! great Heavens, listen !
Lane. It's only some milkman.
Lloyd. Only a milkman ! How do you know? Besides, what do you mean by "only a milkman?" Can't a milkman hang me? Can't a milkman be furious? furious about a man that's killed?
Lane. Pray, sit down, and be easy. Sir John, 'tis true, doesn't appear ; but that's his way. He never stands by a friend, you know; that is to say, openly. But secretly he can do any thing ; and he will. I tell you again, that I woke him directly we came into the house, and he gave me his solemn oath that he would smuggle you into Wales, in the boot of his carriage. It is not a very big boot, but it's better than nothing.
Lloyd. Oh, a paradise, a paradise, if I were but in it. But repeat to me, George. What sort of a man was it that I had the misfortune to — to —. Tell me he was a bad fellow at any rate — a mohawk — a gallows bird, or something of that sort.
Lane. I wish I could. But he was a young gentleman, plainly in liquor himself.
Lloyd. Didn't he carry himself very stiffly?
Lane. Wonderfully, but with a sort of innocence too.
Lloyd. But he said insulting things.
Lane. Not he. That was your fancy.
Lloyd. What, didn't he tell me to go to the devil, and all that?
Lane. Not a bit. He was quite silent, and, in fact, evidently did not hear a word you uttered.

Lloyd. How strange, how horribly strange! and that I should have had all those drunken fancies!

Lane. That's your way, you know, owing to your confounded temper. I beg your pardon.

Lloyd. Oh, I beg yours — everybody's — his.

Lane. You do? Roderick Lloyd beg pardon! Is it positively come to that? to that, which you have sworn a thousand times you would never do to any man living, be the circumstances what they might. Well, this is a change. Ah, ha! (*Laughing.*) A change and a lesson, eh, Rory? And you'll be a good boy, and never do the like again, I suppose?

Lloyd. (*Astonished.*) What has come to you? Is this kindness? Is this humanity?

Lane. Yes, Rory, very good kindness indeed, and very good humanity; for I have now a piece of news to tell you, that will pay you for all you have suffered, and me for all that you have ever made me suffer; for what with frights for you, and perils of *fights* for you, and some three or four flounderings in the gutter, there has been no mean balance, let me tell you, on the side of your old friend. So, mark me, you didn't leave your sword in the man, for I've got it; and you didn't do him any mischief at all, for you couldn't; and he was no man whatsoever, Rory, for he was a Pump.

Lloyd. A Pump? — Swear it. Shout it. Make me sure of it somehow or other, and I'm in heaven.

Lane. (*Tenderly.*) Do you think I'd play with you, Rory, any longer, and in a way like this?

(*Here* Mr. RODERICK LLOYD, *Prothonotary of North Wales, after embracing his friend, jumps and dances in ecstasy about the cellar.*)

Lloyd. By Heaven, it's almost worth going through misery, in order to taste of such happiness.

Lane. That's one of the very points I have so often insisted on in our disputes. Hail to your new metaphysics, Rory; — to your enlightened theosophy.

Lloyd. Come; let's to breakfast then somewhere, out of this infernal cellar. I own my lesson, George. You might have let me off too, a little sooner, I think, eh? Spared me a few sharp sentences. (*They prepare to go.*)

Lane. I'm afraid you're growing a little disconcerted, Rory.

Lloyd. No, I ain't; but —

Lane. A little contradictory again.

Lloyd. No, I ain't; but —

Lane. You contradict me, however, as usual.

Lloyd. No, I don't. Oh, damn it, come along. (*Looking red, and laughing with his companion.*) You won't tell anybody, will you, George?

Lane. Haven't I the blood of the Lloyds in me. Am I not a gentleman, Rory?

Lloyd. You are, you are. So we will drink gallons of tea to settle that

confounded punch; and, I think, I'll never say "No, I don't" as long as I
live; at least not to you, my boy; that is to say, if you behave yourself.
  Lane. Ah, you feel a little angry with me still.
  Lloyd. No, I—(LANE *laughs.*) Damn it. Well, I do; but not half so
angry as happy, either. So, come along.   [*Exeunt.*

CHRISTMAS EVE AND CHRISTMAS DAY.

F the three great annual holidays, Christmas
day is, for many reasons, the greatest; and
one reason among others is, that it stands out
of the winter-time, the first and warmest of
them. It is the eye and fire of the season, as
the fire is of Christmas and of one's room. We have always loved it, and ever shall; first (to give a child's reason, and a very good one, too, in this instance), because
Christmas day is Christmas day; second (which is included
in that reason, or rather includes it, for it is the greatest),
because of a high argument, which will more properly
stand by itself at the close of this article; third, because
of the hollies and other evergreens which people conspire
to bring into cities and houses on this day, making a kind
of summer in winter, and reminding us that —

 "The poetry of earth is never dead;"

fourth, because we were brought up in a cloistered school,*
where carols had not gone out of fashion, and used to sit
in circles round huge fires, fit to roast an ox, making inconceivable bliss out of cakes and sour oranges; fifth,
because of the fine things which the poets and others have

---

* Christ's Hospital.

said of it; sixth, because there is no business going on, — "Mammon" is suspended; and seventh, because New-Year's-day and Twelfth-day come after it; that is to say, because it is the leader of a set of holidays, and the spirit is not beaten down into commonplace the moment it is over. It closes and begins the year with cheerfulness. We have collected, under the head of "The Week,"* some notices of the other principal points connected with Christmas. Most of them are now losing their old lustre, only to give way, we trust, by and by, to better evidences of rejoicing. The beadle we can dispense with, and even the Christmas-boxes; especially as we hope nobody will then want them. And the "Bellman's Verses" shall turn to something nobler, albeit we have a liking for him; ay, for his very absurdities; there is something in them so old, so unpretending, and so reminiscent about him. As long as the bellman is alive, one's grandfather does not seem dead, and his cocked hat lives with him. Good "Bellman's Verses" will not do at all. There have been some such things of late, "most tolerable and not to be endured." We have even seen them witty, which is a great mistake. Warton and Cowper unthinkingly set the way to them. You may be childlike at Christmas; you may be merry; you may be absurd, — in the worldly sense of the term; but you must write with a faith, and so redeem your old Christmas reputation somehow. Belief in something great and good preserves a respectability, even in the most childish mistakes; but it feels that the company of banter is unworthy of it. The very absurdity of the "Bellman's Verses" is only bearable, nay, only pleasant, when we sup-

---

* A column of original and selected miscellany published under this caption in the "London Journal." — ED.

pose them written by some actual doggerel-poet in good faith. Mere mediocrity hardly allows us to give our Christmas-box, or to believe it nowadays in earnest; and the smartness of your cleverest worldly-wise men is felt to be wholly out of place. No, no; give us the good old decrepit "Bellman's Verses," hobbling as their bringer, and taking themselves for something respectable like his cocked-hat, or give us none at all. We should not like even to see him in a round hat. He would lose something of the old and oracular by it. If in a round hat, he should keep out of sight, and not contradict the portrait of himself at the top of his sheet of verses, with his bell and his beadle's staff. The pictures round the verses may be new; but we like the old better, no matter how worn-out, provided the subject be discernible; no matter what blots for the eyes, and muddiness for the clouds. The worst of these old wood-cuts are often copied from good pictures; and, at all events, they wear an aspect of the old sincerity.*

Give us, in short, a foundation of that true old Christmas sincerity to go upon (no matter under what modification of belief, provided it be of a Christian sort), and, like the better sort of Catholics, who go to church in the morning and to their dance in the evening, we can begin the day with a mild gravity of recollection, and finish it with all kinds of forgetful mirth, — forgetful, because realizing the happiness for which we are thoughtful. It is a pernicious mistake among persons who exclusively call themselves religious,

---

* We learn from Hone's "Every-Day Book" that for the use of this personage there was a book, entitled "The Bellman's Treasury, containing above a hundred several verses, fitted for all Humours and Fancies, and suited to all times and seasons." London, 1707, 8vo. — ED.

to think they ought never to be cheerful, without calling to mind considerations too vast and grand for cheerfulness; thereby representing the object of their reverence after the fashion of an officious and tyrannical parent, who should cast the perpetual shadow of his dignity over his children's sports. Those sports are a part of the general ordinance of things. Man is a laughing as well as a thinking creature; and "there is a time ," says the wise man, "for all things." Formal set times for being religious and thoughtful are, to be sure, not the only times; but a perpetual formality is merely the same mistake rendered thoroughgoing and entire! It might be thought unnecessary to touch upon this point nowadays, and a violation of our own inculcations of seasonableness to notice it in the present article; but a periodical writer who is in earnest is much hampered by certain inconsistencies in the demands of some of his readers; and what we feel, we express.

To have a thorough sense, then, of Christmas, grave and gay, and to reconcile as much as possible of its old times to the new, one ought to begin with Christmas Eve, to see the log put on the fire, the boughs fixed somewhere in the room, and to call to mind what is said by the poets, and those beautiful accounts of angels singing in the air, which inspired the seraphical strains of Handel and Corelli. Those who possess musical instruments should turn to these strains, or procure them, and warm their imaginations by their performance. In paintings from Italy (where the violin, on account of its greater mastery, and the enthusiasm of the people, is held in more esteem than with us), we often see choral visions of angels in the clouds, singing and playing on that instrument as well as the harp; and certainly, if ever a sound which may be supposed to resemble them, was yet heard upon earth, it is in some of the harmonies of Arcangelo Corelli. And the recitative of Handel's divine strain, "There were shepherds abiding in the fields," is as exquisite for truth and simplicity as the cheek of innocence. See what Milton has sung of these angelic symphonies in the ode "On the Morning of Christ's Nativity." Shakespeare has touched upon Christmas Eve with a reverential tenderness, sweet as if he had spoken it hushingly.

> "*Some say* that ever 'gainst that season comes,
> Wherein our Saviour's birth is celebrated,
> *The bird of dawning* singeth all night long.
> And then, they say, no spirit dares stir abroad;
> The nights are wholesome; then no planets strike,
> No fairy takes, nor witch hath power to charm;
> So *hallow'd* and so *gracious* is the time."

Upon which (for it is a character in Hamlet who is speaking) Horatio observes, in a sentence remarkable for the breadth of its sentiment as well as the niceness of its sincerity (like the whole of that apparently favorite character of the poet, who loved a friend),

> "So have I heard, *and do in part believe it:*"

that is to say, he believed all that was worthy, and recognized the balmy and Christian effect produced upon well-disposed and sympathetic minds by reflections on the season.

The Waits, that surprise us with music in the middle of the night, evidently originated in honor of the heavenly visitation. They are, unfortunately, not apt to be very celestial of their kind. There is a fellow in particular, that plays the bass, who seems to make a point of being out of tune. He has two or three notes that are correct enough, that enable him to finish in a style of grandeur and self-satisfaction, but his "by-play," for the most part, is horrible. However, the very idea of music is good, especially in the middle of the night; and a little imagination and Christian charity, together with a consideration of his cold fingers, will help us to be thankful for his best parts, and slip as we can over his worst. When the English become a more musical people, zealous amateurs will volunteer their services on fine nights, and, going forth with their harps and guitars, charm their friends and neighbors with strains rendered truly divine by the hour and the occasion, —

> " Divinely-warbled voice
> Answering the stringed noise."

(See Milton's ode, as above-mentioned.)

> " Soft stillness and the night
> Become the touches of sweet harmony."
> MERCHANT OF VENICE.

A Christmas day, to be perfect, should be clear and cold, with holly branches in berry, a blazing fire, a dinner with mince-pies, and games and forfeits in the evening. You cannot have it in perfection, if you are very fine and fashionable. Neither, alas! can it be enjoyed by the very poor; so that, in fact, a perfect Christmas is impossible to be had, till the progress of things has distributed comfort more equally. But when we do our best, we are privileged to enjoy our utmost; and charity gives us a right to hope. The completest enjoyer of Christmas (next to a lover who has to receive forfeits from his mistress), is the holiday school-boy who springs up early, like a bird, darting hither and thither, out of sheer delight, thinks of his mince-pies half the morning, has too much of them when they come (pardon him this once), roasts chestnuts and cuts apples half the evening, is conscious of his new silver in his pocket, and laughs at every piece of mirth with a loudness that rises above every other noise. Next day what a pegtop will he not buy ! what string, what nuts, what gingerbread ! And he will have a new clasp-knife, and pay three times too much for it. Sour oranges also will he suck, squeezing their cheeks into his own with staring eyes ; and his mother will tell him they are not good for him, — and let him go on.

A Christmas evening should, if possible, finish with music. It carries off the excitement without abruptness, and sheds a repose over the conclusion of enjoyment.

A word respecting the more serious part of the day's subject alluded to above. It is but a word, but it may sow a seed of reflection in some of the best natures, especially in these days of perplexity between new doctrines and old. It appears to us, that there is a point never enough dwelt upon, if at all, by those who attempt to bring about a reconciliation between belief and the want of it. It is addressed only to the believers in a Providence, but those who have that belief, if they have no other, are a numerous body. The point is this, — that Christianity, to say the least of it, is a GREAT EVENT. It has had a wonderful effect on the world, and still has, even in the workings of its apparently unfilial daughter, modern philosophy, who could never have been what she is but for the doctrine of boundless sympathy, grafted upon the elegant self-reference of the Greeks, and the patriotism of the Romans, which was so often a mere pretext for the most unneighborly injustice. Now so great an event must have been in the contemplation of Providence, — one of the mountain-tops of its manifestation ; and, if we say, even of a Shakespeare and a Plato (and not without reason), that there is something "divine" in them, that is to say, something partaking of a more energetic and visible portion of the mysterious spirit breathed into mankind, how much more, and with how much more reverential a love, ought we not to have a divine impression of the nature of Him, who drew the great line between the narrowness of the Old World and the universalities of the New, and uttered to the earth, through the angelical organ of his whole being, life and death, that truly celestial doctrine, "Think of *others!*"

NEW YEAR'S GIFTS.

ORMERLY, everybody made presents on New Year's Day, as they still do in Paris, where our lively neighbors turn the whole metropolis into a world of cakes, sweetmeats, jewellery, and all sorts of gifts and greetings. The Puritans checked that custom, out of a notion that it was superstitious, and because the heathens did it; which was an odd reason, and might have abolished many other innocent and laudable practices — eating itself, for one — and going to bed. Innumerable are the authorities which (had we lived in those days) we would have brought up in behalf of those two customs, in answer to the New-Year's-Day-knocking-down folios of Mr. Prynne, the great "blasphemer of custard." Unfortunately if the Puritans thought gift-giving superstitious, the increasing spirit of commerce was too well inclined to admit half its epithet, and regard the practice as, at least, *superfluous* — a thing over and above — and what was not always productive of a "consideration." "Nothing is given for nothing nowadays," as the saying is. Nay, it is doubtful whether next to nothing will always be given for something. There are people, we are credibly informed, taken for persons "well to do" in the world, and of respectable character, who will even turn over the pages of the "London Journal," and narrowly investigate whether there is enough wit, learning, philosophy, lives, travels, poetry, voyages, and romances in it, for three halfpence.*

This must be mended, or there will be no such thing as a New Year by and by. Novelty will go out; the sun will halt in the sky, and prudent men sharply consider whether they have need of common perception.

Without entering into politics, something is to be said, nowadays, for an Englishman's being averse to making presents; and, as it behooves us to make the best of a bad thing, reasons might be shown also why it is not so well to have a formal and official sort of day for making presents, as to leave them to more spontaneous occasions. Besides, if everybody gives and everybody receives, where, it may be asked, is the compliment? And how are people to know whether they would have given or received anything, had it not been the custom?

How are they to be sure, whether a very pretty present is not a positive insult, till they compare it with what has been received by others? And how are men in office and power to be sure that in the gifts of their inferiors there is anything but self-seeking and bribery? It was formerly

---

* Such a one was not Walter Savage Landor, who thus wrote, from Italy to a friend in England: "Let me recommend to you Leigh Hunt's 'London Journal,' three halfpence a week. It contains neither politics nor scandal, but very delightful things in every department of graceful literature." — ED.

the custom in England to load princes and ministers with
New-Year's Gifts. Queen Elizabeth, who had the soul of
a mantuamaker as well as of a monarch, received whole
wardrobes of gowns and caps, as well as caskets of jewellery. What a day must she have passed of it, with all the
fine things spread out before her! And yet with all her
just estimation of herself, and her vanity to boot, bitter
suspicions must occasionally have crossed her, that all
this was but so much self-interest appealing to self-love.
But suppose a Duke or an Earl did not send a gift good
enough. Here was ground for anger and jealousy, and
all the pleasure-spoiling self-will which see no good in
what is given it, provided something be wanting. Dryden
addressed some verses on New-Year's Day to Lord Chancellor Hyde (Clarendon), which he begins as follows:—

> " My Lord,
> While flattering crowds officiously appear
> To give *themselves*, not *you*, a happy year,
> And by the greatness of their presents, prove
> How much they hope, but not how well they love," &c.

Here was a blow (not very well considered, perhaps) at
the self-complacency induced by the receipt of "great
presents." Suppose Lord Chancellor Lyndhurst, or Lord
Chancellor Brougham, had similar presents sent them on
the like occasion. How could the one be sure that his
great legal knowledge, or the other, that even his great
genius and tact for all knowledge, had anything to do with
the compliment? Or that it was not as mere a trick for
court-favor as anything which they would now despise?
We grant that (where there is any right to bestow it at all)
a present is a present; that it is an addition to one's stock,
and, at all events, a compliment to one's influence; and
influence is often its own proof of a right to be compli-

mented; as want of influence is sometimes a greater. But, for the sake of fair-play among mankind, every advantage must have its drawback; and it is a drawback in the power to confer benefits, that it cannot always be sure of the motives of those who do it honor. If a day is to be set apart for such manifestations of good-will, the birthday would seem better for them than New-Year's Day. The compliment would be more particular and personal; others might not know of it, and so would not grudge it; and real affections would thus be indulged, not mere ceremonies.

We own that we think there is something in that distinction. Yet our sprightly-blooded neighbors would no doubt have replies to all these arguments; and, for our part, we are for cutting the knot of the difficulty thus: Make us all rich enough, and then we could indulge ourselves both with New-Year's Day and the birthday, both on the general occasions and the particular one. For, to say the truth, we people who are not rich, and who, therefore, have nothing perhaps worth withholding, are long in coming to understand how it is that rich people can resist these anniversary opportunities of putting delight into the eyes of their friends and dependants, and distributing their toys and utilities on all sides of them. Presents (properly so called) are great ties to gratitude, and therefore great increasers of power and influence, especially if they are of such a kind as to be constantly before the eye, thus producing an everlasting association of pleasant ideas with the giver.* They tell the receiver that he is worth something in the giver's eyes, and thus the worth of the giver becomes twenty-fold. Nor do we say this sneer-

---

* Presents endear absents. — CHARLES LAMB.

ingly, or in disparagement of the self-love which must of necessity be, more or less, mixed up with every one's nature; for the most disinterested love would have nothing to act upon without it; and the most generous people in the world, such as most consult the pleasure of others before their own, must lose their very identity and personal consciousness before they can lose a strong desire to be pleased.

Oh! but rich people, it will be said, are not always so rich as they are supposed to be; and even when they are, they find plenty of calls upon their riches, without going out of their way to encourage them. They have establishments to keep up, heaps of servants, &c., their wives and families are expensive, and then they are cheated beyond measure.

Making allowances for all this, and granting in some instances that wealth itself be poor, considering the demands upon it, nevertheless for the most part real wealth must be real wealth; that is to say, must have a great deal more than enough. You do not find that a rich man (unless he is a miser) hesitates to make a great many presents to *himself*,—books, jewels, horses, clothes, furniture, wines, or whatever the thing may be that he most cares for; and he must cease to do this (we mean of course in its superfluity) before he talks of his inability to make presents to others.

SALE OF THE LATE MR. WEST'S PICTURES.

IT is a villanous thing to those who have known a man for years, and been intimate with the quiet inside of his house, privileged from intrusion, to see a sale of his goods going on upon the premises. It is often not to be helped, and what he himself wishes and enjoins; but still it is a villanous necessity, — a hard cut to some of one's oldest and tenderest recollections. There is a sale of this kind now going on in the house we spoke of last week.* We spoke of it then under an impulse not easy to be restrained, and not difficult to be allowed us; and we speak of it now under another. We were returning the day before yesterday from a house, where we had been entertained with lively accounts of foreign countries, and the present features of the time, when we saw the door in Newman Street standing wide open, and disclosing to every passenger a part of the gallery at the end of the hall. All our boyhood came over us, with the recollection of those who had accompanied us into that house. We hesitated whether we should go in, and see an auction taking place of the old quiet and abstraction; but we do not easily suffer an unpleasant and vulgar association to overcome a greater one; and, besides, how could we pass? Having passed the threshold, without the ceremony of the smiling old porter, we found a worthy person sitting at the door of the gallery, who, on hearing our name, seemed to have

---

* In an article entitled "A Nearer View of Some of the Shops," in "The Indicator." — ED.

old times come upon him as much as ourselves, and was very warm in his services. We entered the gallery, which we had entered hundreds of times in childhood, by the side of a mother, who used to speak of the great persons and transactions in the pictures on each side of her with a hushing reverence as if they were really present. But the pictures were not there, — neither Cupid with his doves, nor Agrippina with the ashes of Germanicus, nor the Angel slaying the army of Sennacherib, nor Death on the Pale Horse, nor Jesus Healing the Sick, nor the Deluge, nor Moses on the Mount, nor King Richard pardoning his brother John, nor the Installation of the old Knights of the Garter, nor Greek and Italian stories, nor the landscapes of Windsor Forest, nor Sir Philip Sidney, mortally wounded, giving up the water to the dying soldier. They used to cover the wall; but now there were only a few engravings. The busts and statues also were gone. But there was the graceful little piece of garden as usual, with its grass plat and its clumps of lilac. They could not move the grass plat, even to sell it. Turning to the left, there was the privileged study, which we used to enter between the Venus de Medicis and the Apollo of the Vatican. They were gone, like their mythology. Beauty and intellect were no longer waiting on each side of the door. Turning again, we found the longer part of the gallery like the other; and in the vista through another room, the auction was going on. We saw a throng of faces of business with their hats on, and heard the hard-hearted knocks of the hammer, in a room which used to hold the mild and solitary Artist at his work, and which had never been entered but with quiet steps and a face of consideration. We did not stop a minute. In the room between this and the gallery, huddled up in a corner, were the busts and statues which had given us a hundred thoughts. Since the days when we first saw them, we have seen numbers like them, and many of more valuable materials; for though good of their kind, and of old standing, they are but common plaster. But the thoughts and the recollections belonged to no others; and it appeared sacrilege to see them in that state.

> " Apollo from his shrine
> Can no more divine:
>
> * * * * *
>
> And each peculiar power foregoes his wonted seat."

Into the parlor, which opens out of the hall and into the garden, we did not look. We scarcely know why; but we did not. In that parlor we used to hear of our maternal ancestors, stout yet kind-hearted Englishmen, who set up their tents with Penn in the wilderness. And there we learned to unite the love of freedom with that of the graces of life; for our host, though born a Quaker, and appointed a royal painter, and not so warm in his feelings as those about him, had all the natural amenity belonging to those graces, and never truly lost sight of that love of freedom. There we grew up acquainted with the divine humanities of Raphael. There we remember a large colored print of the old lion-hunt of Rubens, in which the boldness of the action and the glow of the coloring overcome the horror of the stuggle. And there, long before we knew any thing of Ariosto, we were as familiar as young playmates with the beautiful Angelica and Medoro, who helped to fill our life with love.

May a blessing be upon that house, and upon all who know how to value the genius of it!

TRANSLATION FROM MILTON INTO WELSH.

E are going to do a thing very common with critics; — we are about to speak of a work we do not understand. What is not so common, however, we are not going to condemn it. On the contrary, the evident spirit under which it is written, gives it a very advantageous character in our opinion; and we shall proceed to show those eminent and dissatisfied persons, how possible it is by the help of a little good humor and modesty to be pleased instead of provoked, and to enjoy one's imagination instead of resenting one's ignorance.

The reader is aware perhaps, that there is a kind of Poetical Order existing among our Welsh brethren, the object of which is to keep up the genius as well as remembrance of their ancient Bards. The members look upon themselves, in love at least, as their successors; take the same title of Bards; distribute harps as prizes; and endeavor to catch the reflection of their old fire on the same mountains. Nor is this second-hand inspiration, we dare say, without the occasional production of something fine. In a populous modern city, with its sophistications, such an establishment might be regarded as a mere game at antiques. But in persons of simplicity of life and earnestness of intention, especially in solitudes peopled with grand human recollections, it is difficult to love anything fervently, and never speak of it in a worthy manner. We have seen poems in the English language written by Welshmen of this character, which were as good as some of the English productions of Burns; and the inference is, that in their own language, and on the subject of their own affections, they have not always produced poetry unworthy of ranking with his Scotch. Even upon subjects of mere antiquity, the inspiration above mentioned may act upon them as that of the great poets of Greece and Italy has acted upon their own. Great times and men may literally be said never to die in point of effect. Their touch reaches us from afar. Their eye is upon us out of the clouds of time. We feel their memory in our ears, like the tremble of an eternal song. If their own works help to divert us from the more natural soil out of which they drew the flowers and fountains of their immortality, they serve to create a new stratum of fertility, not so fine indeed as the other, but still fine and abundant, and full of a second vitality. Death itself helps to beautify them. We walk among their memories, as we do among the leaves of autumn, or the ruins of great places; and supply the want of present perfection with the love of that which is past.

In our youth, we met with one of the Modern Welsh Bards, who had all the character we speak of. He was a man of primeval simplicity of manners; that is to say, one who without any of the conventional substitutes for the humanities of intercourse, possessed that natural politeness of benignity, which is so instantly felt to be their vital spirit. He had the true Welsh face improved by information, hair and eyes black as a raven, and an expression of great candor and good nature. If we remember rightly, we gathered from his conversation, that he had risen, by dint of his love of letters, and much to the credit of those who noticed him, from an humble origin; which origin he neither affected to hide nor to boast of. He occasionally came up to London; took his meals with the best society among his countrymen or at his own hermit-like table; and hired an humble lodging near the Museum, where it was his delight to go and study Welsh antiquities. Thus if he came to London, he brought his country with him; found his bards and his very quiet about him, wherever he pleased, in the shape of books; and in default of his goats and mountains, could get among animals and things which perhaps he loved as well, and thought almost as real, the dragons and golden fields of Cambrian heraldry. Among other advantages of the remoteness and romantic nature of the sphere in which he grew up, it had kept him free from the small pedantry and self-sufficiency so often observable in the leading wits of country towns and minor cities, who think their own amount of knowledge the sum of all that is accomplished, and have a particular fancy for setting Londoners in the right. He had the humanity to think well of what he did not know. He loved his country's music and its poets, and in our fondness for an air on the piano-forte and an ode of Horace was pleased to discover something which he thought worthy both of his sympathy and his respect.

This pleasant Cambro-Briton, of whom we are speaking, once took us to see a countryman of his, whose taste in urbanities and antiquities resembled his own. He lived in a small quiet house near the fields; and we found him up to the eyes in good humor, books, and a Welsh harp. If we are not much mistaken, this is the author of the Welsh Milton.

There is something very beautiful to us to see the whole souls of men yearning in this manner towards their native country, when its power has long ceased to exist. They have all the merit of adhering to a great friend in adversity; and yet the friend is perhaps greater than ever he was, and can reward them more. The ancient Britons had in them the seeds of a great nation, even in our modern sense of the word. They had courage; they had reflection; they had imagination. When driven from their larger possessions by the mere power which the world then adored, they soon found out the two great secrets of adversity, — that of softening reality with romance, and of turning experience to reformation. They possessed, in an extraordinary degree, the spirit of legislative improvement. Power at last made a vassal of their prince. There were writers in those times; harpers and bards, who made the instinct of that brute faculty turn cruel out of fear. But there were no presses to let all the world know what the writers thought, and to give intellectual power its fair chances with brute. They bequeathed to their countrymen, however, the glory of their memories. They, and time together, have consecrated their native hills, so as they were never before consecrated. Existing, in a manner, no longer as a thing of the common world, the country took an elevation nearer heaven. It lifted up its head in the light of love and poetry, and its tops shine to this day in the reverted eyes of its wanderers.

> " Fond impious man, thinkst thou yon sanguine cloud
> Raised by thy breath, has quenched the orb of day?
> To-morrow he repairs the golden flood,
> And warms the nations with redoubled ray."

Violence is the grown childhood of the world. Its manhood is intellect and equanimity; and part of the grace of manhood consists in recollecting the better things of infancy. Edward the First, who made vassals of the Welsh, is now an inferior person in our eyes compared with Howell the legislator. We would rather see Alfred the Great than the widest-ruling of all the Roman Emperors. We should expect more in his face. We should recognize in him a greater existing man, — a finer contemporary, — or rather a more becoming fellow-creature for the Shakespeares and Bacons: for when we speak of modern times, we mean the intellectual times which such great men have produced for us. Even the smallness of the territory, to which the old Britons were confined, serves to concentrate and make strong the gaze of recollection. Mere greatness acts through the medium of pride or fear. It always inflicts a sort of uneasy consciousness of the gross nature of its pretensions. Break it, and it resolves its compounds into littleness. You can only contrast it with mere smallness, or pity it because it is not entire. It cannot afford to be otherwise. Its compounds have no principle of growth, — no power of voluntary aggrandizement, — no charm with which to call associations about them. But break a heart into a thousand shivers, and every atom shall be reverenced. Love is great enough for itself. Such phrases as the Great King and the Great Nation, even though warranted in point of physical power, are nothing but vanity, and are felt to be so. Both imply a want of individual importance, and by the same reason a want of general humanity. They make the recollections either too vaguely public, or too minutely private. The Persian in Greece, or the Turk in Candia, was angry at being killed by a petty republican, or regretted only his harem or his houris; but the Greek who "dying, thought of sweet Argos,"* and

---

* Sternitur infelix alieno vulnere, cœlumque
Adspicit, et dulces moriens reminiscitur Argos.
VIRGIL, *Lib.* 10, v. 781.

the Florentine who turned at hearing Dante speak in his native language, and felt his heart live again at "the dialect of Arno's vale," thought of his home and his country as one.

It is a feeling connected with this love of country, which most particularly strikes us in the translation of Milton. Here is an author fond of authorship, an author living among Englishmen, and well aware of the universality of their language, and yet he contents his ambition with producing a long work which none but his countrymen shall understand. It is sufficient for him if he can give them a new source of pleasure. It is enough for the true largeness of his spirit if he can give a thousand times more than he can receive, — happy in obtaining the thanks of the modern Howells and Llewellyns, and in being renowned in a country about twice the size of Yorkshire.

On opening the book, we are then struck with the delight it must afford to those who have no other language, and amused with the unreadable face it presents to those who are not acquainted with it. One's familiarity with the original, and utter·inability to make out its expounder, make up a very pleasant perplexity. We will quote a passage from both, which in Milton is like the coming of an army with music, and which must present high associations, of another sort, to the Welsh reader. Satan has just numbered his forces : —

> " And now his heart
> Distends with pride, and hard'ning in his strength
> Glories: for never, since created man,
> Met such embodied force, as named with these
> Could merit more than that small infantry
> Warr'd on by cranes; though all the giant brood
> Of Phlegra with th' heroic race were join'd
> That fought at Thebes and Ilium, on each side

Mix'd with auxiliar gods ; and what resounds
In fable or romance of Uther's son
Begirt with British and Armorick knights ;
And all who since, baptiz'd or infidel,
Jousted in Aspramont, or Montalban,
Damasco, or Marocco, or Trebisond,
Or whom Biserta sent from Africk shore,
When Charlemain with all his peerage fell
By Fontarabia."

    Yna ymfulchïa,
Ei galon, a chaledu yn ei nerth
Ymorfoledda : canys nid erised
Er pan fu dyn, yr ymddygyrchai lu
Wrth y rhai hyn teilyngach fyddent nog
Oedd y peddytos mân â gyrchent gynt
Greyrod ; er pe cawri Phlegra oll
Yn gyflu ag y glewion â gatêynt
Rhag Thebes a rhag Ilïon, cymhlith o
Gyfneirthiaid Dduwiau y ddwy blaid ; a pheth
A soniant chwedlau am fab Uthr ar gyrch
Marchogion Prydain ac Armorica ;
Ac wedi hwynt oll, cred neu anghred lu,
Yn Aspramont neu Montalbar, neu yn
Damasco, neu Marocco, neu Trebisond,
Neu o Affric dorf Biserta, yn y drin
Wrth Fontarabia, pan y syrthiai holl
Urddolion Carlo Mawr ac efe ei hun.

Here are some fine words to the eye : —

    Yna *ymfalchïa*
Ei galon, a *chaledu* yn ei nerth
Ymorfoledda.

And again : —

    Marchogton Prydain ac Armorica :

And, —

    Yn y drin
Wrth Fontarabia, pan y syrthiai holl
Urddolion Carlo Mawr ac efe ei hun.

Charles the Great keeps up his old triumphs. He always

gets well off in every tongue and nation, — Charlemain, Carlo Mano, Carolus Magnus. Even his plain monosyllable, Carl, which Camden tells us is the only appellation on his coins, has a self-sufficing and dominant sound. But we know not that he ever cut a more imperial figure than in this lofty and solemn agnomen of Carlo Mawr. It reminds one of the mountain.* The names that abound in this passage serve only to show to greater effect the obscurity of the rest. Uthr and Prydain we can make out: Damasco and Marocco, and Trebisond, are as familiar to us as the sounds of a trumpet; but "what the devil," as Brantome would say, is "oedd y pedditos mân?" There happens to be a note to these words; and the idea of explanation is so united with that of a note, that one looks involuntarily for some instruction on the point. The following is the elucidation. "*Odd y pedditos mân.*"]— Syniad yw hyn am y ddammeg o ryfel rhwyng y *crðrod* ac y *creyrod.*" Even the Preface, we find, has nothing in it for us Saxons; nor the Index either. At last, in the former, we hit upon some Greek letters, and thought that some light was going to break in upon us, when lo! we know not for what cause, but these Greek letters contained only Welsh words. This was "the unkindest cut of all." But they look like some memorial about a lady, perhaps an affectionate one ; and we return to our gravities.

The only remaining observation we have to make, is the

---

* Those rogues the punsters, who will be levelling every thing, and laying every language double, have already got hold of the translation of Mr. Owen Pughe. One of them, the other day, seeing the words "Mr. Tomkins" at the head of an advertisement, and finding that it concerned that late eminent writing-master, said that he was the greatest man that flourished during the last century, and that he ought to be called Penman-Mawr.

pleasure with which the great poet himself would have witnessed a translation of his work into this language: there has lately been an Icelandic version of Paradise Lost. This would have gratified him, from feelings common to all writers. The Italian ones were a matter of course. But a translation into old British would have been particularly curious to one, who had meditated an epic poem on the exploits of King Arthur, and had no doubt made himself as well acquainted as possible with Welsh antiquities, for that purpose. The overflowings of this first intention of his, when it was afterwards diverted, are visible in the little streams of romance which occasionally run into its other sphere. Among the subjects also which he has left on record for tragedy, are passages from the same period; and when he began a History of Britain, he delighted to go as far back as possible, and do justice to Briton as well as Saxon. He speaks of the intended epic poem in various parts of his writings, and talks of his subject with a zeal and even a *British* sort of partiality, which is as striking as the ardor of his verse. See particularly the famous passage in his Latin poem to Tasso's friend, Manso, where after expressing his wish to meet with so understanding a patron, and to write about the Round Table and Arthur, who "at that moment was preparing his wars under ground," he bursts out in a strain like the clang of metal : —

<blockquote>
Et, O modo spiritus adsit,
Frangam Saxonicas Britonum sub Marte phalangas !

And oh, did spirit come on me but fit for those high wars,
I'd crash the Saxon phalanxes beneath the British Mars !
</blockquote>

Perhaps considering what a proud patriot Milton was, notwithstanding all his cosmopolitical qualities, it affords some additional explanation to this British part of his enthusiasm, to find that his mother was of Welsh origin. His connections were probably a good deal among the countrymen of her family. His first wife was the daughter of a Powell. That he did not do what he intended, has been regretted by every poet who has alluded to it, from Dryden to Walter Scott. We remember a note in the latter's edition of Dryden, where he asks, what would not have been done with such subjects as the Perilous Chapel and the Forbidden Seat? So much, that being compelled to bring this article to a close, we dare not trust ourselves with dwelling upon it, — with fancying a thousandth part of the grand and the gorgeous things, the warlike and the peaceful, the bearded and the vermeil-cheeked, the manly, the supernatural, and the gentle, with which his poem would have burnt brightly down to us, like windows painted by enchantment.

THE BULL-FIGHT;

OR, THE STORY OF DON ALPHONSO DE MELOS AND THE JEWELLER'S DAUGHTER.

VERYBODY has heard of the bull-fights in Spain. The noble animal is brought into an arena to make sport, as Samson was among the Philistines. And truly he presents himself to one's imagination, as a creature equally superior with Samson to his tormentors; for the sport which he is brought in to furnish, is that of being murdered. The poor beast is not actuated by a perverse will,

and by a brutality which is deliberate. He does but obey to the last the just feelings of his nature. He would not be forced to revenge himself, if he could help it. He would fain return to the sweet meadow and the fresh air, but his tyrants will not let him. He is stung with arrows, goaded and pierced with javelins, hewn at with swords, beset with all the devilries of horror and astonishment that can exasperate him into madness ; and the tormentors themselves feel that he is in the right, if he can but give bloody deaths to his bloody assassins. The worst of it is, that some of these assassins, who are carried away by custom, are persons who are otherwise among the best in the kingdom. They err from that very love of sympathy, and of the admiration of their fellows, which should have been employed to teach them better.

The excuse for this diabolical pastime is, that it keeps up old Spanish qualities to their height, and prevents the nation from becoming effeminate. To what purpose ? And in how many instances ? Are not the Spanish nobility the most degenerate in Europe ? Has not its court, for three generations, been a scandal and a burlesque ? and would any other nation in Christendom consent to be made the puppets of such superiors ? What could Spain have done against France without England ? What have all its bull-fights, and all its other barbarities, done for it, to save it from the shame of being the feeblest and most superstitious of European communities, and of having no voice in the affairs of the world ?

Poor foolish Matadore ! Poor, idle illiterate, unreflecting *cavallero !* that is to say, " horseman ! " which, by the noble power or privilege of riding a horse (a thing that any groom can do in any decent country), came to mean "gentleman !" (and no other country has derived its idea of a gentleman from that of a centaur), can you risk your life for nothing better than this? Must you stake wife, children, mistress, father and mother, friends, fortune, love, and all which all of them may bring you, at no higher price than the power of having it said you are a better man than the butcher? Is there no sacred cause of country to fight for? No tyrant to oppose? No doctrine worth martyrdom? that you must needs, at the hazard of death and agony, set the only wits or the best qualities you possess on outdoing the greatest fools and ruffians in your city? And can you wonder that your country has no cause which it can stand to without help, or to any purpose? that your tyrants are cruel and laugh at you? and that your very wives and mistresses (for the most part) think there is nothing better in the world than a flaring show and a brutal sensation?

Bull-fights are going on now, and bull-fights were going on in the wretched time of King Charles the Second, of the House of Austria, whose very aspect seemed ominous of the disasters about to befall his country; for his face was very long, his lips very thick, his mouth very wide, his nose very hooked, and he had no calves to his legs, and no brains in his skull. His clemency consisted in letting assassins go, because passion was uncontrollable; and his wit, in sending old lords to stand in the rain, because they intimated that it would be their death. However, he was a good-natured man, as times went, especially for a King of Spain; and it is not of public disasters that we are to speak, but of the misery that befell two lovers in his day, in consequence of these detestable bull-fights.

Don Alphonso de Melos, a young gentleman of some five-and-twenty years of age, was the son of one of those

Titulados of Castile, more proud than rich, of whom it was maliciously said, that "before they were made lords, they didn't dine; and after they were made lords, they didn't sup." He was, however, a very good kind of man, not too poor to give his sons good educations; and of his second son, Alphonso, the richest grandee might have been proud; for a better or pleasanter youth, or one of greater good sense, conventionalisms apart, had never ventured his life in a bull-fight, which he had done half a dozen times. He was, moreover, a very pretty singer; and it was even said, that he not only composed the music for his serenades, but that he wrote verses for them equal to those of Garcilaso. So, at least, thought the young lady to whom they were sent, and who used to devour them with her eyes, till her very breath failed her, and she could not speak for delight.

Poor, loving Lucinda! — We call her poor, though she was at that minute one of the richest as well as happiest maidens in Madrid; and we speak of her as a young lady, for such she was in breeding and manners, and as such the very grandees treated her, as far as they could, though she was only the daughter of a famous jeweller, who had supplied half the great people with carcanets and rings. Her father was dead: her mother too; she was under the care of guardians; but Alphonso de Melos had loved her more than a year; had loved her with a real love, even though he wanted her money; would, in fact, have thrown her money to the dogs, rather than have ceased to love her; such a treasure he had found in the very fact of his passion. Their marriage was to take place within the month; and as the lady was so rich, and the lover, however noble otherwise, was only of the lowest or least privileged order of nobility (a class who had the misfortune of not being able to wear their hats in the king's presence, unless his majesty expressly desired it), the loftiest grandees, who would have been but too happy to marry the lovely heiress, had her father been anything but a merchant, thought that the match was not only pardonable in the young gentleman, but in a sort of way noticeable, and even in some measure to be smilingly winked at and encouraged; nay, perhaps, envied; especially as the future husband was generous, and had a turn for making presents, and for sitting at the head of a festive table. Suddenly, therefore, appeared some of the finest emeralds and sapphires in the world upon the fingers of counts and marquises, whose jewels had hitherto been of doubtful value; and no little sensation was made, on the gravest and most dignified of the old nobility, by a certain grandee, remarkable for his sense of the proprieties, who had discovered "serious reasons for thinking" that the supposed jeweller's offspring was a natural daughter of a late prince of the blood.

Be this as it may, Don Alphonso presented himself one morning, as usual, before his mistress, and after an interchange of transports, such as may be imagined between two such lovers, about to be joined for ever, informed her, that one only thing more was now remaining to be done, and then — in the course of three mornings — they would be living in the same house.

"And what is that?" said Lucinda, the tears rushing into her eyes for excess of adoring happiness.

"Only the bull-fight," said the lover, affecting as much indifference, as he could affect in anything when speaking with his eyes on hers. But he could not speak it in quite the tone he wished.

"The bull-fight!" scarcely ejaculated his mistress, turning pale. "Oh, Alphonso! you have fought and conquered in a dozen; and you will not quit me, now that we can be so often together? Besides —" And here her breath began already to fail her.

But Alphonso showed her, or tried to show her, how he must inevitably attend the bull-fight. "Honor demanded it; custom; everything that was expected of him;" his mistress herself, who would "otherwise despise him."

His mistress fainted away. She fell, a death-like burden, into his arms.

When she came to herself, she wept, entreated, implored, tried even with pathetic gayety to rally and be pleasant; then again wept; then argued, and for the first time in her life was a logician, pressing his hand, and saying with a sudden force of conviction, "But hear me;" then begged again; then kissed him like a bride; reposed on him like a wife; did everything that was becoming and beautiful, and said everything but an angry word; nay, would have dared perhaps to pretend to say even that, had she thought of it; but she was not of an angry kind, or of any kind but the loving, and how was the thought to enter her head? Entire love is a worship, and cannot be angry.

The heart of the lover openly and fondly sympathized with that of his poor mistress; and, secretly, it felt more even than it showed. Not that Don Alphonso feared for consequences, though he had not been without pangs and thoughts of possibilities, even in regard to those; for to say nothing of the danger of the sport in ordinary, the chief reason of his being unpersuadable in the present instance was a report that the animals to be encountered were of more than ordinary ferocity; so that the cavalleros who were expected to be foremost in the lists in general, now felt themselves to be particularly called on to make their appearance, at the hazard of an alternative too dreadful for the greatest valor to risk.

The final argument which he used with his mistress was, the very excess of that love, and the very position in which it stood at that bridal moment, to which he in vain appealed. He showed how it had ever and irremediably been the custom to estimate the fighter's love by the measure of his courage; the more "apparent" the risk (for he pretended to laugh at any real danger), the greater the evidence of passion and the honor done to the lady; and so, after many more words and tears, the honor was to be done accordingly, grievously against her will, and custom triumphed. Custom! That "little thing," as the people called it to the philosopher. "That great and terrible thing," as the philosopher justly thought it. To show how secure he was, and how securer still it would render him, he made her promise to be there; and she required little asking: for a thought came into her head, which made her pray with secret and sudden earnestness to the Virgin; and the same thought enabled her to give him final looks, not only of resigned lovingness, but of a sort of cheered composure; for, now that she saw there was no remedy, she would not make the worst of his resolve, and so they parted.

How differently from when they met! and how dreadfully to be again brought together!

The day has arrived; the great square has been duly set out; the sand, to receive the blood, is spread over it; the barricadoes and balconies (the boxes) are all right; the king and his nobles are there; Don Alphonso and his Lucinda are there also; he, in his place on the square, on horseback, with his attendants behind him, and the door out of which the bull is to come, in front; she, where he will behold her before long, though not in the box to which he has been raising his eyes. All the gentlemen who are to fight the bulls, each in his turn, and who, like Alphonso, are dressed in black, with plumes of white feathers on their heads, and scarfs of different colors round the body, have ridden round the lists a quarter of an hour ago, to salute the ladies of their acquaintance; and all is still and waiting. The whole scene is gorgeous with tapestries, and gold, and jewels. It is a theatre in which pomp and pleasure are sitting in a thousand human shapes to behold a cruel spectacle.

The trumpets sound; crashes of other music succeed; the door of the stable opens; and the noble creature, the bull, makes his appearance, standing still awhile, and looking as it were with a confused composure before him. Sometimes when the animal first comes forth, it rushes after the horseman who has opened the door, and who has rushed away from the mood in which it has shown itself. But the bull on this occasion was one that, from the very perfection of his strength, awaited provoking. He soon has it. Light, agile footmen, who are there on purpose, vex him with darts and arrows, garnished with paper set on fire. He begins by pursuing them hither and thither, they escaping by all the arts of cloaks and hats thrown on the ground, and deceiving figures of pasteboard. Soon he is irritated extremely; he stoops his sullen head to toss; he raises it, with his eyes on fire, to kick and trample; he bellows; he rages; he grows mad. His breath gathers like a thick mist about his head. He gallops, amidst cries of men and women, franticly around the square, like a racer, following and followed by his tormentors; he tears the horses with his horns; he disembowels them; he tosses the howling dogs that are let loose on him; he leaps and shivers in the air like a very stag or goat. His huge body is nothing to him in the rage and might of his agony.

For Alphonso, who had purposely got in his way to shorten his Lucinda's misery (knowing her surely to be there, though he has never seen her), has gashed the bull across the eyes with his sword, and pierced him twice with the javelins furnished him by his attendants. Half blinded with the blood, and yet rushing at him, it should seem, with sure and final aim of his dreadful head, the creature is just upon him, when a blow from a negro who is helping one of the pages, turns him distractedly in that new direction, and he strikes down, not the negro, but the youthful, and in truth wholly frightened and helpless, page. The page, in falling, loses his cap, from which there flows a profusion of woman's hair, and Alphonso knows it on the instant. He leaps off his horse, and would have shrieked, would have roared out with horror; but something which seemed to wrench and twist round his very being within him, prevented it, and in a sort of stifled and almost meek voice, he could only sobbingly articulate the word, "Lucinda!" But in an instant he rose out of that self-pity into frenzy; he hacked wildly at the bull, which was now spinning as wildly round; and though the assembly rose, crying out, and the king bade the brute be dispatched, which was done by a thrust in the spine by those who knew the trick, (ah! why did they not do it before?) the poor youth has fallen, not far from his Lucinda, gored alike with herself to death, though neither of them yet expiring.

As recovery was pronounced hopeless, and the deaths of the lovers close at hand, they were both carried into the nearest house, and laid, as the nature of the place required, on the same bed. And, indeed, as it turned out, nothing could be more fitting. Great and sorrowful was the throng in the room: some of the greatest nobles were there, and a sorrowing message was brought from the king. Had the lovers been princes, their poor insensible faces could not have been watched with greater pity and respect.

At length they opened their eyes, one after the other, to wonder — to suffer — to discover each other where they lay — and to weep from abundance of wretchedness, and from the difficulty of speaking. They attemped to make a movement towards each other, but could not even raise an arm. Lucinda tried to speak, but could only sigh and attempt to smile. Don Alphonso said at last, half sobbing, looking with his languid eyes on her kind and patient face — "She does not reproach me, even now."

They both wept afresh at this, but his mistress looked at him with such unutterable love and fondness, making, at the same time, some little ineffectual movements of her hand, that the good old Duke de Linares said, "She wishes to put her arm over him; and he too — see — his arm over her." Tenderly, and with the softest caution, were their arms put accordingly; and then, in spite of their anguish, the good Duke said, "Marry them yet." And the priest opened his book, and well as he could speak for sympathy, or they seem to answer to his words, he married them; and thus — in a few moments, from excess of mingled agony and joy, with their arms on one another, and smiling as they shut their eyes — their spirits passed away from them, and they died.

LOVE AND WILL.

INDING, upon inquiry, that Steele's little periodical paper, called "The Lover," is still less known than we supposed, we shall here give some account of it, and then proceed to some other reflections to which it has given rise. We have already intimated,* that it was one of the numerous publications of the kind to which Steele's necessities and lively impulses united gave birth, and which, for similar reasons, were speedily brought to a close. Tonson collected the forty papers of which it consisted into a duodecimo volume, in which he included a political paper entitled "The Reader," which reached only its ninth number; and this is the book now before us. The dedication to Garth is surmounted by one of those rude little wood-cuts or copperplates, half flower and half figure, formerly, we believe, called head-pieces (perhaps still so, otherwise we know not the technical word). It presents us with Sir Samuel's coats of arms (two lions passant gardant between three-cross crosslets) supported, or rather attended, by two Cupids: one with a lyre for the doctor's poetry, and the other holding his professional emblem, the staff of Æsculapius. The first number is, in like manner, graced with a head of Queen Anne, and so is that of "The Reader." We reckon upon our own reader's not being averse to the mention of these amenities, partly from his love of anything connected with books, and

---

* In an article on "Garth, Physicians, and Love-Letters," in "Men, Women, and Books." — E.D.

partly because they help to show the manners and feelings of the times; and we confess we have another regard for them ourselves, owing to school recollections, and to the minutes of bliss we snatched, during the hardness of our tasks, from those figures of Venuses and Amphitrites, which sail along the tops of Ovid and other classics in the edition of Mattaire.

Steele, whether as an attraction, or a blind (if the latter, it was the most transparent of all blinds), puts forth his "Lover," as "written in imitation of the 'Tatler.'" He supposes himself to be one "Marmaduke Myrtle," a tender-hearted and speculative gentleman "about town," crossed in love, assisted in his lucubrations by four others, who have met with various good or ill success in their honorable passion for some lady, particularly one Mr. Severn, a young gentleman who is his "hero," and whom he describes in the most exquisite manner of the "Tatler," as one that treats every woman of a "certain age" so respectfully, "that in his company she can never give herself the compunction of having lost anything which made her agreeable." Of this hero, however, we hear nothing further but in one paper, and the author makes but the like mention of one of his other assistants. In short, beautiful as some of the papers are, and touched with equal knowledge of the world and delicacy of feeling, it did not "take," and Steele soon got tired. It went upon too exclusive a subject, and professed too open an intention of discountenancing the town ideas of love, to be acceptable to those who could have brought a man of wit his greatest number of readers; while, on the other hand, Steele had such a healthy and unhypocritical sense of the corporeal as well as spiritual part of the passion, that he offended such of his readers as had chosen to take him for a kind of sermonizer on love. In one of his papers is an account of an accident which happened to a young lady on horseback in the cross-country road, between Hampstead and Highgate, and which with an exquisite mixture of playfulness and delicacy, he represented as furnishing a sort of compulsory, but charming, reason why the young gentleman who happened to be with her was to be accepted as her husband. With this anecdote some "heavy rogue," as he truly calls him in a contemporary publication, chose to pick one of those quarrels which, by the degrading turn of their thoughts and the stupidity of their ostentation, create the indecency of which they complain; and this, no doubt, did him a disservice with the dull and commonplace, and added to the perplexity arising from his own mixed pretensions. To complete his causes of failure, he was a zealous politician, and, before he had written a dozen papers, could not help falling foul of the Tories; which in a gentleman so absorbed in the *belle passion* as Mr. Myrtle, was certainly not so well, and must have frightened such of his fair readers as patched their cheeks on the Tory side, and could only fall in love on high-church principles.*

---

* About the Middle of Last Winter I went to see an Opera at the Theatre in the Haymarket, where I could but take notice of two Parties of very fine Women, that had placed themselves in the Opposite Side-Boxes, and seemed drawn up in a kind of Battle-Array one against another. After a short Survey of them, I found they were Patched differently; the Faces on one Hand being spotted on the Right side of the Forehead, and those upon the other on the Left. I quickly perceived that they cast hostile Glances upon one another; and that their Patches were placed in those different Situations, as Party-Signals to distinguish Friends from Foes. In the Middle-Boxes, between those two opposite Bodies, were several Ladies who patched indifferently on both Sides of their Faces, and seemed to sit there with no other Intention but to see the Opera. Upon inquiry I found that the Body of the Amazons on my Right Hand, were Whigs, and those on my Left, Tories; And that those who had

In our last number, we extracted from this book two charmingly pathetic letters, which brought the reader acquainted with a pair of real lovers.* It shall now furnish us with a tragedy of a different sort, though pretending to be equally founded on love, and (as the paragraph advertisements say) of "startling interest." Steele says he had it from a gentleman who was "an eye-witness of several parts of it." The relief which the feelings experienced amidst the terrors of the former story arose from the sweetness of its affections. In the present, the love is of as bitter a sort as the catastrophe, but consoles us by driving matters to a pitch of the ludicrous in the very excess of its will. The heroine is a great spoiled child, who insists upon tearing her lover's breast open, and taking him with her into the other world, just as a smaller one might its drum.

"About ten years ago," says Steele, "there lived at Vienna a German count, who had long entertained a secret amour with a young lady of a considerable family. After a correspondence of gallantries, which had lasted two or three years, the father of the young count, whose family was reduced to a low condition, found out a very advantageous match for him; and made his son sensible, that he ought in common prudence to close with it. The count, upon the first opportunity, acquainted his mistress very fairly with what had passed, and laid the whole mat-

---

placed themselves in the Middle-Boxes were a Neutral Party, whose Faces had not yet declared themselves. These last, however, as I afterwards found, diminished daily, and took their Party with one Side or the other; inasmuch as that I observed, in several of them, the Patches which were before dispersed equally, are now all gone over to the Whig or Tory Side of the Face. — ADDISON, *The Spectator*, No. 81. — ED.

* See the article on "Garth, Physicians, and Love-Letters," in "Men, Women, and Books." — ED

ter before her with such freedom and openness of heart, that she seemingly consented to it. She only desired of him that they might have one meeting more, before they parted for ever. The place appointed for this their meeting was a grove, which stands at a little distance from the town. They conversed together in this place some time, when on a sudden the lady pulled out a pocket-pistol, and shot her lover into the heart, so that he immediately fell dead at her feet. She then returned to her father's house, telling every one she met what she had done. Her friends, upon hearing her story, would have found out means for her to make her escape; but she told them she had killed her dear count, because she could not live without him; and that, for the same reason, she was resolved to follow him by whatever way justice should determine. She was soon seized, but she avowed her guilt; rejected all excuses that were made in her favor, and only begged that her execution might be speedy. She was sentenced to have her head cut off, and was apprehensive of nothing but that the interest of her friends would obtain a pardon for her. When the confessor approached her, she asked him where he thought was the soul of her dead count. He replied that his case was very dangerous, considering the circumstances in which he died. Upon this so desperate was her frenzy, that she bid him leave her, for that she was resolved to go to the same place where the count was. The priest was forced to give her better hopes for the deceased, from considerations that he was upon the point of breaking off so criminal a commerce, and leading a new life, before he could bring her mind into a temper fit for one who was so near her end. Upon the day of her execution she dressed herself in all her ornaments, and walked toward the scaffold more like a bride than a condemned criminal. My friend tells me that he saw her placed in the chair, according to the custom of that place, where, after having stretched out her neck with an air of joy, she called upon the name of the count, which was the appointed signal for the executioner, who, with a single blow of his sword, severed her head from her body."

What a woman! and what a love, to stick to the poor devil of a count to all eternity! very lucky for him was it, that she could not settle matters in the next world with the same tragical nonchalance as in this! though, in the excess of her vanity, she seems to have taken for granted that she could; and that the *angels* were all to tremble before her, as the poor foolish people had been accustomed to do in her father's house. For, observe, she reckons confidently upon going to heaven, instead "of the other way." The very mention of the latter puts her in a frenzy, to which the priest himself is obliged to accommodate his last offices, before he can bring her mind to a temper fit to die in. It is impossible her "dear count" can go to the devil, precisely because she has made up her mind to go elsewhere; such an erroneous proceeding is not to be thought of: she has taken him from his new mistress (upon the contrast of whose mild manners he had just been hugging himself)—has given him his directions with a pocket-pistol which way to go, as much as to say, "There, get you along first,"—and then sets out for heaven after him by the execution-stage, shaking her loving fist towards the stars, and resolved to have him all to herself, till time and termagancy shall be no more!

This is, perhaps, the most extraordinary sample on record of the modesty and tenderness of self-will—of the having the "reciprocity" (as the Irishman said) "all on one side." I love you, says the lady, therefore you must love me; or it is no matter whether you do or not, compared with my treating you as if you did, and tormenting you if you don't. You are very amiable, therefore be so to me above anybody else, whether I am amiable or not. You have a will and wishes of your own, perhaps, as well as other people; but yours and all other people's must of course give way to mine; for that is but reasonable: all are fools and scoundrels who "offer to believe otherwise," and I could knock them all on the head, if I cared for them enough to do so; but that is a favor which I reserve for yourself. So there (*shoots him through the body*) — and now, with this new wound in your heart, come you along with me, and be delighted with me and my company, world without end!

To go to the other extreme of lovely generosity, how different is the wish expressed by Shakespeare, in the contemplation of his own death: of Shakespeare *himself*, observe — not of the dramatist speaking in the person of another, but of the great poet and human being speaking in his own person — of the creator of the characters of Imogen and Desdemona — and of the man who *could* create those characters, because he felt as he spoke in uttering these sentiments. How else, indeed, could he *so* have spoken them? Observe the simple words — the pure and daring trust in the belief of his reader — the great and good mind, that in spite of its having run the whole round of experience, or rather because it had done so, could retain feelings so enthusiastic and generous above all worldly price.

> "No longer mourn for me when I am dead,
> Than you shall hear the surly sullen bell
> Give warning to the world that I am fled
> From this vile world with vilest worms to dwell:
> *Nay, if you read this* LINE, *remember not*

The hand that *writ it;* FOR I LOVE YOU SO,
THAT I IN YOUR SWEET THOUGHTS WOULD BE FORGOT,
IF THINKING ON ME THEN SHOULD MAKE YOU WOE.
Oh, if, (I say), you look upon this verse,
When I, perhaps, compounded am with clay,
Do *not so much as my poor name rehearse,*
But let your love even with my life decay;
Lest the wise world should look into your moan,
And mock you with me after I am gone."

What beautiful writing! What common, every-day words made divine by love! But it may be said that the poet may have written all this, without exactly feeling what he said; that other poets have done as much who were notoriously no very admirable lovers; that it is imagination — an art — fiction.

Do *not believe* it. Put no faith in the envy, or the *want* of faith, that thus attempts to level performance with pretension. You might as well proclaim truth to be a lie. No poets have so written who have not thoroughly felt what they professed to feel. If they had, if incompleteness could thus be completeness, we should have had a thousand Shakespeares instead of one — a thousand Chaucers, a thousand Homers, a thousand Burnses — for we do not mean to say that in every instance the very greatest genius must accompany the truest feeling. It is sufficient that there is entire truth in the feeling to be expressed, and genius enough to express that truth.

" Here's a health to ane I lo'e dear !
Here's a health to ane I lo'e dear !
Thou art sweet as the smile when fond lovers meet,
And soft as their parting tear — *Jessy* !

" Although thou maun never be mine,
Although even hope is denied,
'Tis sweeter for thee despairing,
Than aught in the world beside."

And so he goes on through the whole of that exquisite

song, the last but one that he wrote (so unwitherable is the heart of a true poet). Hear the verse of another:—

> "Yestreen when to the trembling string,
> The dance gaed through the lighted ha',
> To thee my fancy took its wing,
> I sat, but neither heard nor saw.
> Though this was fair and that was braw,
> And you the boast of a' the town,
> *I sigh'd, and said among them a':*
> *'Ye are na Mary Morrison.'*"

And again in a lighter strain, —

> "The deil himself he could na scaith
> Whatever wad belang thee;
> *He'd look into thy bonnie face,*
> *And say, 'I canna wrang thee.'*"

Burns and Ariosto had here hit upon the same thought, because they had received the same truthful impression of the power of a beautiful face to turn away from injury.

> Stese la mano in quella chioma d'oro,
> E strasimollo a se con violensa;
> Ma come gli occhi a quel bel velto mise,
> Gli ne venne pietade, e non l'uccise.
>   ORLANDO FURIOSO, Canto 19.

"The warrior thrust his hand into those locks of gold, and fiercely dragged back the youth; but when he set eyes on that sweet face, pity came into his heart, and he did not kill him." Which Mr. Hoole (the most presumptuous of translators, but the most pardonable in his presumption, because the dullest), thus *defaces*, as if no such feeling had existed. (It should be mentioned that the youth had been begging a respite from death, in order to bury his prince's body; otherwise the reader would see *no reason at all* for his being spared !)

> "Zerbino soon, *his wrath decreasing,* felt
> His manly soul *with* love and *pity melt!*'

Not a word of the face! not a word of the dragging back, nor the locks of gold, nor the whole beautiful picture! (When will the booksellers cease to give us editions of this absurd versifier?) We have not at hand the old translation of Sir John Harrington (better, at all events, than Hoole's), nor the new one by Mr. Stewart Rose, who is a man full of sympathy with his species, and therefore has doubtless loved this passage as it deserves.*

What has made Marot, almost the only French poet till the days of Beranger, that an Englishman or Italian can read with thorough faith in *his* faith, but such passages as the following, simple and straightforward as those of Shakespeare:—

> " Où sont ces yeux, *lesquels me regardozent*
> *Souvent en ris, souvent avecques larmes ?*
> Où sont les mots, qui tant ni ont fait d'alarmes ;
> Où est la bouche aussi qui ni appaisoit,
> Quand *tant de fois et si bien me baisoit ?*"

" Where are those eyes which used to look at me, often in smiles, often with tears? Where are the words which made my heart beat so? Where the mouth which gave me peace, when it kissed me so often and so well?"

Compared with such writing as this, and some passages in their very greatest dramatic poets and Madame des Houlieres, the whole French Parnassus up to the present

---

* Here is Mr. Rose's version of the passage:—

" In furious heat, he springs upon Medore,
    Exclaiming, ' Thou of this shalt bear the pain.'
One hand he in his locks of golden ore
    Enwreathes, and drags him to himself amain ;
But, as his eyes that beauteous face survey,
Takes pity on the boy, and does not slay."

Hunt, however, in the preface to the "Stories from the Italian Poets," says that although Rose was a man of wit and a scholar, " he has undoubtedly turned the ease and animation of Ariosto into inversion and insipidity."— ED.

day, in their most serious moments, seem never to have
had a thorough belief in what they were saying, apart from
that curse of all half-performance, the wish to produce an
effect! They could not love a woman, without beseeching
some by-standers to admire them! nor go into solitude
itself, unaccompanied by a pocket-mirror to adjust their
wigs in!

It is thus, whether in word or deed, that the something
true is spoiled by the something impertinent — something
that does not belong to it. The writer, who is only half
in earnest, wishes to produce a whole true effect, and of
course cannot do it, any more than half a motive is sufficient for what is wholly to be moved. The love that is
not wholly love pieces itself out with vanity, with will, with
fury, perhaps is more than half made up of it, and yet expects wholly to be loved. Nay, the more expects it in proportion as it is violent instead of strong, and demands
instead of deserves. It is for this reason we ought always
to be cautious how we bestow our sympathy on the profession of one passion, while the demand is evidently
made us by another. Even in those unhappy cases of
suicide, for instance, which so frequently appear in the
newspapers, how manifest is it that, in nine cases out of
ten, the claim is of very equivocal worth indeed! The
hasty pity of society (we are the last to quarrel with it, we
would only have it not misbestowed) is too apt to take
for granted, that so violent an end proves whatsoever is
charged against the party living; whereas, all which it
unanswerably proves, is the violence (one way or other)
of the suicide's feelings; and it would be generally found,
we suspect, on due inquiry, that this was the very feature
in the character which produced the alienation on the part
of the supposed offender. Often do these poor wretches,

whether male or female, threaten the catastrophe long beforehand, in order to substitute their will for that of the person threatened. Often do they declare, in loud sullen tones, their determination to repeat the attempt when it is prevented. Sometimes they abuse the people that help them out of it, and not seldom are suicides committed out of avowed spite and revenge, and for the most trivial contradiction. We have read of a girl who threw herself into the water because her sister had refused her some more bread and butter! All this has nothing to do with so gentle, and generous, and enduring, and sweet-seeing a passion as love; which, like charity, makes the best of what it cannot help, tends to repose on all loving aids and patiences, and desires above everything the happiness of its object—not indeed as its every-day wish (that would be too much to expect of human nature), but certainly as its preference in the last resort, if it is to bequeath miserable or consolatory thoughts to its object.

> "For I love you so,
> That I in your thoughts would be forgot,
> If thinking on me then should make you woe."

Not that he desired to be forgot; oh no,—he desired infinitely to be remembered, but not

> "If thinking on me then should make you woe."

In that case he desired that the object of his love, whom he would fain think of in his grave to his last dust, should clean forget that ever there was such a being as one William Shakespeare, whose love had brought tears into her eyes, and with whose memory she might associate, perhaps, something to blame in her own treatment of him.

The newspapers now and then give an account, sometimes touching, sometimes provoking, sometimes as ludicrous as a scene in a farce, of some enamored youth or female who follows the beloved object about with an inveteracy of passion that leaves it no repose, — some romantic post-boy or milkmaid that besets the other's door or person, and at length brings the neighbors about it, to the destruction of business on both sides, and sometimes of the windows. In proportion to the violence or gentleness of the suffering in these cases, you may know whether there is any real love or otherwise. If there is, the object is pursued in so much the better taste accordingly, and the pursuer is content with eternal gazing and a reasonable quantum of the self-pity of tears: in short, the love may be altogether true in that case, however fantastically set; for love is in the heart and imagination of the lover, and not of necessity founded on real merit in the object. But if there is no real love, but simply a childish or fierce desire of having "one's way," then the tears, the noise, the visitations, are violent accordingly, and the happiness of the object is clearly of no importance whatever in the persecutor's eyes, compared with the ridiculous assumption that it must and shall arise from nothing but the happiness of the persecutor! — of that sole and modest individual, who is taking such pains to show an utter unfitness for the task of making happy.

Love, in every mind, is colored by the prevailing passion or quality of that mind; and in proportion as the latter is more or less, so is the love. Thus pride will fall in love (as far as it can) on account of something to be proud of in the object; mere animal passion for mere animal beauty; sentiment with sentiment; and a violent will shall ardently desire to become master or mistress of a character totally the reverse of itself, out of the same will and pleasure with which it shall please it to desire anything else that is best of its kind, and the attainment of which is a confirmation of power. "How dearly I love *my own sweet Will!*" said the lady in the epigram; and the husband doubted her not. "I would rather see my husband *dead*, than guilty of the crime of infidelity," said a lady of what has been happily termed "outrageous virtue."* It was the selfish Abelard who made Eloisa shut herself up in a convent, when she could no longer be his property. The stupid monster Caligula delighted to handle the little throat of his favorite wife Cæsonia, and to think of the power which his throne gave him to order it to be cut off, wishing that all Rome had but one such throat, that he might enjoy the greater idea in the less. Henry VIII., the beast of prosperity, did cut off *his* wife's, — nay, two of them; and was within an ace of doing as much for a third; — in the last instance, for the lady's differing with him in theology! Yet all these people, when it suited them, thought themselves in love; and they were so after their respective fashions; that is to say, with their own "sweet will." It is impossible for such natures to love anybody but themselves. When the question comes, which is to get the better, the sense of their own self-importance, or the happiness of the supposed beloved object, down goes the happiness, like a thing kicked and despised. Its very worth becomes an aggravation of the offence. The despot's charming little beauty is sent to the scaffold. The heart that would have endeared thousands is thrust into the nunnery, —

"Chanting faint hymns to the cold fruitless moon."

God forbid, for our own sakes as well as theirs, that any one's fellow-creatures should be denied such merits or

---

* By Steele: "Will Honeycomb calls these over-offended Ladies, the Outrageously Virtuous." *The Spectator*, No. 266. — ED.

excuses as they may have, let their natures otherwise be as provoking, or even revolting, as they may — much less that all impulses to suicide should be confounded, and the fascinated terror of a gentle mind like Cowper's be dealt with like vulgar rage and resentment, or the desperation of a Nero. The Neros and Henrys themselves were the growth of circumstances. Many a disturber of the peace of private life — nay, all — *must* have had causes for being what they are, apart from their full-grown wills and mistakes ; otherwise there would be no such things in the world as parents and ancestors, and educations and breedings, and nurses, and imperfect laws, and all that makes society what it is — a commonplace so obvious, that it would be ridiculous to repeat it, did not intelligent people sometimes startle you with arguing as if the case was otherwise, only showing, all the while, one of the consequences of their own breeding, and thus confirming every word they think they are refuting. Our heroine who murdered her "dear count," had an energy which might have been turned to better purpose ; she evinced a taste for a companionship better than her own (for we may suppose the count to have had no mean attractions that way); and, at all events, she did not mind going through pain and death, to secure, as she thought, the society of another fellow-creature. There was probably no little need of our charity on the count's own part, if we knew all the story. Where indeed is the fellow-creature who shall say he has none ? And how ill would it become those whose need is the least, to be finally bitter against such as have had the misfortune to want more. The editor of the new " Pictorial Edition " of Shakspere (by the way, we adopt with him that new spelling of the name, happy to do the least and most trivial thing as Shakspere himself appears to have done it) has well defended the great poet from the strange charge brought against him of being too charitable. The sky might as well be accused of bending too equally "over all." If the very representative of Nature must not be as charitable as he is inclined to be, then would it be no inclination of Nature herself; and what an awful consideration for us, in the last resort, would that be! But the great mother is "justified of her children;" and no depth of the human heart was ever sounded to its extreme point, in which the rod did not pierce through sweet waters as well as through stubborn clay.

www.ingramcontent.com/pod-product-compliance
Lightning Source LLC
Chambersburg PA
CBHW031423230426
43668CB00007B/413